"You have the Words of Eternal Life."

Transformative Readings of the Gospel of John from a Lutheran Perspective

Edited by
Kenneth Mtata

on behalf of
The Lutheran World Federation
– A Communion of Churches

Lutheran University Press
Minneapolis, Minnesota

"You have the Words of Eternal Life."
– Transformative Readings of the Gospel of John
from a Lutheran Perspective
Documentation No. 57, October 2012

Kenneth Mtata, editor
on behalf of The Lutheran World Federation – A Communion of Churches

Editorial assistance: Department for Theology and Public Witness

Layout: Department for Theology and Public Witness

Design: LWF-OCS

Cover photo: © Peter Williams/WCC

Published by Lutheran University Press under the auspices of:
The Lutheran World Federation
150, rte de Ferney, PO Box 2100
CH-1211 Geneva 2, Switzerland

Also available in Europe under ISBN 978-2-940459-25-4

Parallel edition in German available from, Evangelische Gemeindepresse, Stuttgart, Germany, under ISBN 978-2-940459-26-1

Library of Congress Cataloging-in-Publication Data

You have the words of eternal life : transformative readings of the gospel of John from a Lutheran perspective / edited by Kenneth Mtata.
     p. cm.
  "On behalf of The Lutheran World Federation-a communion of churches."
  Includes bibliographical references.
  ISBN 978-1-932688-83-2 (alk. paper) -- ISBN 1-932688-83-8 (alk. paper)
  1. Bible. N.T. John--Criticism, interpretation, etc. 2. Lutheran Church--Doctrines. I. Mtata, Kenneth.
  BS2615.52.Y68 2012
  226.5'06--dc23
                        2012041792

Lutheran University Press, PO Box 390759, Minneapolis, MN 55439

Manufactured in the United States of America

Contents

Preface

Martin Junge

Reading and the proclamation of the Holy Scriptures awaken and strengthen faith communities in their belief and practices in the world. Reading sacred texts is closely related to the ability to "read" the world, and vice versa. As faith communities sharpen the way in which they interpret both the Scriptures and world around them, their actions become increasingly refreshing and life giving. In other words, biblical interpretation contributes to solidifying Christian commitment to social transformation.

In 2011, the Lutheran World Federation (LWF) embarked on a hermeneutics program in order to nurture this desire to "read" shared sacred texts and contexts. The Bible not only connects today's Christians but also provides a bridge to preceding generations of faith. As such, it is vital to take seriously the witness of past interpretations and to relate them to contemporary ones. Since our contexts are interconnected, we need to find ways not only of communicating our differences but also to use our interaction as an opportunity for mutual enrichment and challenge.

The LWF decided to embark on this process in order to connect contemporary faith communities with the rich cloud of witnesses from the past and to hear afresh God's Word. Moreover, in view of the 500th Anniversary of the Reformation in 2017, it is appropriate to remember the prominence of the Bible during the sixteenth-century Reformation. The Bible remains central to the ever growing number of Christians. Worldwide easy access and ready availability of the Bible entail the need to develop comprehensive tools for interpretation, so that the Bible becomes a source of renewal for both the church and society. It is in this light that I commend to you this publication, which is the result of the LWF's first, international hermeneutics consultation.

Introduction

Kenneth Mtata

Transformative hermeneutics

While "literacy" tends to be associated with the ability to read written texts, it is also helpful to look at it as a general ability to "read" texts and contexts that is, "reading" in a broader sense. On the one hand, "reading" is one's ability to make sense and make the best of (maximize) one's environment. "Misreading," on the other, is the tendency to perceive inadequately. Reading plays a significant function in faith communities since they are endowed with sacred texts that must be read or made sense of in order to shape beliefs and model the community's life. As such, churches have a pressing responsibility not only to read the Bible properly, but also to apply it to the shaping of the life of the believing community within itself and its relationship with those outside it. The challenge is how to read such fixed biblical texts in the rapidly changing contemporary contexts of the faith community. The difficulty not only lies in the fact the Holy Scriptures are the basis of life and faith, and hence are to be taken seriously, but how the churches, separated in space and time, can appropriate these texts for themselves without misreading them. Closely related to misreading biblical texts is also the misreading of the context in which these texts are being appropriated. There tend to be two extremes emanating from such a dilemma. The first is to assume that what is written in the biblical texts should be taken literally and applied directly to contemporary life. The second is to assume that, due to their antiquity, the sacred texts are too alien to be relied on for shaping contemporary faith and life. Maneuvering between these two extremes is one task of the Lutheran World Federation (LWF) hermeneutics process of which this volume is the first product.

The Lutheran churches subscribing to the LWF have committed themselves to "confess the Holy Scriptures of the Old and New Testaments to be the only source and norm of its doctrine, life and service."[1] These churches of the Reformation locate themselves within the ecumenical tradition going back to the early church. They therefore take the three ecumenical creeds (Apostles', Nicene and Athanasian creeds) and the Confessions of the Lutheran Church, particularly

---

[1] "Constitution of the Lutheran World Federation," Article II, in *From Winnipeg to Stuttgart 2003–2010, The Report of the General Secretary on Behalf of the Council* (Geneva: The Lutheran World Federation, 2009), 146.

the unaltered Augsburg Confession and Martin Luther's "Small Catechism," as the lens through which appropriately to interpret the Holy Scriptures.[2] If the Holy Scriptures constitute the basis for "doctrine, life and service," it becomes necessary that this function be clarified for each generation and in the specific local existence of the church. While such clarification will always at best be tentative, attempts should be made to establish some level of functional clarity of the relationship between the Bible, diversity of reading contexts and the unifying hermeneutical lens of a particular theological tradition in order to forge common action in the world today. This clarity will not only help to strengthen the unity of the churches belonging to the Reformation tradition, but also in their ongoing dialogue with other faith traditions and their shared witness to the world.

In a bid to move toward this clarity, the LWF has embarked on the hermeneutics program, conceived against the backdrop of tensions of biblical interpretation regarding various ethical issues, the obvious one being that of human sexuality. While this background is instructive, the deliberately chosen overarching background of this hermeneutics program is the envisaged commemoration and celebration of the 500th Anniversary of the Reformation in 2017. The sixteenth-century Reformation was characterized by a new commitment to the Holy Scriptures. The relationship between God's Word and religious, social, political and economic renewal is not unique, but also evident in God's speaking to Moses and the giving of the law and the discovery of the book (scroll) during Josiah's reforms (2 Kings 22–23). Another good example is the reestablishment of temple worship after the exile;

> So they read from the book, from the law of God, with interpretation. They gave the sense, so that the people understood the reading. And Nehemiah, who was the governor, and Ezra the priest and scribe, and the Levites who taught the people said to all the people, 'This day is holy to the Lord your God; do not mourn or weep.' For all the people wept when they heard the words of the law (Neh 8:8–9).

At the beginning of his ministry, Jesus saw the establishment of God's reign as founded on the promises in God's Word,

> and the scroll of the prophet Isaiah was given to him. He unrolled the scroll and found the place where it was written: "The Spirit of the Lord is upon me, because he has anointed me to bring good news to the poor. He has sent me to proclaim release to the captives and recovery of sight to the blind, to let

---

[2] Ibid.

the oppressed go free, to proclaim the year of the Lord's favor." And he rolled up the scroll, gave it back to the attendant, and sat down. The eyes of all in the synagogue were fixed on him. Then he began to say to them, "Today this scripture has been fulfilled in your hearing" (Lk 4:17–21).

Examples of hearing the Word of God afresh resulting in the renewal of religious and social institutions abound. In the context of the Reformation, we can see that the Holy Scriptures played a central role, not only in legitimizing that "new" thing which God was purported to be doing, but also as a means for a renewed appropriation of the early Christian traditions in a new context. As a catalyst for renewal, the Scriptures appear to have contributed to the process due to the widespread availability of the Bible in the vernacular and also by proposing new ways of interpretation. The previous period was characterized by only the Latin text in addition to a few German translations, based on inferior manuscripts and not on the original languages. Martin Luther managed to achieve much since he happened to have access to superior manuscripts and worked with the original languages in addition to Latin. Luther found the time to put his German translation together while he was in hiding at the Wartburg Castle between 1520 and 1522. Luther also took advantage of Johannes Gutenberg's newly inaugurated printing press to print many copies of the German Bible. In addition, the emphasis on the primacy of the Holy Scriptures over tradition and personal revelation called for an increased reading and study of the Bible. If God spoke primarily through the written word, one was obliged to commit to its reading and study.

The papers presented in this book seek to attend to three interpretive poles of the biblical text, the interpretation of the Bible in the Reformation tradition and the diversity of contexts informing the manifold interpretations. Some do not simply describe, but also propose, in a modest way, how these three interpretive poles might be fruitfully related so that reading the Bible becomes a transformative process. The basic biblical text used is the Gospel of John. In other words, the Gospel of John is being read in light of different contexts through the lens of the ecumenical, Lutheran and Reformation traditions. The aim is not to emphasize the variety of reading contexts, but to find shared reading practices, regulated by the common reading lens of the Lutheran and ecumenical traditions. It is this perspective of relating the three interpretive poles that the future volumes of this hermeneutics series will seek to deepen from various angles. In the following, we do not give a summary of the papers, which should be read in their individual integrity, but a broad overview of the relationship of these three hermeneutical poles.

The biblical text

One of the major contributions of Martin Luther and the Reformation was the rediscovery and exaltation of the materiality and the historical nature of the text as the medium through which God would speak and give the Holy Spirit to human beings. God would only address individuals and communities from outside through the reading and hearing of the Word and the sacraments. In his context, Luther opposed other positions that either exalted individual, intuitive or internal spiritual revelation apart from the external Word. In emphasizing the written Word, Luther tried to subvert Rome's claim to exclusive authority over the interpretation of the Word or to put the tradition of the church at the same level as the Word of God. This emphasis on the written word called for the Bible to be available in the vernacular. This would in no way undermine the necessity of rigorous study requiring mastery of the original languages, Hebrew and Greek. The translatability of the word into the vernacular was viewed as reminiscent of the incarnation, as has been pointed out by several African theologians such as Kwame Bediako and Lamin Sanneh.

The fact that the Word of God is translatable differentiates the Bible from the sacred texts of other religions in a number of ways. From the onset, it becomes necessary to take seriously the distinction between the Bible, the Holy Scriptures and the Word of God, as shown in this volume by Hans-Peter Grosshans, according to whom, the "*Bible* is a book (like other religious books)" but "becomes *Holy Scripture* in its use in the church and which may become the *Word of God* when people are addressed by it in a salvific way" (Grosshans in this volume, emphasis added). This distinction of the physical book and its objective content from its subjective appropriation puts the responsibility on the reader without denying the Spirit behind the content. The appropriation of the Bible as the Holy Scriptures opens up the church to the opportunity of hearing the Word of God. Received with this positive attitude, the Holy Scripture unleashes the power from its contents, written in ordinary human language in the past, to move the church to the future. In order to acclimatize with its language and master its *habitus* beyond technical expertise, the biblical text must be read and studied regularly at home, in church, in private and in community. It must be critically studied, meditated upon, discussed, argued over, enacted, preached on and shared. In this way, it can shape belief and life. Read and lived in this attitude, the ordinary words of the Holy Scriptures become the "words of eternal life" (ῥήματα ζωῆς αἰωνίου Jn 6:68). It is through this diligent search of the Scriptures that the encounter with Christ, the Word of God and eternal life, is made possible.

Several essays seek to hear the address of the biblical text of the Gospel of John by looking at it as a whole but also through its themes or different sections. This approach comes from the recognition that the entire Gospel of John is composed of several traditions that go back to Jesus and the early Christian communities via several routes. But it is this single focus (Jesus Christ) of the traditions that gives the final text of the Gospel its wholeness, not only within itself, but also with the books of the Christian Old Testament and the rest of the New Testament. This single focus, "the nuclear event" to use Paul Ricoeur's terminology, "possesses at once a historical significance and a kerygmatic dimension."[3] While such early genealogy of the individual *pericopes* can only be identified with very little confidence, as Craig Koester shows in this publication, they provide the coherence characteristic of the Gospel of John. He singles out the notions of the "Word," "life," "actions or signs," the "crucifixion and resurrection," and the "Spirit." Koester emphasizes that one way of reading a biblical text is to look at its overarching themes characterized by recurring ideas or motifs across the whole book. In so doing, one can discern, albeit only tentatively, the context from which the gospel itself emerges. Such a position that one could approximate the community behind the gospel based on its content has lately been challenged but nonetheless remains plausible to a certain extent.

Commendable reading practices emphasize the "otherness" of biblical texts, which must be allowed to speak both familiar and unfamiliar language to the contemporary reader. This can be achieved by creating both distance and proximity to the text. By creating proximity, one is open to what the biblical text has to say and willing to be "converted." By creating distance, the readers allow the text to speak to its past audience while trying to eavesdrop on that conversation, fully aware of the limitation that they only eavesdrop on a small part of that past conversation.[4] If the text is to be honored as worthy of speaking today, the reader has the responsibility to take up this historical task of "journeying between" the "strangeness" of the past and the "familiarity" of the contemporary world.[5] Only such a committed and open engagement with the past is likely not only to confirm what the reader is familiar with, but also to bring some surprises.

---

[3] Paul Ricoeur, *From Text to Action: Essays in Hermeneutics*, vol. II, transl. Kathleen Blamey and John B. Thompson (Illinois: Northwestern University Press, 1991), 89.

[4] David L. Bartlett and Barbara Brown Taylor (eds), *Feasting on the Word* (Louisville: Westminster John Knox Press, 2008), 15.

[5] Stefan Collini, et al (eds), *History, Religion and Culture: British Intellectual History 1750-1950* (Cambridge: Cambridge University Press, 2000), 15.

This historical task involves the investigation of the words, sentences and their combinations in the whole text in relationship to contemporaneous use of language. It is in this historical sense that the biblical text can speak afresh and renew doctrine for the life of the church.[6] This was one of Martin Luther's major contributions. For Luther, the historical materiality of the biblical text was to be prized above the allegorical sophistications of creative interpretation. The historical distance of the biblical text will also reveal its continuity and discontinuity with previous religious traditions as Denis Olson shows in this publication. This is how the Word of God can renew. It is based on God's past speaking in ways that address contemporary questions. It has been observed that renewal was possible in the Jewish faith because there was always a written and fixed text that governed the parameters within which interpretive creativity could take place.[7]

Context

The fact that "the Word became flesh and lived among us" (Jn 1:14) is God's recognition of context. The incarnation of the Word took place in first-century Palestine, that is, in space and time. The reason why God can speak to all people at all times is because God speaks to local situations as well as to human beings' existential needs. The reason why God's utterance awakens the hearers to new commitments and life is because it does not simply condone or condemn their context, but speaks to them in order to strengthen, renew and to spur them to their highest possible authenticity—God's Word is creative; God's utterance awakens. According to John, when Jesus says, "Lazarus, come out!" (Jn 11:43), Lazarus comes to life. But in this same understanding, this promise of life from God's pronouncement is not only limited to the single case of Lazarus; Jesus says, "everyone who lives and believes in me shall never die" (Jn 11:26). In this sense, abundance of life is both immanent and transcendent; the good news must address the local and immediate but also promise something more profound.

This immediate and transcendent potential of God's communication becomes evident in the fact that biblical texts, written for specific audiences and local contexts, could, with the same effectiveness, be encountered in other contexts separated in space and time. In his essay, Vítor Westhelle distinguishes between different contexts that directly impact the interpretation of the Holy Scriptures.

---

[6] Jaroslav Pelikan (ed.), *Luther's Works*, vol. 1 (Saint Louis: Concordia Publishing House, 1958), 233.

[7] See, Bernard M. Levinson, *Legal Revision and Religious Renewal in Ancient Israel* (Cambridge: Cambridge University Press, 2008).

The first is the context that occasioned the writing of the text itself but may also include the context for which the text was written in the first place. The second context is the context of reception, that is, how existential concerns of different eras have shaped the questions brought to the text. These two broad categories of contextual approaches to the Bible should be taken into consideration. We have already pointed out above that language and idioms used in the composition of the biblical text were comprehensible to the particular context in which the text emerged or the audience for whom it was initially written. We are also aware that while the biblical text was written with a specific context in mind, there is also a general assumption in much biblical literature that the text could also be read by those the text was not initially directed to.

The assumption of both the particular and general understanding of context is evident in John as, for example, in the confrontation of Thomas' doubt.

> Then he said to Thomas, "Put your finger here and see my hands. Reach out your hand and put it in my side. Do not doubt but believe." Thomas answered him, "My Lord and my God!" Jesus said to him, "Have you believed because you have seen me? Blessed are those who have not seen and yet have come to believe." Now Jesus did many other signs in the presence of his disciples, which are not written in this book. But these are written so that you may come to believe that Jesus is the Messiah, the Son of God, and that through believing you may have life in his name (Jn 20:27–31).

In this example, we can observe an early situation in which belief was at stake as characterized by the ubiquitous presence of the notion of belief and unbelief in the whole fourth gospel. From the onset, the Gospel points out that John the Baptist was "a witness to testify to the light, so that all might believe through him" (Jn 1:7) while the concluding part affirms that the Gospel was written so that "you may come to believe that Jesus is the Messiah, the Son of God, and that through believing you may have life in his name" (Jn 20:31).

While we may be uncertain as to whether believing is the "intention" of the "author," we can be certain that believing is the very important voice of the text in its early context of reception. In this early context of the Gospel of John, the community is confronted with the choice of publicly confessing its faith or losing its credibility by hiding its identity; "many, even of the authorities, believed in him. But because of the Pharisees they did not confess it, for fear that they would be put out of the synagogue; for they loved human glory more than the glory that comes from God" (Jn 12:42–43). In other words, the word of the Gospel of John confronts a confessional context, one in which one must make a choice between faith in Jesus and losing one's position in society, or hiding one's identity and losing one's place in the Father's household (ἐν τῇ οἰκίᾳ τοῦ πατρός) (Jn 14:2). It is this power and ingenuity of the biblical text to address immediate hearers with such broadness that make this text reach subsequent contexts of believing communities with singular power and influence.

The missiological implication here is that the written Word of God, which transformed lives in the past generations, has the power to do the same today and in different contexts. Transformative hermeneutics stimulate this critical engagement with the Word of God so that it transforms the lives of today's readers. If it is contextual, then biblical interpretation seeks to move beyond the technical readings of the past while seeking to embody the transformation of the past into the present (Eve-Marie Becker in this volume). As Anni Hentschel shows, "one and the same text may be understood in a completely different way by different people, because reading and understanding depend on the reader's context, especially in terms of historical situation, cultural assumptions, literal knowledge, age and gender."

Another contextual question has to do with what the text means to contemporary society. This is one difficult aspect of interpretation because there are no clear rules as to how one moves from the message to the early recipients to applying the same message to contemporary situations. One must already decide *a priori* what aspects of the text correspond to contemporary questions. As will be shown below and throughout the essays in this volume, this *a priori* classification of corresponding issues from the biblical text to the contemporary context is shaped by one's theological or even "ideological" orientation, whether one is aware of it or not. As such, an interpretation of the Bible that seeks to take context seriously is inherently ethical. As Monica Melanchthon shows in this book, "One cannot miss discerning the strong ethical component in contextual biblical interpretation." But the shape of ethical questions emerges from questions arising from the text itself and also questions from one's context. As has been pointed out above, as enough distance is created for the text to speak, it raises questions that the reader may not have had in the first place. But, also, as readers carefully look at their own context, they bring questions to the text which another person, who has made different experiences, could not bring. Is there a general way of categorizing these commonly shared existential questions?

Both Bernd Wannenwetsch and Sarah Hinlicky Wilson underline the ethical dimension of contextual hermeneutics as they draw on Luther's law and gospel categories. For Wannenwetsch, this existential, ethical category belongs to a general understanding of citizenship participation in the economy, politics and faith community (*oeconomia, politia, ecclesia*) characteristic of all societies. Wannenwetsch points to the Johannine understanding of law as the "law of love," which is the "ethic of belonging" that must govern the relationships of the whole human family but especially those of the household of faith. He criticizes ethics interested in identifying what often appears as the principled and infinite art of determining degrees of compatibility between distinct moral principles, or of weighing them up against each other according to circumstance; but if the basic question is about our belonging, the rivalry between various agencies and powers that claim our allegiance will be much more obvious, and hence the need to become clear about where we really belong. Our actions and overall conduct of life will then simply "tell the tale" of where we actually belong (Wannenwetsch in this volume).

If one takes "belonging" as central to ethical living in the community, one also has to take "belonging" as central to the general quest for citizenship in the spheres of economics, politics and the faith community (*oeconomia, politia, ecclesia*), all of which are governed by the political function of the law (*usus politicus legis*) and the theological function of the law (*usus theologicus legis*). From this Lutheran understanding, these spheres of human existence (at least *oeconomia* and *politia*) are shared by all people separated in space and time, making it possible for biblical interpretation from a contextual perspective to prepare Christians for participation in the public space. In other words, at an existential level, the human quest for belonging underlies the possibility for relating contextual questions of the past to those of the present (Eve-Marie Becker in this volume).

We can observe that many contextual approaches to the Bible have tended to engage with the economy and politics, thereby emphasizing the political rather than the theological function of the law. In this volume, Monica Melanchthon refers to the context of human rights abuses in India for which she invites "organic intellectuals" to work with the local marginalized. These organic resource persons provide tools to "give a transformative or life giving impetus to biblical study and interpretation" since they are not only focusing on the text in its past, but are willing to engage with pressing issues today. These contextual theologians do not only "critique but also engage in constructive theological reflection that is public in nature," says Monica Melanchthon.

There are a number of challenges to contextual hermeneutics. One such challenge has to do with its over-dependency on the political function of the law in which the Bible and theology become indistinguishable from any other secular discourse. It should be pointed out that good hermeneutics should equip God's people appropriately to engage with Pontius Pilate, the Romans, tax collectors as well as the priests, scribes, the Pharisees and the Sadducees. Yet, they should be able to do this on the basis of their own theological resources. Christians should, through reason, be able to engage in public space. They should be able to tackle the challenges of injustice, power and marginalization. The political function of the law (*usus politicus legis*) helps them in this regard. Nonetheless, in their engagement with one another, Christians should use the law as it draws attention to sin for the sake of repentance. For this reason, the law should be thought of in relationship to the gospel, the promise and gift of God. The interpretation of the Bible becomes transformative when law and the gospel are related as they function together as the Word of God. The danger of simply being driven by a political agenda is that one loses the theological dimension of humanity's sinfulness, including the sinfulness of the poor and marginalized. This became evident during the struggle against apartheid when, during the day, black women and men would march together against racism and, during the night, some black men would rape black women.

The second criticism leveled against a contextual approach is related to the one above. It is the tendency to generalize that which constitutes context. If it is not every experience that has a direct implication on biblical interpretation, then what has? In other words, what experience constitutes effective context for hermeneutical purposes? Contextual hermeneutics usually does not provide methodological clarity on this, hence the need for Westhelle's essay in this volume. What complicates this aspect of context is that contemporary context is always fluid. If there are several contextual issues, which issue is privileged as the basis for theological reflection? For Paul Tillich, context or "situation" "as one pole of all theological work, does not refer to the psychological or sociological state in which individuals or groups live."[8] Rather, for him it refers to the "scientific and artistic, economic, political, and ethical forms in which they express their interpretation of existence."[9] Tillich uses examples from politics and health to illustrate this point. He suggests that "theology is not concerned with the political split between East and West, but is concerned with the political interpretation of the split" and that theology "is not concerned with the spread of mental diseases or awareness of them, but it is concerned with the psychiatric interpretation of these trends."[10] In other words, Tillich sees context as the "totality" in which human beings find themselves in reading their situations. The context that is central for hermeneutics relates to human self-understanding in moments that

---

[8] Paul Tillich, *Systematic Theology*, vol. 1 (Chicago: Chicago University Press, 1951), 3.

[9] Ibid., 4.

[10] Ibid., 4.

threaten their existence and well-being. Tillich's "situation" is the category which contextual approaches have labeled the "poor" and "marginalized" as their context for doing theology or reading the Bible. The question is how the contextual biblical interpretation of the "middle class" could be of any benefit to the poor or the "marginalized."

Contextual Bible study scholars such as my former teachers, Gerald West and Jonathan Draper, have made valuable contributions to addressing this relationship between what West calls the "untrained" and "trained" readers of the Bible corresponding to the "middle class" scholars reading the Bible in solidarity with "marginalized" communities.[11] Draper has shown the close connection between the biblical text and the context by emphasizing the necessity for positioning oneself contextually. For Draper, the "Word of God is not to be found in the letter of the Scripture. Nor is it in the spirit of the hearing or reading community. It is precisely between these two, in the mutual, dynamic relationship, in a back-and-forth that is never perfectly objectifiable."[12] The challenge of the relationship between contextual "margins" and solidarity with their "socially engaged" or "organic intellectuals," to use West's language, remains a fruitful area for further exploration in contextual hermeneutics. This is especially true because most of the essays in this volume are written by trained theologians and can therefore be fully utilized by other theologians or students of theology at seminaries. Transformative hermeneutics seeks to find ways of linking the experiences and expertise of congregations and academic theologians, an effort demonstrated to an extent by some of the above mentioned scholars. This engagement comes from the realization that the Bible is read for different purposes by scholars who read it for their academic work and "ordinary" readers who read it for their devotional life. However, there is inexhaustible mutual fecundation in bringing these diverse purposes into deliberate dialogue.

One crucial contribution of contextual hermeneutics is in this "recognition of the validity of another *locus theologicus*: present human experience" that is, the experiences of the reading community. Contextual theology seeks to consider "culture, history, contemporary thought forms" together with "'Scripture and tradition, as valid sources for theological expression."[13] The question remains whether this foregrounding of human experience does not

---

[11] Gerald O. West, *Biblical Hermeneutics of Liberation*; *Modes of Reading the Bible in the South African Context* (Maryknoll, NY: Orbis, 1995; originally published by Pietermaritzburg: Cluster, 1991).

[12] Clodovis Boff, *Theology and Praxis: Epistemological Foundations* (Maryknoll, N.Y: Orbis Books, 1987), 136, cited in Jonathan Draper, " 'For the Kingdom is Inside You and it is Outside of You': Contextual Exegesis in South Africa," in Patrick J. Hartin and J. H. Petzer (eds), *Text and Interpretation: New Approaches in the Criticism of the New Testament* (Brill: Leiden, 1991), 243.

[13] Stephen B. Bevans, *Models of Contextual Theology* (Maryknoll, N.Y.: Orbis Books, 2002), 4.

weaken efforts toward objectivity. Vítor Westhelle shows here the fruitfulness of Latin American contextual approaches in which the Exodus narrative gave hope of deliverance to the local Christian communities in times of political oppression. He demonstrates how similar texts were used by the oppressors in apartheid South Africa who contextually appropriated the same Exodus narrative to legitimate their own quest for the land of promise. The Book of Exodus became the basis of the white supremacists' domination of the black South Africans as they assumed to be Israelites in representing themselves in the narrative.

One significant challenge for contextualization lies in this subtle function of endorsing a particular earthly political establishment in the name of God. In other words, contextualization falls into the trap of being too concrete when proposing what the kingdom of God should look like on earth. This can be explained by the fact that most contextual approaches tend to employ a hermeneutical key from social, economic or political theories with clear proposals and then use the biblical text or theological reflection to legitimate such theories. This was the case in Latin American Liberation Theology's use of Marxist theory, with the result that some extreme theologians engaged in violent military activities with the hope of establishing the "classless" godly society.

The above critique was common among some Western theologians because of their sense of custodianship of the theological enterprise and hence trying to defend its traditional methods. This notwithstanding, the history of Western theological scholarship evinces a contextual commitment that has not continued with the same vigor in recent times. There is evidence that in nineteenth-century Germany, such scholars as Adolf von Harnack, Martin Rade and others were contextual theologians in that they sought to "confront" their "audience with the opportunities of the Christian faith in the social, political, and cultural challenges of their day."[14] For them, theology was "founded in a historical way in the gospel as the origin for life and faith of Christianity."[15] Even though contextual approaches to theology and the Bible largely flourished in the global South, they pointed out that this way of approaching theology and the Bible "is not an option, nor is it something that should only interest people from the Third World"[16] because the "old content of faith-the same yesterday, today, and forevermore is always received under the conditions of a new context of life."[17]

---

[14] Hans Schwarz, *Theology in a Global Context: The Last Two Hundred* (Grand Rapids: Eerdman, 2005), 136.

[15] Ibid.

[16] Tom Powers, *The Call of God: Women Doing Theology in Peru* (New York: State University of New York Press, 2003), 8.

[17] Carl Braaten, *Principles of Lutheran Theology*, second edition (Minneapolis: Fortress, 2007), 2.

Theological orientation

Words such as "confessional," "dogmatic" and "theological" tend to be viewed with suspicion in biblical studies. They are associated with rigid orientation to studying the Bible in ways that only serve to buttress the hegemony of the hierarchy of the church, hence as curtailing the freedom of scholarship. From some postcolonial and postmodern perspectives, explicit confessional and theological orientations are seen as endorsing the oppressive ideology and the patriarchal *status quo*. Such views are not completely correct. What we know is that everyone has an entry point to the biblical text, which is shaped by their theological or what Gerald West calls "ideological-theological" or "ideo-theological" orientation.[18] Every reader has this orientation whether or not they are conscious of it. The greatest danger is to be unaware of it and when that orientation is oppressive and contradicts the broader witness of the gospel. It is for this reason that the transformative hermeneutics opted for here have a deliberate confessional or theological orientation of the Lutheran and Reformation tradition.[19]

An explicit confessional hermeneutical orientation recognizes that the

> earliest creedal traditions preserved already in the Old and New Testaments served to unify the people of God, orient God's people their identity in the history of God's saving intervention, and clarify the faith of God's people in the context of its challengers, so ecumenical creeds speak to the unity, identity, and integrity of Christian church and its faith.[20]

The principle of orientation has been acknowledged as an important perspective in hermeneutics. For example, Rudolf Bultmann used the same principle when he talked about "pre-understanding" (see Becker in this volume). As Bultmann put it, the reader's orientation should not be understood in "terms of psychological introspection. Rather, it is essential to determine one's own position, so that the exegete does not yield to an inappropriate identification

---

[18] Gerald West, "Interpreting 'the Exile' in African Biblical Scholarship: An Ideotheological Dilemma in Postcolonial South Africa," in Bob Becking and Dirk Human (eds), *Exile* and *Suffering*, Old Testament Studies 50 (Leiden: Brill, 2009), 247–68.

[19] LWF member churches view the three ecumenical creeds (Apostles', Nicene and Athanasian creeds) and the Confessions of the Lutheran Church, particularly the unaltered Augsburg Confession and Martin Luther's "Small Catechism" as true interpretations of the Holy Scriptures and hence as useful hermeneutical lenses through which these churches can read the Scriptures together.

[20] Joel Green, *Seized by Truth: Reading the Bible as Scripture* (Nashville: Abingdon Press, 2007), 137.

between what the text says and the exegete's predetermined expectations."[21] In contextual hermeneutics, "pre-understanding" or "hermeneutical self-awareness," is the recognition that readers have a "formation" that puts weight in their reading but also that this weight is impacted as they encounter the text in its "otherness." For example, for Martin Luther, the hermeneutical key was Jesus Christ; it was that which "drove Christ" that shaped the evangelical reading of Scriptures. The same principle can also be observed at work in John. "You search the scriptures because you think that in them you have eternal life; and it is they that testify on my behalf" (Jn 5:39).

The question is whether confessional or theological orientation stifles exegetical creativity and hence theological renewal. One's orientation affects interpretation whether one is aware of it or not. The greatest danger does not come from having an orientation but from being unaware of it. Hans-Peter Grosshans shows here that actually the challenge begins even before one starts reading. One must decide on the nature of the biblical text. One's engagement with the text is determined by whether one is simply reading the "Bible," the "Holy Scriptures" or encountering the "Word of God." These distinctions are important within the Lutheran and Reformation traditions in which the Bible can be looked at like other religious books but "becomes Holy Scripture in its use in the church and … may become the Word of God when people are addressed by it in a salvific way" (Grosshans in this volume). Our choices determine how we encounter the biblical text. If readers need to be explicit about their orientation, how does the confessional orientation affect efforts toward some objectivity regarding the Bible?

Bernd Wannenwetsch encourages "reading Scripture as a sort of critical interlocutor of our tradition, so as eventually to trigger a fresh reading of both." This is what it means to belong to a faith tradition, it means "taking seriously the traditional deposit for the present" (Wannenwetsch in this volume). As Carl Braaten has pointed out, Christian tradition cannot be taken wholesale. "There is a lot of rotten stuff in the history of Christianity," he asserts.[22] Communities,

> in their struggle with their faith in their context come up with explanations
> that provide them with appropriate language to these situations; they pass on
> such explanations that may be useful for subsequent generations. But subse-
> quent generations need to relate to these previous explanations in light of the

---

[21] Rudolf Bultmann, *Glauben und Verstehen*, III, 142-150 in Hans Conzelmann and Andreas Lindemann, *Interpreting the New Testament: An Introduction to the Principles and Methods of N.T. Exegesis* (Peabody: Hendricks Publishers, 1988), 2.

[22] Braaten, op. cit. (note 17), 3.

demands of their times. In bequeathing the tradition to the next generation and in the contextualization of such tradition, tradition becomes living. But in taking tradition in its fixed form with no efforts to relating it to contemporary questions, it becomes traditionalism that kills.[23]

Does identifying a shared hermeneutical framework remove plurality and conflicting interpretations? Not necessarily because readers' contexts remain different, so their appropriation of the Holy Scriptures will not be identical. However, clarifying theological starting points could move readers far closer to one another than if they remain ignorant of their theological positions or unwilling to engage with others. It is for this reason that members of the LWF must always find ways of orienting their hermeneutics to their shared theological traditions, i.e., the three ecumenical creeds (Apostles', Nicene and Athanasian creeds) and the Confessions of the Lutheran Church, particularly the unaltered Augsburg Confession and Martin Luther's "Small Catechism." One reason why these confessions are taken very seriously as the lens through which Scripture can be read is the recognition that contemporary Christian communities read the Bible in the community of past Christian traditions. This is done in the awareness that these confessions were responding to particular questions of the time so that no one should expect these confessions to "yield concretely binding directives for all concrete situations."[24] It is also accepted that there have been periods in which the "confessions and dogmatics were improperly placed above Scripture" for example in the era of Lutheran orthodoxy.[25] It is however possible for the rich deposit of the tradition of the faith community to be taken seriously in the contemporary interpretation of Scriptures, where tradition is renewed and Scripture is illuminated. As Jaroslav Pelikan said, "Tradition is the living faith of the dead; traditionalism is the dead faith of the living."[26] This critical engagement between tradition and Scripture would contribute immensely to the unity of the church and to the church's public witness.

---

[23] Jaroslav Pelikan, *The Vindication of Tradition* (New Haven: Yale University Press, 1984), 65, in Olson in this publication.

[24] Edmund Schlink, *Theology of the Lutheran Confessions* (Philadelphia: Fortress Press, 1961), xxi.

[25] Ibid., xxi–xxii.

[26] Jaroslav Pelikan, *The Emergence of the Catholic Tradition (100–600)* (Chicago: University of Chicago Press, 1971), 9.

Way to the future

As Hans-Peter Grosshans points out,

> the way in which we deal with the plurality of understandings of God's Word and address requires a methodological answer. The churches have to work out procedures of communicating the various understandings with each other and have to enable such cross-cultural and cross-contextual communication in various ways by creating possibilities for people from various contexts to communicate their respective understandings of biblical texts and to reflect theologically on this.

All the proposals in this publication cannot take the place of that constant communication among the churches. Such communication requires openness that recognizes the complexity of "reading" and of making sense of the Scriptures in our time (see Anni Hentschel in this volume). Such communication also requires humility that comes from the recognition of the work of Spirit who illuminates the reading of the Holy Scriptures. This Spirit is the wind that "blows where it chooses" (Jn 3:8). We can only see with hesitation where the Spirit is transforming lives and sometimes only in retrospect. For our part, we should be diligent in our task of reading our contexts and the Holy Scriptures in light of our own tradition. For the rest, it "is the spirit that gives life; the flesh is useless. The words that I have spoken to you are spirit and life" (Jn 6:63).

Lutheran Hermeneutics: An Outline

Hans-Peter Grosshans

Do Lutherans have a distinctive hermeneutic on which they can draw in order to strengthen the internal bonds of the communion and to deepen the quality of their engagement with other Christians and the world? Can this hermeneutic be synthesized from the "effective" reading contexts, the Lutheran theological heritage and the Holy Scriptures into manageable texts about this hermeneutic, which can help the understanding and communication in the various situations biblical texts are read and used within the churches?

In order to arrive at an answer to these questions, some major paradigmatic contributions within the development of Lutheran hermeneutics—or what may be called "Lutheran" hermeneutics—spring to mind. Such retrospection may be helpful to establish whether there may be a specific Lutheran profile in hermeneutics—at least from a historical perspective. Even if Lutheran communities and theologians do not follow former Lutheran ways of reading and understanding biblical texts, they should be aware of the tradition they depart from or they try to update in light of today's problems and understandings.

In the process of finding out what hermeneutics is about, it is helpful to remember the origin of the term "hermeneutic" in Greek (ἑρμενευτική). As far as we know, this term was first used by Plato. According to the most ancient sources, hermeneutic means the interpretation of the signs of the gods—rather like the interpretation of dreams. Interpretation here is used in the double sense of "translating" and "giving meaning" to signs from elsewhere. In European philosophy, from Plato to Martin Heidegger, the origin of hermeneutic was connected with the god "Hermes."[1] Hermes's role was to interpret divine messages to human beings.[2] In later Greek antiquity, the god Hermes was seen as the mediator *per se*, as a magician and the inventor of language and scripture. All this shows that hermeneutics is seen as interpretation in the strict sense (as translating) and in a figurative sense. In the later history of Protestant hermeneutics we find these two sides, especially in Friedrich Schleiermacher's hermeneutics at the beginning of the nineteenth century. According to Schleiermacher, in understanding texts

---

[1] Despite the similarity of the words this is etymologically questionable.

[2] According Plato, Hermes especially had the competence of speech (περὶ λόγου δύναμι̣j – Platon, Kratylos 408 a2).

we have, on the one hand, a grammatical analysis and, on the other, a divination, a prophetic reconstruction of a given text or speech.[3]

Hermeneutical developments in the early church

We have to remember two major developments in the early church in order to understand the peculiarity of Lutheran hermeneutics. In Christianity, hermeneutics, or what we call hermeneutics, is present from the beginning. We can already see processes of interpretation and understanding, mainly of texts of the Old Testament but also of texts produced within the new Christian communities in the texts of the New Testament. With Jesus Christ's ascent to heaven Christianity became a text-based religion. Two questions then became important: Which are the relevant texts? How should these texts be interpreted?

The first question was answered in the process of canonization. In an informal process a number of texts were selected for the canon of Holy Scripture. Canon is the Greek word for *norma* (norm). A set of texts was assigned the role of being the norm and the rule for deciding what was Christian.

The second question was addressed with the concept of the fourfold sense of Scripture, which was first proposed by Origen. In chapter two of the fourth book of his *De principiis*, Origen (185–254) answers the question regarding how we should read and understand divine writing. He believed that the reason for misunderstandings and wrong interpretations was that people understand Scripture literally and not in a spiritual way. According to Origen, the literal sense of biblical texts is for the simple-minded, while believers who are progressing in their faith should read the Bible according to its spiritual, allegorical sense. Furthermore, those who are perfect in faith should read the biblical text in its eschatological sense. This concept is a way of consistently interpreting the Holy Scripture as a whole, avoiding contradictions and making sense of passages in the Bible that at first may seem obscure. Therefore, one has to distinguish between the literal and spiritual meanings of the biblical text. Subsequently, the spiritual meaning was further refined as the allegorical, moral and anagogical (eschatological) sense. The idea was that beside or beyond or within the literal meaning, a biblical text can be read in an allegorical way, as an allegory of the human soul's spiritual life; or, the text can be read in a moral way, disclosing something about Christian life; or, the text can be read in an

---

[3] See Friedrich Schleiermacher, *Hermeneutics and Criticism and Other Writings*, transl. Andrew Bowie (Cambridge: Cambridge University Press, 1998); Jean Grondin, *Introduction to Philosophical Hermeneutics* (New Haven/London: Yale University Press, 1994).

eschatological way, revealing something about Christian hope. It is obvious that the interpretation of the biblical text's spiritual sense emphasizes the role of the interpreter and is not controlled by the biblical text alone.

These two developments have to be borne in mind when we come to Martin Luther's understanding of Holy Scripture in general and to his hermeneutical principles in particular.

Bible—Holy Scripture—Word of God: Distinctions in Martin Luther's writings

In the first instance, Luther considered Holy Scripture, in its role in the process of salvation, to be one of the divine media of salvation. In the second instance, this also became important for theological epistemology. For Luther, the Holy Scriptures were the source and norm of human knowledge of God.

God speaks to human beings and to God's people—the church—through the words of the Bible in various ways. God is present in the world through God's Word—and it is this subject that interests Luther as a theologian.

Therefore, it is important to distinguish three ways of understanding: The Bible—Holy Scripture—the Word of God. The Bible is a book (like other religious books) which becomes Holy Scripture in its use in the church and which may become the Word of God when people are addressed by it in a salvific way. Such address may happen in the way of a commanding divine law or in the way of the saving gospel. "No book may comfort except the Holy Scripture ...; because it includes the Word of God."[4]

But, for Luther, it was essential that the Holy Scripture, as source and norm of the church's teaching and God's saving Word, should not be separated from the literal biblical texts in their wholeness as one book. Therefore, the humanist motto of his time *ad fontes*, "back to the sources," became important for Luther. *Ad fontes* means going back to the original sources of the church's teaching and preaching, that is, to the original text of the Bible in Greek and Hebrew. Such humanists as Erasmus were convinced that Christianity could be renewed by returning to its roots. Luther shared this opinion and therefore translated the New Testament from the original Greek into German in 1521. Throughout his life, he cooperated with other scholars, such as his friend Philipp Melanchthon, on translating the Old Testament from Hebrew into German. In order fully to grasp texts in a foreign language from historical,

---

[4] *WA* 10/1, 2, 75, 3–7 ("trosten mag keyn buch, denn die heyligen schrifft...; denn sie fasset gottis wortt"). Author's own translation.

geographical, cultural, political and religious contexts other than one's own, one has to read them in their original language and translate them into one's own mother tongue. Christian communities need some people in their midst who are able to do this translation and interpretation. For most people who do not know the original languages of the biblical text, it is vital that they can rely on the linguistic competence of the translators and interpreters.

However, Luther was convinced that, on the basis of a true understanding of the biblical texts, the preaching of the Word of God was better done orally than in writing. Addressing people with the Word of God (commanding or comforting) is not like informing people with a learned book. For Luther, the fundamental form of the gospel was the oral message, which he did not regard as being inferior to the written or printed word: "Christ did not write his doctrine himself ... but transmitted it orally, and also commanded that it should be orally continued giving no command that it should be written."[5]

> In all places, there should be fine, goodly, learned, spiritual, diligent preachers without books, who extract the living word from the old Scripture and unceasingly inculcate it into the people, just as the apostles did. For before they wrote, they first of all preached to the people by word of mouth and converted them ... However, the need to write books was a serious decline and a lack of the Spirit which necessity forced upon us... For when heretics, false teachers, and all manner of errors arose in the place of pious preachers ..., then every last thing that could and needed to be done, had to be attempted ... So they began to write in order to lead the flock of Christ as much as possible by Scripture into Scripture. They wanted to ensure that the sheep could feed themselves and hence protect themselves against the wolves, if their shepherds failed to feed them or were in danger of becoming wolves too. [6]

Luther was fully aware of possible false interpretations of Holy Scripture; this necessitates theological discourse and the writing of theological books. But how can we discern which interpretations are true and which ones are false? From where do church leaders and theologians obtain their wisdom in order to ascertain which interpretations are true and which ones are false? In the quote above, Luther gives us only one hint, namely that these writing should lead the reader by Scripture into Scripture. But this is only a very general criterion for knowing which interpretation may be true and needs to be developed more fully.

---

[5] *LW* 52, 205.

[6] Ibid., 206.

With respect to the above mentioned canon of Holy Scripture, it is important that Luther did not understand every biblical text to be of relevance for Christians and to be of equal value. Crucial when reading a biblical text is whether or not it proclaims Christ who was crucified and rose from the dead for the salvation of all people. Luther believed this to be the Bible's own measure of the truth, which makes a critique of biblical texts possible. Luther claimed Christ to be the only content of the Holy Scripture, "Without doubt the entire Scripture is oriented toward Christ alone."[7]

With this criterion, Luther radically criticized entire biblical books. According to him, the Letter of James, the Letter to the Hebrews and the Book of Revelation to John do not belong to the main books of the New Testament because these texts are not oriented toward Christ alone. Nevertheless, out of his respect for the tradition and its selection of the biblical canon, Luther did not eliminate these biblical books from the German Bible. He did, however, alter the sequence of the Scriptures in the New Testament and put those texts at the end of the Bible.

In dealing with the biblical texts critically, Luther did not judge biblical texts by external criteria, but in the context of the Bible as a whole. He claimed that,

> Christ is the Lord, not the servant, the Lord of the Sabbath, of law and of all things.
>
> The Scriptures must be understood in favor of Christ, not against him. For that reason, they must either refer to him or must not be held to be true Scriptures.[8]

In his writing "On the Bondage of the Will" (*De Servo Arbitrio*), Luther developed his understanding of the Holy Scripture and its interpretation in discussion with the traditional Catholic understanding, the (so-called) Anabaptist movement, which became especially strong in 1525, and with Erasmus of Rotterdam.

Luther's main hermeneutical principle: Holy Scripture interprets itself

What is the authority of the Holy Scripture and who guarantees its truth?

In his early disputes with the authorities of the Roman church, Luther had emphasized the authority of the Holy Scripture against other authorities within

---

[7] *WA* 10/2, 73, 15.

[8] *LW* 34, 112.

the church and some of the doctrines and practices of the Roman church. The church's official claim was that the church and its representatives guarantee the authority of the Holy Scripture.

Luther, however, did not agree to this subordination of Scripture to the church and its tradition. Instead, he believed the Holy Scripture to be self-authenticating: Holy Scripture has and needs no guarantor other than itself.

Luther did not only base this insight on the New Testament's claim to be inspired by God, such as 2 Timothy 3:16: "All scripture is inspired by God." Such a circular argument was far too weak. Luther's position was that of a realist: the authority of Holy Scripture is wholly founded on its content, which refers to Jesus Christ and the divine process of human salvation. Therefore, the authority of the Holy Scripture depends on the truth of its central contents, namely God's relationship to human beings—nobody and nothing else gives the Holy Scripture authority, not even an institution such as the church. Here, again, we see Luther's emphasis on the truth—the Bible is not true simply because it says so. What makes the Bible true is that it truthfully records God's work of salvation.

Therefore, the authority of the Holy Scripture does not depend on the fact that the church as a community of people has selected and combined the biblical texts as a Holy Scripture. Rather, it is the truth of the Holy Scripture on which the church depends for its authority.

Consequently, the true meaning of biblical texts is to be found in its reference to the loving and just God and God's gracious relation to humanity. This, for Luther, is the same as the reference to Jesus Christ. Therefore, all former and present interpretations of biblical texts have to be evaluated in this light. Luther sums up his position by saying that Holy Scripture interprets itself. The Holy Scripture is, "totally certain ..., quite easy to understand, completely revealed, its own interpreter"[9] and "therefore Scripture is its own light. It is splendid when Scripture interprets itself."[10]

This principle of Holy Scripture interpreting itself is used by Luther against the traditional position, which held that the church's teaching office, guided by the Holy Spirit, has the authority and competence to give a true interpretation of Scripture.

Luther also opposed the understanding of Holy Scripture put forward by the then new, so-called Anabaptist movement.[11] The "radical wing" of the

---

[9] *WA* 7, 97, 23

[10] *WA* 10/3, 238, 10

[11] Nowadays the Lutheran churches have come to the insight that the term "Anabaptist" is wrong.

Reformation, represented by such people as Andrew Carlstadt[12] or Thomas Müntzer,[13] was termed an Anabaptist movement because it rejected infant baptism, as a consequence of which adults had to be baptized again. They stressed the inward and spiritual side of Christian life and the Holy Spirit was set in opposition to the letter of Scripture. Within their religious communities, leadership fell to the spirit-filled, be they clergy or lay. This frequently led to the abolition of the professional ministry. To give an example, Thomas Müntzer clearly expressed this concentration on the divine spirit:

> God does disclose himself in the inner word in the abyss of the soul. The man who has not received the living witness of God really knows nothing about God, though he may have swallowed 100000 Bibles. God comes in dreams to his beloved as he did to the patriarchs, prophets, and apostles... God pours out his Spirit upon all flesh, and now the Spirit reveals to the elect a mighty and irresistible reformation to come.[14]

Anabaptists claimed that the true interpretation of biblical texts needed a special spiritual talent, one which God bestows on particular people. Luther did not ignore the significance of the Holy Spirit for the interpretation of Scripture, but he considered that the spirit in which people are able to give a true interpretation of the Bible has to be the spirit of the Holy Scripture itself.

For Luther, the Catholics and the Anabaptists of his time were "enthusiasts" because, in their interpretations, they subjugated Scripture to external rules. It is for this reason that Luther was suspicious of the allegorical, pictorial interpretation of biblical texts (versus all forms of spiritual interpretation) and instead emphasized that they should be interpreted in a simple, literal sense.

---

[12] Andrew Carlstadt (1480–1541) was one of the inspiring figures for the "radical wing" of the Reformation. In 1522, Carlstadt and others introduced reforms such as the marriage of priests and the rejection of divine orders. They also destroyed all paintings in the churches and abolished church music because it was considered that the divine spirit could dispense with all external aids, whether art or music. Luther did not agree with all of these reforms. In particular, he himself loved church music and thought it had an important place in worship to which he contributed many hymns of his own composition.

[13] Thomas Müntzer was another prominent figure of the "radical wing" of the Reformation. Ordinary people expected that, with the coming of the Reformation, their living conditions would improve. "Prophets" such as Müntzer preached the end of the world. In 1525, he proclaimed the kingdom of God was at hand and he formed a rebellion of peasants in Saxony.

In fact, all over Germany the peasants rebelled but their rebellions were crushed by the armies of the princes. Müntzer himself was caught and beheaded. In 1525, Martin Luther wrote two essays "Against the Heavenly Prophets" and "Against the Robbing and Murdering Hordes," which were the starting signal for the princes with their armies to crush the peasants and radical Christians.

[14] Quoted in Roland H. Bainton, *Here I Stand. A Life of Martin Luther* (Peabody, MA: Hendrickson Publishers, 2009), 204.

Luther assumes this to be possible in most cases because he considers the Bible to be clear in itself and its stories to have simple meanings that follow from their essential content which is Jesus Christ.

In 1525, the same year that Luther was involved in conflicts with the Anabaptists and the peasants, he wrote an extensive essay, "On the Bondage of the Will," answering Erasmus's substantial critique of his theological ideas, which had been published in 1524 with the title, "On the Freedom of the Will." Luther's essay deals with the understanding of the Holy Scripture and it is at this point that Luther introduced the new distinction between the external and internal clarity of Scripture.

> To put it briefly, there are two kinds of clarity in Scripture, just as there are also two kinds of obscurity: one external and pertaining to the ministry of the Word, the other located in the understanding of the heart. If you speak of internal clarity, no man perceives one iota of what is in the Scriptures unless he has the Spirit of God. All men have a darkened heart, so that even if they can recite everything in Scripture ..., yet they apprehend and truly understand nothing of it... For the Spirit is required for the understanding of Scripture... If, on the other hand, you speak of the external clarity, nothing at all is left obscure or ambiguous.[15]

Erasmus had claimed that Scripture contains obscure parts which necessitate interpretation by the church authorities or interpretation according the tradition of the church. Responding to this, Luther put forward the following distinction: on the one hand the inner clarity (or obscurity) of the message of the biblical texts, located in the understanding of people's hearts, on the other, external clarity (or obscurity) of the biblical texts, located in the understanding of the signs and meanings in the texts by human reason. While when reading biblical texts with an open mind nothing is obscure or ambiguous for human reason, the message of the text may be obscure for somebody's heart.

Some philosophers acknowledge that the theologian Martin Luther defended the freedom of human reason to a greater extent than the philosopher Erasmus of Rotterdam as well as his followers. This use of human reason for the interpretation of the Bible was further developed by the second-generation Lutheran Matthias Flacius Illyricus in his hermeneutical writing (in the *Clavis Scripturae Sacrae—Key to Holy Scripture*). Flacius shared Luther's interest that readers of a biblical text can by themselves reach a plausible and faithful

---

[15] *LW* 33, 28.

understanding of the text by following generally acknowledged rules—rules for reading and interpretation that follow from the insights of human reason.[16]

Nonetheless, when using biblical texts the limits of human reason also become clear. Human reason can grasp the meaning and insights of biblical texts but has no access to their inner clarity and cannot convince the human heart to trust in their message, especially in the promise of the gospel in the Old and New Testaments. With regard to the role of biblical texts in terms of creating trust in God, Luther believed that this could only be done by God. God creates trust in Godself when God speaks to people via the biblical texts.

Luther distinguished two ways in which God speaks to people: through commandments and promises. In Luther's terminology, God speaks to people in the way of the law and in the way of the gospel.

In dealing with Luther's hermeneutics we have to consider this Lutheran distinction, although it may not directly be part of Luther's hermeneutics. We cannot separate the question of the interpretation of biblical texts from its role as a means of God communicating Godself to human beings in order to save them and let them partake in God's life.

Luther considered himself to be following St Paul in his distinction between law and gospel. This distinction expresses a fundamental twofold experience with the Word of God: "There are two things that are presented to us in the Word of God: either the wrath of God or the grace of God, sin or righteousness, death or life, hell or heaven."[17]

Luther's did not intend to separate the Word of God into two opposing parts or to divide the Bible into two parts: the texts of the law and the texts of the gospel. The distinction between law and gospel stands for different ways of interpreting God's relationship to human beings and two ways of God addressing people: demanding from and commanding people and making promises to people and comforting them.

With respect to the divine law, Luther distinguished at least two different uses. First, God's Word as law convicts people of their sins and, secondly, God's commandments are concerned with the proper ordering of human life—i.e., by framing rules helping to regulate and govern human society. Luther called the first function of the divine law its theological use, the second the political use of the law of God.

The first use of divine law refers to the experience of God's holiness and justice setting the standards for human life and opening the way for it to be-

---

[16] Jure Zovko, "Die Bibelinterpretation bei Flacius (1520-1575) und ihre Bedeutung für die moderne Hermeneutik," in *ThLZ*, 132. Jg. (Leipzig, 2007), 1169–80.

[17] *WA* 39/1, 361, 4–6

come holy and just. In God's presence everyone, even a prophet, experiences their life as being unholy and worthless—a life that has to end and pass away. God's holiness sets such a high standard that people feel unable to fulfill it. God's Word as law, therefore, causes individuals to realize that their lives do not meet the demands of the true, divine life. God's law convicts people as sinners. In this sense, it does not directly lead to righteousness but exposes human sin and with this uncovering of sin enables people to see themselves in their true state.

But God's commandments also serve a political purpose and contribute to the proper ordering of human life. God, as part of God's creative activity, resists chaos in our social world. For one who knows the Bible it is obvious that this function of the divine law has to be further differentiated. There is a major difference between the Ten Commandments and, for example, the laws of political and civil life in old Israel, or the ordering of some procedures and rituals in the temple in Jerusalem. Thus Luther assumed that God's law, expressly revealed to Moses, is a general law applicable not only to Jews but to all people. This divine law is also written into people's hearts. Moreover, in the biblical texts there is also the law of the Jewish people, valid only for the ordering of the lives of the Jewish people.

God's law, which God has written into people's hearts, is known by all (cf. Rom 2:14–15) and is therefore older than Moses' Ten Commandments. Luther considered that human beings know by nature that one has to worship God and love one's neighbor. This living law in people's hearts is identical to the law given by Moses and the ethical commandments of the New Testament (especially Mt 7:12, "In everything do to others as you would have them do to you; for this is the law and the prophets.")

> Therefore, there is one law which runs through all ages, is known to all men, is written in the hearts of people, and leaves no one from beginning to end with an excuse, although for the Jews ceremonies were added and the other nations had their own laws, which were not binding upon the whole world, but only this one, which the Holy Spirit dictates unceasingly in the hearts of all.[18]

This universal law defines human conscience. The law, which is written in the heart of human beings by nature, speaks to their conscience. In accordance with their conscience, individuals implicitly know the conditions that must be fulfilled for life to be worthy. Thus, conscience is a divine voice in the midst

---

[18] *LW* 27, 355.

of human life, but it is God as a legislator and a severe judge who speaks in conscience. In that sense, the voice of conscience cannot be the final Word of God for Luther. By their conscience people are inexorably confronted with God's demands and accused and judged according to the measure of divine law—probably ending up in desperation and death.[19] God, the author of divine law, speaks in conscience and therefore conscience is part of the law to which human beings are subject. Conscience expresses the individual's high dignity as well as the fact that humans are not free. It is through failure to live up to one's conscience that one becomes aware of the need for God's grace.

But, what are the demands of the law God has written in human hearts? Surely, God not only makes demands on people by accusing and convicting them of sin but has introduced rules, such as the Ten Commandments, to lay down the principles for an ordered life. For Luther, one of the functions of the political use of divine law is to restrain crime in our sinful world, which is possessed by the devil, and thus to secure public peace. Such commandments as "You shall not kill," "You shall not commit adultery," or "You shall not steal" (Ex 20:13–15) are examples of that. Other functions of the political use of divine law are to order education and also, and most importantly, to enable the preaching of the gospel. Luther believed God to have installed authorities and institutions that have to transfer those fundamental laws into daily life and political order. These institutions and authorities are the governments of cities and countries, civil law and, especially, parents and teachers because it is in the education of young people that the foundations for the future are laid. With the help of these institutions and authorities human beings can fulfill God's fundamental requirements for a peaceful and just order in society because the alternative would be characterized by violence and chaos. For Luther, it was of great importance that God has provided a positive and beneficial order for human life in our fallen and sinful world. It is God's will that people should live peacefully and in harmony with their neighbors. Reason, conscience and the law in human hearts are given by God, the Creator, as the conditions necessary for an ordered, just and peaceful society.

Luther deemed it to be essential that people confront God's demands and the threat of God's judgment in their lives. This confrontation with the divine law highlights the fact that human beings are incapable of entering into a right relationship with God through their own efforts. Only when people come

---

[19] Luther lived his own life based on conscience as the final and only judge—for example in his conduct before the Diet of Worms in 1521. Luther rendered the freedom of conscience a great service in the history of humankind. Like Thomas More (1477–1535), Luther took a stand on conscience in the consciousness that before God he could not act otherwise.

to realize the inadequacy of these efforts will they then be ready to receive the gospel. Only when an individual comes to despair and realizes that they cannot rely on their own strength does God give them everything that they themselves could not produce by their own efforts, that is, life in its fullness as proclaimed in the gospel.

In the gospel, God addresses human beings as a gracious and kind God. We have to notice that God has not set the gospel in opposition to the law as if God were saying, "My dear child, you do not manage to fulfill my law, but I forgive your failure and shall accept and love you as you are." This would be a false understanding of Luther's position. When offering forgiveness, justice and love in the gospel, God not only accepts people's actual situation but wants to change it for the better. The gospel does not legitimate the present situation of life. Instead, in the gospel God sticks to the same aims he puts forward in his law:

> Here, the second part of Scripture comes to our aid, namely, the promises of God which declare the glory of God, saying, "If you wish to fulfill the law and not covet, as the law demands, come, believe in Christ in whom grace, righteousness, peace, liberty, and all things are promised you. If you believe, you shall have all things; if you do not believe, you shall lack all things."[20]

The objectives of divine law and the gospel are justice, peace and freedom, which are important for a person's life. But the gospel not only formulates these aims, it already includes the realization of these aims because they are realized in God. Once a person believes and trusts in God's promise, then they will have everything God has promised because in faith they partake in divine life. The gospel therefore requires the response of faith, and it is faith alone that is needed to achieve the objectives. Luther held that in believing the gospel believers have the "spiritual" goods of peace, justice and freedom because they are made just, free and peaceful by God.

I have described Luther's soteriological concept of God speaking in a two-fold way, law and gospel; this is part of Luther's understanding of the Bible. It is through the message of the Bible—in reading or in preaching—that God speaks to human beings. There is nothing through which God speaks to people that is not witnessed in the Bible. Without keeping this soteriological dimension and role of the biblical texts in mind, we would end up with a technical understanding of Lutheran hermeneutics.

---

[20] *LW* 31, 348–49.

Luther underlined the authority of the Holy Scripture for the life of the church and that of every single believer. But he also presented a very reflective and differentiated understanding of the Holy Scripture, its role within the church and the rules and processes of its interpretation. This has been the starting point for an ongoing discussion dealing with questions of hermeneutics and the processes of interpreting and understanding biblical texts. In order to identify the emphases of a specifically Lutheran hermeneutics, I shall look at a few paradigmatic contributions which Lutheran theologians have put forward.

Taking the literalness of the Bible seriously: The first complete modern hermeneutics by Matthias Flacius

In 1567, the Croatian Lutheran theologian Matthias Flacius Illyricus (1520–1575) published a hermeneutic with the title, *Clavis Scripturae Sacrae—Key to Holy Scripture*. According to the philosopher Hans-Georg Gadamer, Flacius's truly Lutheran hermeneutic is the starting point of the history of modern hermeneutics.[21]

Luther's principle that Holy Scripture is its own interpreter increasingly came to be considered as a mainly polemical assertion rather than a helpful description of biblical interpretation. Therefore, Protestant scholars saw the need to develop a hermeneutical theory and to define the procedure of interpretation according to Luther's general hermeneutical principle. Since in Protestantism the interpretation of biblical texts could not rely on external authorities, such as the authority of inspired teachers or church leaders, but had to be done alone, it became necessary to clarify the process of interpretation academically. Therefore, Protestant scholars developed a scientific biblical hermeneutics. Matthias Flacius was the first to publish such a hermeneutics. His hermeneutic is faithful to the divine dignity of the Holy Scripture while taking the academic insights in other academic fields (mainly in philosophy) into account. In 1546, at the Council of Trent, the Roman Catholic Church had attacked the Protestant principle of Holy Scripture being its own interpreter by teaching that Holy Scripture is hermeneutically insufficient and needs to be supplemented with the authority of tradition. Therefore, Protestant scholars had to show that Holy Scripture is sufficient and comprehensible. In order to do so they had to clarify the hermeneutical method and the means needed for the interpretation of biblical texts when presupposing the sufficiency and

---

[21] Cf. Hans-Georg Gadamer, "Einführung," in Hans-Georg Gadamer and Gottfried Boehm (eds), *Seminar: Philosophische Hermeneutik* (Frankfurt: Suhrkamp, 1976), 7–40.

comprehensibility of Holy Scripture. Flacius's extensive work fulfilled exactly this. He answered his Roman Catholic critics by insisting that the reason for not understanding Holy Scripture (or parts of it) is not its incomprehensibility but the lack of linguistic skills of its interpreters and their questionable method of interpretation. On the basis of the coherence of Holy Scripture, Flacius highlighted the normative autonomy of Holy Scripture by showing all the elements of the process of exegesis and interpretation. In using philology, exegesis, rhetoric, logic and other academic insights every biblical text can be comprehensibly interpreted within the coherence of the whole Bible.

We cannot here go into the details of Flacius's elaborate hermeneutics. Instead, I shall illustrate his general hermeneutical intention by referring to the debate he was involved in the 1550s and which can be considered as one of the reasons why he wrote his elaborate hermeneutics.

During the 1550s, Flacius engaged in an extensive controversy with Kaspar of Schwenckfeld (1489–1561), originally a follower of Luther, who developed what we may refer to as a "spiritualistic" theology after having been disappointed by the course of the Reformation.[22]

Schwenckfeld distinguished strictly between the Holy Scripture, which remains outside the faithful, and the Word of God, which is effective inside the faithful. For Schwenckfeld, the true and proper Word of God was Jesus Christ alone. He was convinced that only the born again human being is able to give in faith a proper and adequate interpretation of the Holy Scripture. In its written form as a text, even in preaching, Holy Scripture cannot get to the heart of human beings, where the fundamental decisions about life are made. For him, therefore, the central question was how human beings can come to believe in their hearts.

According to Schwenckfeld, biblical texts did not suffice for this. Only God and the Holy Spirit can reach people's hearts in such a way that the heart is transformed and faith is called forth. Words, signs, symbols or fellow human beings (e.g., pastors) cannot do this but remain outside the heart. The Word of God is Jesus Christ himself, who communicates himself through the Holy Spirit to the very heart of human beings. This Word of God is effective inside the believing hearts without any outer means, instrument or medium.

For Schwenckfeld, a new hermeneutical constellation of Scripture and faith followed from these insights. True faith does not follow the Holy Scripture. Rather, it is the other way round: Scripture has to follow faith. The Holy

---

[22] The writings of Caspar of Schwenckfeld are published in the 19 volumes of the "Corpus Schwenckfeldianorum" (publication started 1907 in Leipzig). Followers of Caspar of Schwenckfeld nowadays can be found in the US, see **www.centralschwenkfelder.com**

Scripture can only be interpreted adequately if a human being already believes; because only this trust in the heart has the proper reference to Holy Scripture. According to Schwenckfeld,

> The proper vivid gospel is not the history of Christ, voice, sound, letter. It is also in its essence not an outer word, like the oral gospel is not God's power or Godself, but it is an inner word of faith, the vivid Word of God, the word of truth.[23]

Contrary to Schwenckfeld, Matthias Flacius emphasized that there is no immediate knowledge of God and salvation, but that both are always mediated. For Flacius, these media, in which God communicates Godself, are determined by God.

Against all individual reinterpretations of the divine Word, which became flesh and language, Flacius insisted that "God will not act with us human beings except by his outer Word and sacrament. Everything that is praised by the spirit without this Word and sacrament is the devil."[24] God realizes God's goals, namely to save the world, not immediately but with outer, visible and graspable means.

Flacius's interpretation of Romans 10:17 is strict: "So faith comes from hearing, and hearing by the word of Christ." God has devised a series of actions to bring forth eternal salvation such as Scripture, the sacraments, the preachers and listening with the ear. Flacius shows that "faith comes from the outer listening to the preached word" and not "from an inner revelation" by an immediate touching of the Holy Spirit.[25]

For Flacius, also the Holy Spirit is at work when human beings believe in God and, thus, are true Christians: According to Galatians 4:6, it is the Holy Spirit who makes people say in their hearts, "Abba! Father!" But Flacius did not agree that God immediately gives God's Spirit into the heart of a human being. As he pointed out, "in these questions, concerning the outer word, we have to insist, that God gives his Spirit or grace to nobody without giving it through and with the preceding outer word."[26]

---

[23] M. Flacius Illyricus, *Aus den Schmalkaldischen heubt artickeln wider den Schwenckfeld, in welchen die gelertesten Prediger aufs ganz Deutschlandt sich haben unterschriben* (Magdeburg, 1553), 3. Author's own translation.

[24] M. Flacius Illyricus, ibid., 3.

[25] M. Flacius Illyricus, "Vom fürnemlichem stücke, punct oder artickel der Schwenckfeldischen schwermerey" (Magdeburg 1553), 3.

[26] Flacius, op. cit. (note 23), 1.

In contrast, Schwenckfeld and his followers praised themselves for having the Spirit without and before the Word—with the consequence, according to Flacius, that they judge and interpret the Scripture and the spoken word as they like.

Thus, the Holy Scripture becomes the means for self-interpretation. If God gives faith to human beings without the means of written or spoken word and, therefore, faith is not the result of the preached Holy Scripture and its teaching of Christ, then, according to Flacius, we no longer have the possibility to verify and identify the Christian faith. Rather, we would then have to presuppose that people of other faiths, who do not know about the preaching of the Word of God and the sacraments, can be saved like Christians. If the human heart is prepared for the knowledge of God and salvation and transformed by inner revelation, then the Holy Scripture as well as the preachers are unnecessary and in vain. We are then no longer able to identify Christian faith because we lack set criteria.

If we identify with the debate between Flacius and Schwenckfeld regarding the difference between letter and spirit (2 Cor 3:6: "for the letter kills, but the Spirit gives life") and the talk of the new heart and spirit (Ez 11:19), then, in the one instance, neither the Holy Scripture ("letter"), the sacraments nor anything else created can reach people's hearts. All this only touches the outer senses not the heart. Therefore, Holy Scripture itself has to be understood as a "dead letter" which kills rather than saves. The Holy Scripture, according to this understanding, is an uncertain thing: it is subject to human discussion and interpretation and therefore not really reliable. Faith therefore cannot be founded in and justified by Holy Scripture. Rather, it is the other way round: Scripture has to be directed and oriented toward faith—faith, which is immediately called forth by God.

For Flacius, such an understanding clearly did not respect Holy Scripture and the consequences are dramatic for the principles of Christian faith and life. In the last instance, this implies that it is impossible to identify the Christian life and church because there is no public and reasonable criterion and norm for being a Christian and a church and by that to distinguish Christians from non-Christians.

Today we can observe that the position opposed by Flacius is very popular in all Christian churches. Putting faith first and the literal and preached Holy Scripture second is popular because it allows for a greater openness of the Christian faith toward other religions. The intuitive and immediate self-certainty of the hearts of the followers of other religions can be interpreted as being the result of God's immediate work. Moreover, this understanding seems to respect the autonomy of every single believer to a greater extent than the truly Lutheran position of putting Holy Scripture first.

In today's interpretation of the Holy Scripture we can also observe a lack of respect for Scripture's concrete materiality. Texts are frequently subjected to eisegesis rather than exegesis. Contextual and culture related interpretations subjugate biblical texts to recent cultural conditions. Ideologies as well as doctrinal theories use the biblical text to justify their own position and Scripture is used rather like a self-service cafeteria, where one picks and chooses those parts and elements that one likes and that seem useful. Holy Scripture is subordinated to people's and communities' inner self-understandings and used to confirm one's certainties of life and self-interest as well as old traditions. Texts that do not fit are ignored or denied.

This is even the case with the very popular endeavor to look for the centre of Holy Scripture. In faith people claim to know the essential and central message of the Holy Scripture, which sets the criteria for all interpretation. In a strict hermeneutical sense, however, the centre of the Holy Scripture has to be worked out through the interpretation of all the texts of the Holy Scripture. Flacius spoke of the *scopus* of the whole Holy Scripture, which is the goal envisaged in the entire Bible and the red line running through all its texts. This is not a dogmatic construction of the Bible's central message, but the result of the interpretation of all the texts. Precisely this creates the first circle of hermeneutics: between interpretation of the single biblical text and the *scopus*, the goal taken into sight in the whole Bible. Both have to be related to each other and both may change in this process of interpretation. Then a second moment becomes important: the coherence between all the various texts of the Bible. Therefore, the Bible in its literal form becomes important. For Schwenckfeld (and according to Flacius as well as the Roman Catholic Church) the service of Holy Scripture was to create a reference to Jesus Christ, who then communicates himself—beyond the texts—to human beings (for example in tradition or in an immediate way). But if we distinguish Jesus Christ from the biblical texts, then we cannot control whether we are really referring to Jesus Christ or to the Triune God when reading the biblical texts. Therefore, Schwenckfeld's concept needs an inspired interpreter, who relates the readers and listeners beyond the interpretation of the texts to the reality witnessed to in the texts. Flacius, on the other hand, insists on the lingual unity of form and content. According to his understanding, biblical texts—like other texts—already include their own spirit and the reality they are talking about. Therefore, Flacius does not need a problematic spiritual interpretation of the biblical texts because the interpretation of their literal sense is superior. With the literal meaning of biblical texts comes external as well as internal clarity in the heart. For Flacius, internal clarity about the message of the biblical texts cannot be called forth, except through interpretation on the basis of the literal meaning of the text.

This understanding of the Holy Scripture was supported by the doctrine of inspiration (even literal inspiration)—making clear that the author of the Holy Scripture was God, using human beings as a means to communicate Godself.[27] At the same time, theologians became increasingly aware that there were further aspects in the process of understanding Holy Scripture that had to be considered.

From the Reformation to today: Awareness of contexts and historical-critical understanding

Johann Conrad Dannhauer's work, *Hermeneutica sacra sive methodus exponendarum sacrarum litterarum*, published in 1654, marked a further major step in the development of hermeneutics as a theory of interpretation. For the first time, hermeneutics appeared in the title of a book. Dannhauer applied hermeneutics to all texts, which at his time meant biblical, theological as well as legal texts. Dannhauer was writing at the end of the long-drawn-out religious wars in Europe, and some people regard his hermeneutics as a result of the reflection on the religious wars in Europe. A methodologically developed theory of interpretation produced many possible meanings of texts where before there had been only the one, absolute meaning of the Holy Scriptures and laws for which people had taken up arms.

The discussion of the learned replaced the fighting on the battlefield. We can learn from this period that hermeneutics is developed further and becomes important when a tradition loses its reliability and when people seek to correct it or to begin anew. This already applied to the time when the doctrine of the fourfold sense of biblical texts was further developed to make use of old texts in the new (Christian) tradition. Furthermore, during the Reformation a new methodology was developed which could be used to free oneself from oppressive traditions and to bring forth a general understanding of reason, which enabled all those able to read to interpret biblical texts.

---

[27] Because God is the author it makes no sense to ask for the author's intentions in the interpretation of biblical texts. This only becomes relevant when the writers of biblical texts are not seen as mere instruments of God, but rather as media through which God communicates Godself and God's teaching.

A significant development in hermeneutics came from one of the heterodox sidelines of the Lutheran churches, from Pietism, especially from the Pietism of Halle. For people such as August Hermann Francke and his followers, Lutheran dogmatics had become an inflexible system which had lost its vitality. Therefore, the interpretation of biblical texts not only had to satisfy the academic standards of the learned and well-educated, but also needed to contribute to the deepening of the piety and spirituality of the people reading the Bible. According to Johann Jakob Rambach (1693–1735), who developed a hermeneutic in the eighteenth century, hermeneutics is a practical habit with which a theologian learns to discover the meaning of Scripture, to interpret it for others and to use it intelligently. Rambach included a theory of human emotions and affections in his hermeneutics in order to probe more deeply into the spiritual movement of the biblical authors' emotions so as to experience in this way the effects of the Holy Spirit. The context of the reader and listener became important in Pietist hermeneutics. Fully to understand biblical texts means that people, who read or listen, are affected at the level of their emotions as well as their concrete existence. Reflection on the processes of understanding had to take into account the situation of the readers and listeners in their respective contexts.

As a result of the Lutheran insistence that Holy Scripture was one of God's worldly means to communicate Godself to human beings, the Bible increasingly became the object of historical interest. How did God really communicate Godself and God's will into these texts? What do we learn about God when we perceive how God communicated Godself in our understanding and communication?

The development of the historical-critical method was and remains the major challenge for reading and listening to the Bible within the church. The differences between historical-critical exegesis and the Reformers' biblical interpretation seem to be radical. The following survey will call to mind the major insights of the development.

During the seventeenth and eighteenth centuries the awareness for the historical character of the Bible increased considerably. The Jewish philosopher Baruch Spinoza (1632–1677) showed the historical character of the Old Testament, whose texts were not the timeless sayings of God but reflected history.

Johann Martin Chladenius (1710–1759) followed this insight into the historical character of all writings, emphasizing the perspectives of the interpreter and the writer of a text. Interpreters have their own individual, specific perspective, which is subject to their concrete place in space and time. The writer of a historical text has already looked at a certain object from a specific vantage point from which they conceived what they were writing about.

Georg Friedrich Meier (1718–1777) emphasized the self-interpretation of the author of a text which, for them, is the authentic interpretation. In further defining the historical situation of both interpreter and author the interest shifted from a purely hermeneutical to a historical one.

There was an increasing awareness that God communicated Godself not only into a text (the Bible) but also into history, that is, into a concrete time and place which we have to understand in our interpretation in order to understand God's message for our own time. This is the starting point of the historical-critical method in the interpretation of the Bible.

This critical interest in interpretation went hand in hand with other issues. By knowing the historical setting, interests and perspectives of the biblical texts, one could critically distinguish between that which seems to be historical and that which seems to be the timeless meaning and message of these texts. In this sense, Spinoza had critically examined the Old Testament by distinguishing between the general purpose of the Bible (in his opinion, the teaching of morals) and the historical meaning of individual biblical texts. Many others followed him in this attempt critically to assess the timeless message of the Triune God to humankind (which most of the time was an ethical message and seemed to be identical with those morals that were considered to be reasonable at the time).

The hermeneutical problem with such a procedure is obvious: the general purpose of the Bible was identified from the perspective of reason, but people disagreed as to what was deemed reasonable. So the timeless message of the Bible varied considerably in the various critical interpretations. Thus it became indispensable further to reflect on the multidimensional relationship between history and hermeneutics. This relationship is multidimensional. First, biblical texts have to be conceived as historical texts, written at a certain point in history in a certain part of the world. Therefore, one has to understand the historical conditions under which these texts were produced. Second, the text is given to an interpreter with a tradition of interpretations. An interpreter is not free from this history of interpretation. Third, the interpreter is located at a certain point in history in a certain part of the world. Their interpretation is influenced by the conditions of the context in which they live.

Because of these dimensions of the relationship between history and hermeneutics it became the primary task of hermeneutics to acquire that which has been experienced as truth in the given tradition. With this shift in emphasis, the definition of hermeneutics as a method of interpretation and explication became secondary. Hermeneutics were confronted with the task to bridge the historical gap of 2000 years in order to enable an understanding of the old texts, including the acquiring of the meaning and the truth of the text in the personal existence of the reader and believer. Gotthold Ephraim Lessing (1729–1781) and the Danish philosopher Sören Kierkegaard (1813–1855) are well known proponents of this hermeneutical concept.

Their position was generalized. Hermeneutics became a theory of understanding all written and fixed articulations of life.[28] Hermeneutics has to explain how it is possible objectively to understand (written) articulations of life from other and foreign individuals from former times or foreign cultures. To understand means to comprehend them as possibilities for one's own self-understanding and one's own life (so one has to relate everything one is interpreting to one's own life as the Pietist Johann Jakob Rambach proposed).

The entire history of modern hermeneutics has been summed up excellently by the Lutheran New Testament scholar Rudolf Bultmann (1884–1976) in a seminal essay first published in 1950.[29] While numerous articles deal with more recent contributions to Lutheran hermeneutics, I shall finish my reflections on the development of Lutheran hermeneutics with the presentation Rudolf Bultmann's essay, which I believe better describes the hermeneutical problems and processes than many later hermeneutical writings.

In his essay, "The Problem of Hermeneutics," Bultmann recalls the rules of hermeneutics for the interpretation of texts in general, and especially of biblical texts. Every interpretation—be it brief or lengthy—has to start with a formal analysis of composition and style. In the composition of the text, individual phrases and parts have to be understood in the context of the whole, but the entire text also has to be understood in the light of individual phrases.

This insight creates the first hermeneutical circle of every interpretation. Understanding is progressing in a circle: the more I study a work in its entirety, the more I understand single phrases in and parts of the text; the deeper I go into the analysis of phrases and parts of a text, the better I understand the whole and so on.

The interpretation of texts in a foreign or classical languages has to follow the rules of the respective grammar, which has to be complemented by the knowledge of the individual use of these languages by the author (e.g., to understand a text in the Gospel of John one has to know ancient Greek as well the peculiarities of John's use of Greek). This then may be extended to

---

[28] Wilhelm Dilthey defined hermeneutics as the theory of interpretation that relates to all human objectifications. See Wilhelm Dilthey, "The Rise of Hermeneutics (1900)," in Wilhelm Dilthey, *Selected Works, Volume 4: Hermeneutics and the Study of History*, ed. Rudolf A. Makkreel and Frithjof Rodi (Princeton University Press) 2010, 235–60). Cf. Rudolf Makkreel, "Wilhelm Dilthey," in *Standford Encylopedia of Philosophy*, at **http://plato.stanford.edu/entries/dilthey/** .

[29] Rudolf Bultmann, "Das Problem der Hermeneutik," in *ZThK* 47 (1950), 47–69.

the knowledge of the use of the respective language at the time the text was written. This insight into the historical development of a language then has to be combined with the knowledge of the history of the time.

This insight into the process of interpretation creates another hermeneutical circle: the circle between a text and its time (or context). Part of this hermeneutical circle is the circle between our knowledge of a language and our knowledge of history.

Already Friedrich Schleiermacher (1768–1834) saw that the methodology described above may be too formal for many texts. We may not come to a true understanding of a text or writing by following the hermeneutical rules alone. Therefore, we cannot only look at the literal reality but have to consider the author as well as the interpreter. The formal, grammatical and historical interpretation needs to be supplemented by—as Schleiermacher calls it—a psychological interpretation. One has to understand a text as a moment in the life of a precise person (the author) or a group of people (the author belongs to). To understand this one needs not an objective but a subjective interpretation, in which the interpreter has to reproduce the original production of the text. The interpreter has to empathize with the author of the text for such a reproduction.

In the case of biblical texts, this psychological interpretation differs from the interpretation of a poem where the inner state of the author may be of interest. With regard to interpreting biblical texts, understanding the relationship between author and the object or event, that is, to the content they are writing about is vital. As Bultmann shows, here again we have another dimension of the hermeneutical circle, namely the circle between preconception and understanding. The interpreter of a text has certain preconceived ideas regarding the content of the text they are interpreting because they already have an established relationship with that which the text is talking about. In this relationship we can also find the interest of the interpreter in respect of the text and its content.

This insight creates a further hermeneutical circle between author and interpreter in their respective contexts. In more recent contributions to hermeneutics we find a difference whether this is already a full description of the circle between author and interpreter within their respective contexts or whether this circle is concentrated on the content of the text. (The one position is outlined by the German philosopher Hans-Georg Gadamer in his famous book *Truth and Method* published in 1960).[30] This position concentrates on understanding each other in communication (be it orally or literally, be it

---

[30] See Hans-Georg Gadamer, *Truth and Method*, 2nd rev. edition, transl. J. Weinsheimer and D. G. Marshall (New York: Crossroad, 2004).

with people present or absent, e.g., in a different place or time). The second position that emphasized the content, which is what our communication and understanding are about, is best represented by the French philosopher Paul Ricoeur.[31] It presupposes that we refer to a reality that is not identical to our individual perceptions and understandings when we communicate with each other and that we may reach a consensus regarding the realities we are communicating (literally or orally).

In a circle of interpretation, the interpreter has to establish what the text really wants to express. This process of interpretation is successful when the text reveals to the reader and interpreter human existence in its various manifestations, and questions the reader and interpreter if these possibilities could be their own. According to Bultmann, we come to a true interpretation and understanding of biblical texts when we hear the question the text is posing and discover what the text demands of us. Then the text opens up my own possibilities in life by calling me away from myself.

According to Bultmann, the whole hermeneutical process is a critical one: I (we) have to analyze and interpret the biblical text critically in order to critique ourselves. The main interest of modern Lutheran hermeneutics then is to interpret biblical texts not so as to find self-affirmation and self-reassurance but critically to listen to and hear what the biblical text has to tell us as the Word of God with respect to our lives in the various contexts and situations we live in.

The last part of the hermeneutical process may be the point where people from various contexts and situations share the results of their listening to and hearing the Word of God. It is an empirical experience that has been described frequently over the last decades. Results are not the same in all contexts. Therefore, the awareness of the contextual differences in God communicating Godself to people increased significantly over the last decades. There has been considerable discussion on how we should interpret this contextual plurality and the way in which the churches should deal with it. In my opinion, the first question has to be answered theologically and the second methodologically.

The theological interpretation of the plurality of contextual understandings of God's Word is in fact simple. It witnesses to the vividness and concreteness of God communicating Godself to God's people. The Triune God is not an imperialistic emperor who has only one message for everybody in the world and wants everybody to live their lives in the same way. The life of people

---

[31] See Paul Ricoeur, "The Conflict of Interpretations" in Don Ihde (ed.), *Essays in Hermeneutics* (Evanston: Northwestern University Press, 1974); Paul Ricoeur, *Interpretation Theory. Discourse and the Surplus of Meaning* (Fort Worth: Texas Christian Press, 1976); Paul Ricoeur, *Essays on Biblical Interpretation* (Philadelphia: Fortress Press, 1980); Paul Ricoeur, *From Text to Action. Essays in Hermeneutics II*, transl. K. Blamey and J. B. Thompson (Evanston: Northwestern University Press, 1991).

varies and God addresses the concrete lives of individuals and communities in their peculiarity. Lutheran churches should deal with this plurality of life accordingly. The church tentatively depicts and realizes what Christians hope for: a full, true and eternal life in the kingdom of God, in which we celebrate the full communion of humankind with God and with one another. Such an eschatological communion is possible only when those who are together are not dissolved in an undifferentiated unity or usurped by a few.

The way in which we deal with the plurality of understandings of God's Word and address requires a methodological answer. The churches have to work out procedures of communicating the various understandings with each other and have to enable such cross-cultural and cross-contextual communication in various ways by creating possibilities for people from various contexts to communicate their respective understandings of biblical texts and to reflect theologically on this.

Luther's Relevance for Contemporary Hermeneutics

Anni Hentschel

The words and actions of the medieval monk and scholar Martin Luther, primarily known as the initiator of the sixteenth-century Protestant Reformation in Europe, had far-reaching consequences not only for the church but society at large. Throughout the centuries, he has had his advocates and critics.

One of his own students is quoted as having said,

> Everyone who heard him knows what kind of man Luther was when he preached or lectured at university. Shortly before his death he lectured on ... Genesis. What sheer genius, life, and power he had! The way he could say it! ... in my entire life I have experienced nothing more inspiring. When I heard his lectures, it was as if I were hearing an angel of the Lord. .... Luther had a great command of Scripture and sensed its proper meaning at every point. Dear God, there was a gigantic gift of being able to interpret Scripture properly in that man.
>
> So said Cyriakus Spangenberg, preaching on "the great prophet of God, Dr. Martin Luther, that he was a true Elijah," on 18 February 1546. [...]
>
> His opinion differed from that of Luther's contemporary, Johannes Cochlaeus, theologian and bureaucrat in the service of Duke George of Saxony, who concluded the first (albeit polemical) biography of Luther:
>
> Let the pious consider what Luther accomplished through so many labours, troubles, and efforts of his depraved intention, by whose rebellious and seditious urging so many thousands of people have perished eternally ... and through whom all Germany was confused and disturbed, and let go all its ancient glory... .[1]

Here we have two decidedly different interpretations of one and the same man and the impact of his work: Luther the blessed "angel of God" or a damned and dangerous heretic. Were one to hear these two opinions without knowing the person's name one would probably not expect them to refer to one and the same person. This is a vivid example of the differences in the way in which

---

[1] Robert Kolb, *Martin Luther: Confessor of the Faith* (Oxford: University of Oxford Press, 2009), 1.

people interpret events and words. Interpretation depends on the interpreter's perspective; consequently, there is a wide range of interpretations of texts, even of biblical texts, which is what hermeneutics is all about.

As a theory of interpretation, the hermeneutical tradition stretches back to ancient philosophy. The question of how to interpret the sacred Scriptures was posed by outstanding Jewish and Christian theological thinkers such as Philo of Alexandria, Augustine or Thomas Aquinas, emphasizing especially their allegorical nature.[2] They were convinced that the literal sense of divinely inspired texts may conceal a deeper non-literal meaning that can only be discovered through systematic interpretative work. Scripture tells us something about history (literal sense). It teaches us about faith and belief (allegorical sense). It guides us in moral questions and shows us the way to live a good life (moral sense). After all, it shows us our end and the fulfillment of all things (anagogical sense).[3] Martin Luther started reading the Bible with this sense of the fourfold meaning.[4] Step by step he came to reject allegorical readings and to emphasize the literal sense of Scripture. It is in the wake of his principle of *sola scriptura* that a genuinely, modern hermeneutics gradually developed. Rejecting the authority of traditional interpretations of the Bible, Luther's concern was to set Scripture free to interact with the reader. Since then, it has been up to the individual reader to stake out their own path to the meaning of the text. This created new problems of communal reading and, consequently, hermeneutics in general changed.

While it is impossible to give an exhaustive overview of the main concerns of this huge field of research, one can single out some of the ways in which Luther's reading of Scripture impacted modern hermeneutics. Preoccupied with subjective piety and without developing anything like an explicit hermeneutical theory of understanding, his reflections on interpreting the Bible shaped and gave direction to modern hermeneutics.

Indeed, the task and necessity of interpreting actually begin in the Bible itself, and a part of this essay will give an insight into the Gospel according to John and its special way of handling the problem of hermeneutics. It is obvious that the author narrated and interpreted the story of Jesus in a strikingly different way to the so-called Synoptic Gospels.

---

[2] Cf. Karen Joisten, *Philosophische Hermeneutik* (Berlin: Akademieverlag, 2009), 35–47.

[3] Cf. ibid., 46f.

[4] On the way Luther used and rejected the fourfold meaning of Scripture, cf. Gerhard Ebeling, *Evangelische Evangelienauslegung. Eine Untersuchung zu Luthers Hermeneutik* (Darmstadt: Wissenschaftliche Buchgesellschaft, Fotomechan. Nachdr. der 1. Aufl. München 1942, 1968).

The starting point of the Reformation was Martin Luther's lecture on and exegesis of God's Word. The discovery of God's graciousness revolutionized all aspects of Luther's life and thought, but first and foremost it changed the way in which he read the Bible. Luther became a reformer because he discovered a new meaning to the Bible. Time and again he stressed the constitutive importance of the authority of God's Word. The fact that the Holy Scriptures embody ultimate authority served Luther as the unquestionable basis for all his theological argumentation. First of all, Luther saw his own role as interpreter of God's Word[5] and as a preacher of God's promises.[6]

In our quest for Luther's relevance for contemporary hermeneutics, three points seem to be especially relevant. First, Martin Luther was mainly interested in the literal sense of the text, questioning the authority of traditional interpretations of the Bible and thereby freeing the reader to uncover the meaning of a biblical text on their own. Second, according to him, Scripture alone is sufficient to make someone a Christian, i.e., to create faith by means of the Holy Spirit. Third, in spite of the individual aspects of reading the Bible, Luther pointed out that Scripture was its own interpreter and therefore the criterion of each interpretation and doctrine. It is necessary to recognize that Martin Luther was well aware of the fact, that the Bible often contradicts itself and is not fully coherent.

The literal sense (sensus literalis) of the text

My first point is Luther's appeal to the literal sense of the text. As a medieval scholar, Luther was well versed in scholastic theology and especially in the scholastic way of studying the Bible. At the beginning of his career as a scholar he interpreted the Bible by applying the fourfold meaning. The problem with this way of interpreting the Bible, especially with allegorical interpretations, was, according to Luther, that they tended to be too arbitrary.[7] Thereby, the Bible could too easily be used to confirm its interpreters' preconceived ideas. Especially, the church and its tradition held the authority to decide about the contents of the Bible, in other words, to decide about the truth. By reading

---

[5] See Athina Lexutt, *Luther* (Stuttgart: UTB, 2008), 29.

[6] Cf. The promise is especially singled out by Oswald Bayer, "Luther as an Interpreter of Holy Scripture," in Donald K. McKim, *The Cambridge Companion to Martin Luther* (Cambridge: University of Cambridge Press, 2003), 73–85.

[7] Cf. Ulrich Körtner, *Der inspirierte Leser. Zentrale Aspekte biblischer Hermeneutik* (Göttingen: Vandenhoeck und Ruprecht, 1994), 88–91.

Paul's letter to the Romans, Luther realized that the church's doctrine on God's grace differs from the justification sermon he had found in Paul's letter to the Romans. Luther was convinced that the truth concerning this important point could not be disputed. He came to reject allegorical readings and historical and grammatical aspects of interpretation became more and more important for him.[8]

In the preface to his commentary on Isaiah, he argues that the reader of the Bible needs to be equipped with the knowledge of the historical origins of the text and its author. The reader's efforts to grasp the meaning of a biblical text include grammatical and philosophical training as well as patient meditation. Nevertheless, Luther's aim is not to propose a correct interpretation or truth of the biblical texts, but to place the reader into a proper relationship to Christ. Luther's quest is not hermeneutical but theological and existential. Historical and philological information is the means of answering theological questions. Luther's 1518 *Pro veritate inquirenda et timoratis conscientiis consolandis* (For the Investigation of Truth and for the Comfort of Troubled Consciences) shows that the inquiry into truth aims at comforting troubled consciences. For Luther, the Bible was not in the first place a historical document to analyze what was preached and practiced at the time of Jesus and the first Christian communities and thus setting a norm for the readers' belief. Rather, his main concern was to comfort consciences that feared the last judgment. His theology is about human sin and God's grace, the sinning human being and the justifying God.[9] Through God's Word, God creates faith in the reader, bringing freedom and certainty to the individual. "Luther calls this type of speech act *Verbum efficax*, that which establishes communication, which frees one and gives one confidence: an effective, accomplishing Word."[10] The word of the law kills the sinner and the word of the gospel saves them; thereby reading the Bible can be seen as an event by which text and reader interact.

---

[8] Cf. Jörg Baur, "Sola Scriptura—historisches Erbe und bleibende Bedeutung," in Hans H. Schmid und Joachim Mehlhausen (eds), *Sola scriptura. Das reformatorische Schriftprinzip in der säkularen Welt* (Gütersloh: Mohn, 1991), 19–34, 32.

[9] *WA* 40II, 3281f.; cf. *LW* 12, 311. Cf. Oswald Bayer, *Martin Luther's Theology. A Contemporary Interpretation*, transl. Thomas H. Trapp (Michigan/Cambridge: W. B. Eerdman Co, 2008), 37–39. On the significance of justification for Martin Luther's understanding of Scripture, cf. the results of Ulrich Asendorf, *Lectura in Biblia. Luthers Genesisvorlesung (1535-1545)* (Göttingen: Vandenhoeck und Ruprecht, 1998), 491–503.

[10] Cf. Bayer, ibid., 53. Bayer identifies these promises—sentences spoken in the name of Jesus who brings salvation to the reader or hearer—as performative speech acts. He uses John L. Austin's theory that analyses the function of sentences. Cf. John L. Austin, "Performative und konstatierende Äußerung," in Rüdiger Bubner (ed.), *Sprache und Analysis. Texte zur englischen Philosophie der Gegenwart*, KVR 275 (Göttingen: Vandenhoeck und Ruprecht, 1986), 140–53. Promises such as "Your sin is forgiven," or "To you is born this day a Savior!" (Lk 2:11), can be understood as performative utterances effecting what they say. Cf. Bayer, ibid., 50–54.

It was Hans-Georg Gadamer who in the twentieth century explicitly pointed out that understanding means an event and not only the search for a fixed meaning in a text.[11] He warns us about taking too simply and straightforwardly the idea that a text reflects precisely that which was in the author's mind. It is not uncommon that a person says or writes something and the addressee asks if they really mean what they have said. In general, expressing our thoughts adequately is not easy. Words and phrases often have no clear and unique meaning, but it is the situation that determines their meaning.[12] Thus, texts once written take on a life of their own because they can be read in different contexts by different persons. Based on these insights, reader response theories have shown that one and the same text may be understood in a completely different way by different people because reading and understanding depend on the reader's context, especially in terms of the historical situation, cultural assumptions, literal knowledge, age and gender.[13]

Therefore, Gadamer points out that any act of reading or understanding is itself historical and interpretations are part of the endless stream of historical interpretations.[14] There is no objective perspective on an event or text. With reference to the Bible, this means that we cannot understand it from an objective and stable position. Human beings interpret events and words from their personal perspective which is historically and socially determined. Thus, Gadamer changed the classic hermeneutical circle clearly depicted by Schleiermacher, who had described the circularity of reading.[15] In order to gain the overall meaning of a text, we need to give proper attention to its details. But we can only appreciate the significance of the details if we have an impression of the general idea of the text. Therefore, we suggest a possible interpretation that has not yet been proven to be true. Schleiermacher called this initial

---

[11] Cf. Hans-Georg Gadamer, "Wahrheit und Methode. Grundzüge einer philosophischen Hermeneutik," in *Gesammelte Werke*, Band I (5. durchgesehene und erweiterte Auflage, Tübingen: Mohr, 1986), 476–78. Cf. Günter Figal, "Hermeneutik IV. Philosophisch," in *⁴RGG* UTB 8401 (Tübingen: Mohr, 2005), 1652–54; Joisten, op. cit. (note 2), 141–51.

[12] According to Martin Luther, words gain a new meaning in Jesus Christ if they are understood from the perspective of God's saving action in Christ. Cf. Karl-Heinz zur Mühlen, "Luther II Theologie," in *³TRE* (Studienausgabe, Berlin/New York: Walter de Gruyter, 2000), 530–67, here 543.

[13] Cf. An introduction to reader response theories with further literature is presented by Ralf Schneider, "Methoden rezeptionstheoretischer und kognitionswissenschaftlicher Ansätze," in Vera Nünning and Ansgar Nünning (eds), *Methoden der literatur- und kulturwissenschaftlichen Textanalyse* (Stuttgart: Metzler 2010), 71–90. Concerning the relevance of reader orientated theories for New Testament hermeneutics, cf. Oda Wischmeyer, *Hermeneutik des Neuen Testaments. Ein Lehrbuch*, NET 8 (Tübingen/Basel: Francke, 2004), 154–58.

[14] Gadamer, op. cit. (note 11), 281.

[15] Cf. Ingo Berensmeyer, "Methoden hermeneutischer und neohermeneutischer Ansätze," in Nünning and Nünning, op. cit. (note 13), 29–50, here 34f.

inductive hypothesis formation divination. It is necessary to continue reading the text clearly, using it to falsify or verify the hypothesis with respect to the details, called comparison. Schleiermacher was convinced that, with the help of this method, one could grasp the meaning of a text and that it was possible to understand the text better than its author by means of the psychological interpretation. The central point of this hermeneutical circle was not the dynamic interaction between text and reader, but the verification of the true and normative meaning of the text which is equivalent to the intention of the author.[16] In this way, the study of history becomes an indispensable tool in the process of unlocking the hermetic meaning and use of language.

Gadamer abandoned the idea that a text has a fixed meaning. Understanding does not mean grasping the meaning of a text, but rather to understand ourselves and our own historical situation. Thus, the hermeneutical interest turns to the reader and the reading process. For Gadamer, understanding is not restricted to understanding or interpreting texts, but understanding is the way we are in the world. Living means understanding; a human being is a being in language. In this crucial point, Gadamer, a student of Heidegger, accepted his teacher's ontological and existential turn in hermeneutics. With Heidegger, the hermeneutical circle refers to the interplay between one's understanding of the world and one's self-understanding. Gadamer points out that a human being is a being in language and only through language the world is opened for us.[17] In order to understand ourselves we need to understand that we live in a linguistically mediated historical culture. This has consequences for our understanding of texts. Being part of our own tradition, literary works do not present themselves to us as neutral objects of scientific investigation. They are rather part of our horizon that shapes our worldview. This aspect is not to be seen as a hindrance to our ability to understand or to analyze, but provides the basis for our understanding. In this context, Gadamer rehabilitates the merit of prejudices. Against the conviction of the Enlightenment, Gadamer claimed that it is neither possible nor desirable to set ourselves free from our prejudices in order to come to an objective viewpoint. Prejudices in the sense of being formed and informed by tradition are part of our humanness and the creative and necessary grounding of all processes of understanding.[18]

Because tradition is always alive and in constant productive development, we have no access to a historical text as it originally appeared to its contempo-

---

[16] Cf. Berensmeyer, ibid., 35.

[17] Gadamer, op. cit. (note 11), 387f.

[18] Ibid., 81.

raries. Trying to ascertain a text's exact historical context or the intention of its author is a wasted effort. The text is handed down to us through a complex and ever-changing process of interpretation, which becomes richer and more colorful as time passes. History, Gadamer pointed out, is always effective history, a fact that is not to be seen as a deficiency.[19]

We recognize the significance of a text by explicating and interpreting it and thus entering into a dialogical relationship with the past. Gadamer refers to this as the fusion of horizons. Our own prejudices are brought into a quasi discourse with the text. Through the effort of interpreting we understand that which at first appears alien and, in so doing, we participate in the production of a richer meaning so that we gain a better understanding not only of the text but also of ourselves. This reciprocal determination of text and reader is Gadamer's version of the hermeneutic circle.[20] To obtain a better understanding of a text and of ourselves, we must, in the first place, accept and be aware that our own viewpoint is determined by our own prejudices. In the second place, we have to give the text a chance to express its own conviction. Gaining knowledge of the text and knowing ourselves are interminable processes without determinate endpoints. Indeed, tradition, prejudice and understanding are part of a process, which is neither subjective nor objective, but to be seen as the constant interplay between text and interpreter.[21] Therefore, the hermeneutical circle in the sense of Gadamer is not a method, but it is foremost the description of the ontological basis of understanding.

Clearly, Gadamer is not primarily concerned with the alteration and formation of the subject but with the ongoing process of interpreting texts and the production of an increasingly encompassing context of meaning. Every single act of reception and interpretation is part of this historical process. A text is the result of an interpretation, and it is the initial point of new and other interpretations. Because of the new historical situation and individual prejudices of the reader, each reading brings forth a new understanding. Thus, the reading process does not provide final conclusions about a text's meaning for us, but an endless stimulation to further inquiry. The ideas we start with, our presuppositions and presumptions, determine how significant a text becomes for us. Gadamer primarily investigates the conditions of understanding as such and these conditions are not to be removed or bracketed by appealing to a certain method. Rather, these conditions open up the world to our understanding.

---

[19] Joisten, op. cit. (note 2), 145–47.

[20] Cf. Berensmeyer, op. cit. (note 15), 34–36.

[21] Ibid, 36.

What do his insights imply for the literal meaning of biblical texts? First of all, it shows that the historical interpretation based on Enlightenment ideals of critical reason and rationality does and cannot provide an objective and clear meaning of the biblical text based on the intention of its author. The widespread assumption that literal meaning is to be identified with historical meaning and the author's historical intention is the literal truth of a text is obviously neither reasonable nor valid. Each process of reading is a new event in which the horizon of the text fuses with that of the reader. Therefore no "objective" reading or interpretation is accessible. The consequence is that the reader with their own individual situation and knowledge is an essential part of the reading process in which meaning is produced by the interplay between text and reader.[22]

This theory poses two severe problems with regard to interpreting biblical texts. If—as Gadamer and especially reader response theories suggest—the reader is a necessary part of the reading process in order to produce meaning, how can the Bible be understood as *scriptura sui ipsius interpres* (Scripture clarifying itself)? Can the Bible still be *norma normans* if its meaning depends not only on the text, but also on the reader and the reading process? Secondly, how is it possible to talk about truth if it is not possible to single out one clear meaning of biblical texts? I will deal with these two questions by referring to Martin Luther and to modern hermeneutical and linguistic theories.

Sola scriptura and modern reception theories

The idea that a text may have just one meaning that once grasped remains firm and unchanging for all time is a modern concept, which neither the biblical authors nor Martin Luther subscribed to. Luther did not read the Bible primarily historically, but christologically. Nevertheless, the literal meaning is important for Luther because God has bound himself to God's Word. No one can interpret God's will without reading and interpreting the letters of the Bible. "Therefore we should and must insist that God does not want to deal with us human beings, except by means of his external Word and sacrament. Everything that boasts of being from the Spirit apart from such a Word and sacrament is of the devil."[23] For Martin Luther, "the proper subject of theology is man guilty of sin and condemned, and God the Justifier and Savior of

---

[22] Cf. Wischmeyer (note 13), 20.

[23] "Smalcald Articles (1537)," in Robert Kolb and Timothy Wengert (eds), *The Book of Concord. The Confessions of the Evangelical Lutheran Church* (Minneapolis: Fortress Press, 2000), 323; *BSLK* 455, 31–465.5.

man the sinner."[24] Theology is about the relationship between God and human beings. Therefore a good theologian must discern between law and gospel, the first one accusing and killing the sinners and the second one justifying and saving them.[25] By means of God's Word, God reveals God's wrath and grace. In the law, God speaks against the sinners, and in the gospel God speaks on their behalf. If a word is to be read as law or as gospel depends on the situation of the reader. Indeed, the theological differentiation between law and gospel is to be interpreted as an anthropological category. One and the same Word of God can come across the same reader as law or as gospel as the case may be. The hermeneutical punch line of this differentiation primarily relates to the reader or hearer of the Scripture and the ever new situation of reception. Correspondingly, it cannot be ignored that Luther's *sola scriptura* is not a formal principle denoting that the theological truth can be deduced solely from the letters of the text by using grammatical and philosophical tools. In fact, its content, the gospel of Christ, and its effect, the address of the sinner as the one to be saved by God's grace, show an authority that is highly material.[26] Thereby Luther's foundational thesis about the Holy Scripture as its own interpreter becomes clear. Only in this way can Scripture be the only source of faith, which excludes other authorities deciding about faith and the right interpretation of the biblical text. "[T]here is no book which teaches the faith except the Scriptures."[27] "Christ has two witnesses to his birth and his realm. The one is Scripture, the word comprehended in the letters of the alphabet. The other is the voice or the words proclaimed by mouth."[28] Faith comes by hearing the Word (Rom 10:17). The Augsburg Confession points to this key aspect of Lutheran theology by depicting that God gives the Holy Spirit by means of God's Word, creating faith in those who hear the gospel.[29] "Rather, its authority consists in that it works faith. The Lutheran tradition has articulated this in such a way that its *auctoritas normativa* follows from its *auctoritas causativa*—because of the authority that it has to create faith."[30] This is the obvious meaning of the Holy Scripture, or to state it more precisely, by

---

[24] *LW* 12, 311; cf. *WA* 40II, 3281f.; Cf. Bayer, op. cit. (note 9), 37–39.

[25] *WA* 40I, 207, 17f; cf. Bayer, ibid., 38.

[26] Cf. Lexutt, op. cit. (note 5), 39. Joisten argues for a formal criterion, cf. Joisten, op. cit. (note 2), 69. Concerning this question, cf. Ulrich H.J. Körtner, *Einführung in die theologische Hermeneutik* (Darmstadt: Wissenschaftliche Buchgesellschaft, 2006), 96.

[27] *LW* 52, 176; cf. *WA* 10I/1, 582, 12f.

[28] Ibid., 205; cf. *WA* 10I/1, 625, 14–16.

[29] "The Augsburg Confession," Article V, in *BC*, op. cit. (note 23), 40; cf. *BSLK* 58, 2–10.

[30] Bayer, op. cit. (note 9), 76f; Cf. Baur, op. cit. (note 8), 22, 30f.

means of God's grace becoming flesh in Jesus Christ, God gives us the faith that brings us to a new birth from God (Jn 1:13).[31] Thus the literal meaning of Scripture has a spiritual significance which depends on its reception, that is the situation—the belief or unbelief—of the reader. Its truth is not enclosed in the letters, but it occurs fresh and anew when reading Scripture this way. Because of the need to be applied to the present situation, it is always something new. Understanding occurs as a sort of event that happens where and to whom the Holy Spirit wants.[32]

Luther's differentiation between external and internal word can take us a significant step further. God gives God's spirit to no one except by means of the external word.[33] This explicit reference to Scripture is a quasi protection against theologians or preachers who maintain to possess the Holy Spirit and are convinced that they talk in the name of God. The written word gives each Christian the possibility to prove if such claims are right or wrong. Despite dark passages in the Bible, Luther points out that the external clarity of Scripture is sufficient for the reader to recognize Christ.

> The inner clarity of scripture is the light provided by the Holy Spirit, and thus the power of God himself, which enlightens the darkened heart of human being who is caught up in himself and is thus blind. [...] This light creates the human being anew, so that he confesses and recognizes himself to be a sinner and confesses and recognizes God as the one who justifies the sinner.[34]

The inner clarity of the Word is the process—initiated by the Holy Spirit—in which the reader applies the biblical text to their own life and situation. For Luther, reading Scripture is more than recognizing the letters and words of the biblical text, but there is an application of the text to the heart of each reader initiated by the Holy Spirit. By reading and interpreting the biblical text the reader is also interpreted by the text[35] or, in Gadamer's words, the horizon of the text and that of the reader fuse.

---

[31] Wilfrid Härle points out that the authority of Scripture has its basis in the revelation of Jesus Christ. Scripture is the witness of Jesus Christ, the authority of Scripture is derived from the authority of the revelation of Christ. Cf. Wilfried Härle, *Dogmatik* (Berlin/New York: de Gruyter, 1995), 113–17, 136–39.

[32] Cf. zur Mühlen, op. cit. (note 12), 549f.

[33] Cf. Reinhard Schwarz, "Martin Luther II. Theologie," in ⁴*RGG* UTB 8401 (Tübingen: Mohr, 2005), 573–88, 573. Cf. Baur, op. cit. (note 8), 30.

[34] Bayer, op. cit. (note 9), 84f.

[35] Cf. also Gerhard Ebeling, *Die Anfänge von Luthers Hermeneutik*, in *ZThK* 48 (Tübingen: Mohr, 1951), 172–230, here 175.

In light of Gadamer's central insight and modern reception theories, namely that the reader plays an essential part in producing the meaning of a text, the biblical text itself cannot be seen as complete and sufficient.[36] The external word, consisting of the letters, is necessary but not sufficient. Nonetheless, with Luther the reception of a biblical text, the internal word, can be thought of as having been inspired by the Holy Spirit. Thus, by the power of the Holy Spirit, the biblical text creates the reader needed, so that they can believe in God and understand the Bible as Holy Scripture. Thereby, the biblical text can be conceptualized as the *medium salutis* for the reader whose individual horizon fuses with that of the Bible in the process of reading. Gadamer's conclusion and that of other reception oriented hermeneuticians did not necessarily exclude the *sola scriptura* of Lutheran hermeneutics. But biblical hermeneutics must be grounded in the concept of a reader whose reading process is inspired by the Holy Spirit.[37]

Scriptura sui ipsius interpres and the story of Jesus Christ

From the above discussion, Scripture can still be seen as *medium salutis* that creates faith by the Holy Spirit inspiring the reading process. But how can one talk about the truth of a biblical text if one accepts that a text does not have a clear and objective meaning or content, one that only has to be detected by means of the right grammatical and philosophical methods? Because of the fusion each individual reader's horizon of the text on the one hand, and of the reading process on the other, each reader will construct another sense from a given text and its potential meaning.[38] Can the Bible strictly be seen as interpreter of itself? And, in what sense can the Bible be true if, like other texts, it does not have just one meaning?[39]

---

[36] This is the reason why Bayer clearly states that it is not the interpreter who makes sense of the text, but that the meaning of a text is expressed by the text itself. Cf. Bayer, op. cit. (note 9), 69. This opinion contradicts the insights of modern hermeneutics and of cognitive theories, cf. Peter Stockwell, *Cognitive Poetics. An Introduction* (London/New York: Routledge Chapman & Hall, 2002). Nevertheless, Bayer points out that reading is a circular process by which the reader interprets the text and the text interprets the reader. Cf. Bayer, op. cit. (note 9), 69.

[37] One concept of a reader oriented inspiration theory is proposed by Körtner, op. cit. (note 7), 88–113.

[38] Cf. concerning the process of reading, Peter Müller, *Verstehst du auch, was du liest? Lesen und Verstehen im Neuen Testament* (Darmstadt: Wissenschaftliche Buchgesellschaft, 1994), 120–60.

[39] Jacques Derrida raises the more radical question if a text can even have a meaning at all. Cf. Joisten, op. cit. (note 2), 185–95; Peter V. Zima, *Die Dekonstruktion. Einführung und Kritik* (Tübingen/Basel: Francke, 1994)

Martin Luther was well aware of the fact that reading the Bible literally would not lead to one firm and forever unchanging interpretation and theology. Thus, he pointed to the fundamental content of the Bible in order to establish its validity. Luther holds fast to the conviction that the Bible is clear and has one single meaning in those texts which are decisive for people's belief.

> For what sublime thing can remain hidden in the Scriptures, now that the seals have been broken, the stone rolled from the door of the sepulcher [Matt. 27:66; 28:2], and the supreme mystery brought to light, namely, that Christ the Son of God has been made man, that God is three and one, that Christ has suffered for us and is to reign eternally? Are not these things known and sung even in the highways and byways? Take Christ out of the Scriptures, and what will you find left in them? The subject matter of the Scriptures, therefore, is all quite accessible, even though some texts are still obscure owning to our ignorance of their terms.[40]

According to Luther, the entire Scripture, Old and New Testaments, must be read and interpreted on the basis of Jesus Christ, and each struggle for understanding must primarily examine that which deals with Jesus Christ. Christ himself is the Word that became flesh (Jn 1:14).

> [T]he measuring rod—the "canon"—is set up to establish what is absolutely truth, what is truly new, which will never become old. That which is eternally new has a name: Jesus Christ.
>
> [In this way] all the correct holy books agree, in that every one of them preaches and drives Christ home. That is also the correct touchstone for evaluating all books: to see whether they drive Christ home or not, since all Scripture shows Christ, Rom. 3 [:21], and Saint Paul desires to know nothing but Christ, 1 Cor. 2 [:2]. Whatever does not teach Christ is not apostolic, even if Saint Peter or Saint Paul teaches it. Once again, whatever preaches Christ, that is apostolic, even if it were to be presented by Judas, Annas, Pilate, and Herod.
>
> With absolute clarity one can see where the dividing line falls that distinguishes Christian theology from a Bible fundamentalism. One cannot state it any more incisively than Luther does when he articulates the criterion that uses specific, material content—against a claim for scriptural authority that is established on formal grounds.[41]

---

[40] *LW* 33, 25–26; cf. *WA* 18, 606, 24–31. Cf. Jörg Baur, *Sola scriptura*, op. cit. (note 8), 24f. He points out that Christ and Scripture are not identical, but Christ is the lord over Scripture.

[41] Cf. Bayer, op. cit. (note 9), 82, who is citing Bornkamm, *Luthers Vorreden zur Bibel*, 171. Cf. "The Preface to the Epistles of St. James and St. Jude," in *LW* 35, 396.

Therefore, Luther is far away from teaching a biblicism that treats every biblical text as having equal importance. He is quite aware of the fact that there are writings within the biblical canon promulgating "another theology" as, for example, Paul. He puts the books whose theology he regards as questionable, i.e., James, Jude, Hebrews and Revelation, at the end of the canon, but he does not exclude them from the canon.[42] Thereby, Luther differentiates between the biblical texts without denying one of them its status of being a canonical text. For Martin Luther, the unifying subject of the New Testament texts is Jesus Christ, and the criterion of a text being the Word of God is Jesus Christ.

The texts of the New Testament are neither historical nor biographical in a modern sense, but they describe who Jesus Christ was, they offer interpretations of this person and its relevance for their authors' belief and they present the story of Jesus Christ.[43] The name itself tells a story, identifying Jesus as the Christ, as the one who is sent and anointed by God.[44] Knowing something about Jesus Christ at the same time means learning something about God and God's story—love story—with Israel and the world. The New Testament texts are different interpretations of Jesus' worldly life. They are written by authors who wanted to describe how they experienced God through the story of Jesus and how this story became the foundation of and reason for their life and belief. They were not caught up in seeking to discover the history of Jesus Christ that lies behind the text—they did not even know the word "history" in our modern sense.[45] These texts present the Jesus Christ story that is not identical with the human Jesus and the life he lived, but they are interpretations and the earliest witnesses of Jesus Christ we have.[46] These texts can be seen as the first receptions of the story of Jesus Christ, reception comprehended as an interpretive understanding.

The hermeneutical process described by Gadamer can also be applied to understanding the New Testament texts.[47] The authors of the New Testament

---

[42] Cf. Baur, op. cit. (note 8), 25. Martin Luther was well aware of the fact that neither the Old nor the New Testament is free from errors.

[43] Eckart Reinmuth uses the term "Jesus-Christus-Geschichte" in order to discern the New Testament texts from the life of Jesus itself, from the "Geschichte Jesu Christi." "Jesus-Christus-Geschichte" is Reinmuth's term to describe all the interpretations and memories, which were told or written because of the fact that the narrators came across Jesus Christ who addressed them individually. Cf. Eckart Reinmuth, *Hermeneutik des Neuen Testaments. Eine Einführung in die Lektüre des Neuen Testaments* (Göttingen: Vandenhoeck und Ruprecht, 2002), 21.

[44] Cf. Ibid., 15.

[45] Martin Luther recognized the differences between the four gospels and the differences of their accounts, cf. *WA* 40I, 126, 20–22; Baur, op. cit. (note 8), 26. Luther preferred the Gospel according to John because John is the one who preached especially Jesus' words and his significance for belief. Cf. *WA* DB 6, 10, 25f.

[46] Cf. Reinmuth, op. cit. (note 43), 21.

[47] Cf. the analysis of the Gospel according to John by Takashi Onuki, *Gemeinde und Welt im Johannesevangelium. Ein Beitrag zur Frage nach der theologischen und pragmatischen Funktion des johanneischen "Dualismus,"* WMANT 56 (Neukirchen-Vluyn: Neukirchener Verlag, 1984).

lived in a historical context different from that of Jesus Christ, who was crucified two to nine decades before them. New questions concerning faith and Christian ethics arose, but it was not possible to ask Jesus as his disciples could do. The author of the Gospel according to John is the New Testament writer who approached this problem the most deliberately. He narrated the story of Jesus Christ from the perspective of the situation of his community, answering the community's questions by narrating anew his story, which means at the same time interpreting the Jesus Christ story from a new perspective. John is not primarily interested in historical facts or the chronology of the single events in Jesus' life, but rather points to the significance of Jesus—his life and his preaching and his relation to God who sent him—for the readers of his gospel. He explicitly points out that there is a difference between understanding Jesus and his significance before and after Easter.

After Easter, the Holy Spirit reveals to John's community that crucifixion and resurrection are descriptive of Jesus' life. God sent Jesus to save the world by means of his crucifixion and resurrection, both referred to as elevation in John. As John and his community came to know the significance of Jesus (Jn 8:28; 20:28), they understood Jesus' deeds and words as well as the traditions of his story in a new way (Jn 2:22; 7:39; 12:16; 14:26). If Jesus is revealed as God' Son at Easter, then he must have been God's Son since his birth, even before his birth. With this new insight, the author of John's Gospel perceives Jesus' whole life from a new perspective, that he truly is God's son. This is where according to Gadamer the horizons fuse.[48] The new perspective of the author, inspired by the Holy Spirit, who revealed to him the significance of Easter, led him to a new interpretation of Jesus' life. Now he saw Jesus' divinity also in his human being. But he was very conscious of the fact that this perspective was enabled after Easter by the Holy Spirit (Jn 2:22; 12:16). In theological terms, John's insight and that of his community can be described as revelation; in anthropological terms it can be seen as a new interpretation of the life of Jesus caused by the Easter event. This new insight was brought about by the Holy Spirit and influenced the narration of his story about Jesus Christ. John does not differentiate between events and interpretation because for him the events clearly show the nature of Jesus Christ. Furthermore, Jesus' words and deeds are relevant with regard to the community's current problems. In his narration, the author pays special attention to those aspects of Jesus' deeds, which in his opinion are of special significance for his community's present situation. The accounts about Jesus are seen together and presented together

---

[48] Cf. Ibid. 193–213.

with the experiences of the community. This dialectical way of narration is a consequence of this fusion of the two horizons that is especially obvious when Jesus teaches post-Easter insights before Easter (Jn 3:11; 9:4, 31, 17, 14 et al.).[49] The Gospel according to John can be seen as a new interpretation of the Jesus Christ story for John's community. Thereby the newly narrated and interpreted story can relate to questions and problems the contemporary addressees have. It combines two temporal horizons—that of the time of Jesus and that of the time of John and his community. These two horizons can be differentiated. This differentiation constitutes a hermeneutical tool which can help us better to understand the special construction of John. However, the two horizons cannot be separated because events and interpretation are intermingled.

Given this background, the question remains if this astonishing new interpretation of the Jesus Christ story is theologically legitimate. John repeatedly refers to the Holy Spirit.[50] The Paraclete serves to ensure access to Jesus' words and deeds by teaching the disciples and by reminding them of all his words (Jn 14:26).[51] The essential function of the Spirit according to John is related to proclamation and teaching.[52] The Spirit teaches everything and reminds them of Jesus (Jn 14:26). The Spirit also reminds the disciples that he will be their advocate in conflicts concerning the truth and that he leads them to the truth (Jn 16:8–15). The resurrected Jesus gives the Spirit to his disciples (Jn 7:39; 20:22). The Spirit supports and encourages the disciples in the trials of their belief. The truth of their belief cannot easily be demonstrated or defended against differing opinions. Therefore, the Spirit comforts them and ensures their belief. It is the Spirit who assures the disciples that the unbelief of the world is wrong, that Jesus did not fail but in truth returned to his Father and that the sovereign of this world is already convicted (Jn 16:9–11). In so doing, the Spirit enables the disciples to believe and reassures them that the unbelief and the mockery of the world cannot destroy their belief. He is the godly

---

[49] Onuki, op. cit. (note 47), 204.

[50] Concerning the pneumatology of John, cf. Udo Schnelle, *Theologie des Neuen Testaments* (Göttingen: Vandenhoeck und Ruprecht, 2007), 664–67; Udo Schnelle, *Johannes als Geisttheologe*, NT 40 (Leiden: Brill, 1998), 17–31; Rudolf Schnackenburg, *Das Johannesevangelium*, HThK IV/1 (Freiburg: Herder, 2001), 33–58.

[51] Cf. Schnelle, *Theologie*, ibid., 56, who speaks of a hermeneutical concept of memory in the Gospel of John. Concerning the significance of pneumatology for Martin Luther's hermeneutics, cf. Asendorf, (note 9), 184–89.

[52] Cf. Jörg Frey, *Vom Windbrausen zum Geist Christi und zur trinitarischen Person*, forthcoming. Jerome H. Neyrey, S.J., differentiates between the spirit reminding aspects of the past for the present on the one hand and the spirit teaching everything, i.e., teaching new things in the future. He writes: "Such future words cannot be tested or normed, although later we hear of cries for 'discernment of the spirit' (1 Jn 4:1; 1 Cor 12:10)." Cf. Jerome H. Neyrey, S.J., *The Gospel of John* (Cambridge: University of Cambridge Press, 2006), 250.

creator and preserver of their belief; he opens their eyes to the truth that can only be recognized by means of interpretative retrospection concerning Jesus Christ.[53] He himself leads them to the truth, to Jesus Christ who has gone to his Father (Jn 16:13).

The author of the Gospel according to John thus understands truth always in connection with God. Truth means God's truth that was revealed in Jesus (Jn 1:14, 17). Jesus, John the Baptist, the Spirit, they all testify to the truth which is related to God or to Jesus (Jn 5:33; 8:40-45; 15:26; 16:13; 18:37). The Johannine Jesus himself says, "Jesus said to him, 'I am the way, and the truth, and the life. No one comes to the except through me" (Jn 14:6). "You say that I am a king. For this I was born, and for this I came into the world, to testify to the truth. Everyone who belongs to the truth listens to my voice" (Jn 18:37). That implies that it is not the author of the Gospel who has the truth and can give it to others, but God reveals the truth time and again. And the truth is bestowed on human beings by the Spirit. The Spirit of the truth (Jn 14:17; 15:26; 16:13) testifies to Jesus; he testifies what he hears from God. By means of his teaching, the Spirit continues the teaching of Jesus (Jn 14:26; Jn 16:13–15), and he informs the disciples about the truth (Jn 20:22f). The aim of this teaching is primarily to comfort the disciples and accordingly the readers of the Gospel and to confirm their belief.[54] Since they can no longer see Jesus (Jn 7:39; 14:26), it is necessary that the Spirit recalls Jesus to their mind. According to John, truth is connected with God or Jesus and the witness to him testified by the Spirit. And this witness creates and confirms the faith of the disciples. This implies that the truth is not to be found in the letters of the gospel, but in the message of God freeing the hearers from sin (Jn 8:32ff) and turning their hearts to God and Jesus (Jn 14:6).[55]

This corresponds to Luther's insight that God is the one who works faith and salvation in everyone by means of Jesus Christ and by means of the Spirit who brings the word of Christ to the hearts of human beings. The truth is not included in the letters of the Bible, but the truth is in God and when someone reads the Bible and God's Spirit opens their eyes to the truth during the reading process, then faith can emerge and the reader comes into contact with the

---

[53] Frey, ibid.

[54] Cf. Schnelle, *Theologie*, op. cit. (note 50), 668; Onuki, op. cit. (note 47); Manfred Lang, "Johanneische Abschiedsreden und Senecas Konsolationsliteratur," in Jörg Frey and Udo Schnelle (eds), *Kontexte des Johannesevangeliums: Das vierte Evangelium in religions- und traditionsgeschichtlicher Perspektive* (Tübingen: Mohr, 2004), 365–412.

[55] Cf. Asendorf, op. cit. (note 9), 50f.; Wolf-Dieter Hauschild, "Geist/ Heiliger Geist/Geistesgaben IV. Dogmengeschichtlich," in ³*TRE* Studienausgabe (Berlin/New York: Walter de Gruyter, 2000), 196–217, here 208f.

truth. God's Word can be found there where Christ is preached. This is not only a dogmatic teaching; this is an event which happens ever anew during the reading process when God brings about the justification of the reader or hearer, when God forgives sin and thus frees from the fear of the future. Thus, neither interpretative skills nor hermeneutics can extract the truth from the words of the Bible, but it is only the Holy Spirit who can put the truth into words and create belief and assure salvation. This means that while the external word is necessary, it is the internal word which effects belief in each individual reader by means of the Spirit thereby demonstrating its truth. Therefore, it is not possible to grasp the truth of the Bible once and forever. It is necessary to read the Bible again and again and to let the Holy Spirit speak to one's own situation or, to put it in hermeneutical terms, to let the horizon of the text fuse with that of the reader. Each reading is at the same time an interpretation as we have seen before.

> What is thus of utmost importance [...] is that one take seriously that a *reciprocal relationship* exists between that which is fixed and that which is changeable, between the verbal and the written, between the living Spirit and the fixed literal text. Whoever does not take this to be true misses the point about the unique character of the authority of Holy Scripture, which is none other than the authority of the living God himself. Luther took into account that what is fixed and what is open-ended both exist concurrently.[56]

This is in agreement with modern hermeneutical insights pointing out that a fixed text produces ever new interpretations during each reading process. The material criterion to prove if an interpretation or even a biblical text is good is its agreement with Christ and his message that brings faith and deliverance to human beings. Whatever Jesus Christ teaches in this way is God's Word.

> When Christ is preached as the prophets and apostles present him, then when the preacher speaks, God speaks and the Holy Spirit produces faith, hope, love, and a joyful new life. "The poor Holy Spirit," said Luther, "doesn't want anything else to be preached." [...] "The preachers have no other office than to preach the clear sun, Christ. Let them take care that they preach thus or let them be silent."[57]

---

[56] Bayer, op. cit. (note 9), 80f.

[57] Fred W. Meuser, "Luther as Preacher of the Word of God," in Donald K. McKim, *The Cambridge Companion to Martin Luther* (Cambridge: University of Cambridge Press, 2003), 136–148, here 138.

The inner clarity of the Word shows the truth of the Word, but it is the gift of the Holy Spirit and does not become the possession of the human being. Similarly, a publication of the Protestant Church in Germany states that, from a Christian perspective, truth cannot be understood as a true and verifiable statement about reality, but truth is an event that happens. God reveals Godself by means of God's Word as the one that a person can rely on. From a Christian perspective, truth happens when God is revealed as a God who frees me from sin and who creates belief by the power of the Holy Spirit.[58] The human witness represents this truth, but like every human action this witness is fallible.[59] Each reading, understanding and interpreting is a human reaction to God's saving action in Jesus Christ and therefore fallible and not perfect. This holds true also for the Holy Scripture itself narrating, with human words, experiences with God and especially the story of Jesus Christ.[60] Truth happens when someone reads the Scripture and recognizes that Christ is its center and that Christ offers them salvation and freedom. But every human reading and interpretation is only an approach to the truth, an answer to the message God has spoken to me.

Reinmuth suggests that it is senseless, even dangerous, inhuman and fatal solely to rely on the letters of the New Testament.[61] John 8:44 can serve as an alarming example. The Johannine Jesus accuses his opponents, the Jews, of evildoing, of lying and murder, calling them sons of the Devil. This biblical text was used, or rather misused over the centuries to legitimate crimes against the Jewish people. New Testament texts are themselves interpretations of the story of Jesus Christ and the critical question is if they are consistent with this story of Jesus Christ that they tell in a new way.[62] The Jesus Christ story or in Martin Luther's words "what drives home Christ"[63] is the material criterion to prove Scripture and its interpretations.

> Preaching the Jesus of the Gospels always meant preaching his love for sinners. Notice how gently the Savior deals with wounded spirits, Luther said to the Wittenbergers, how friendly Jesus is to publicans and sinners, how patiently he

---

[58] Cf. EKD Texte 77, *Christlicher Glaube und nichtchristliche Religionen. Theologische Leitlinien* (Hannover 2003), 14, at **www.ekd.de/download/Texte_77.pdf** .

[59] Concerning the relation between human sin and human understanding of scripture, cf. Baur, op. cit. (note 8), 37, 41.

[60] With reference to the differentiation between God and Holy Scripture, cf. ibid., 21.

[61] Cf. Reinmuth, op. cit. (note 43), 37.

[62] Ibid.

[63] Cf. Thomas H. Trapp, "Translator's Preface," in Bayer, op. cit. (note 9), xiii, concerning this translation of Luther's dictum, "Was Jesum Christum treibet."

bears with the disciples who misunderstood him, what compassion for lepers, for the widow whose son had died, for blind Bartimaeus, and for the woman taken in adultery. When Luther preached to people who, like himself, had been taught to think of God and Jesus as threatening and distant [...], Luther delighted in speaking of the Lord as one who made ordinary people feel at home in his presence. Comfort and assurance were high priorities for Luther.[64]

Luther's foundational thesis that Scripture is its own interpreter not only refers to the letters and words, but especially to the effect that a biblical text or its preaching has and which must be brought into agreement with the central message about the subject of theology that "man [is] guilty of sin and condemned, and God the Justifier and Savior of man the sinner."[65]That the essence of the reading process is not solely to be found in the text itself, but especially in the reading process by which a text gains its significance for the reader, is a salient insight of modern hermeneutical and linguistic theories[66] but would not at all be surprising news for Martin Luther. Luther was well aware of the role of the individual reader in the reading process since he considered faith to enlighten the understanding of the Bible while unbelief darkens it. The written word can only create faith when the Holy Spirit works through these very words on the heart of the reader.[67] Therefore, a formal understanding of the Lutheran *sola scriptura* misses the point about his hermeneutical insights for he knew that the texts of the Bible cannot be brought together to form an unambiguous theological system.

Consequences for a responsible Protestant interpretation of Scripture

In dealing with some aspects of modern hermeneutics, we have seen that even such words as "meaning," "reading," "history," or "truth" are not really clear and have changed their meaning over the centuries. The author of the Gospel of John had no concept of what we now describe as "historical." Of course, for John "truth" is not the accordance of the description with the historical facts but

---

[64] Meuser, op. cit. (note 57), 138f.

[65] *LW* 12, 311, cf. *WA* 40II, 3281f.; cf. Bayer, op. cit. (note 9), 37–39.

[66] Cf. Roland Barthes conclusion that writing is a proposal and the reader defines its significance. Roland Barthes, *Literatur oder Geschichte* (Frankfurt/M.: Suhrkamp, 1969), 126.

[67] Cf. e.g., *WA* 5, 537, 12. Cf. concerning the problem of tradition and interpretation Henning Paulsen, "Sola Scriptura und das Kanonproblem," in Hans H. Schmid/ Joachim Mehlhausen, *Sola Scriptura. Das reformatorische Schriftprinzip in der säkularen Welt* (Gütersloh: Mohn, 1991), 61–78, here 65–78.

truth is personal, Jesus Christ himself is the truth. If the meaning of relevant words is ambiguous, how then can a sentence, i.e., a network of words, or even a whole text, a network of sentences, be clear at all? Hermeneutics warns us about taking too simply the idea that a biblical text says what I think it means. Thereby, the insights of modern hermeneutics and linguistic theories help us not to make absolute claims regarding our understanding of a biblical text. But, given this situation, how can we interpret the Bible at all? There was neither a perfect writer nor is there a perfect reader. It was Martin Luther himself who warned us that sin darkens human understanding, even the understanding and interpretation of biblical texts. Indeed, Martin Luther knew that Christ alone can be the teacher of the truth and the master of interpreting God's will. He wished explicitly that

> each person ought to refrain from mentioning my name, and not call one-self a Lutheran, but rather, a Christian. What is Luther? Is it not true that the teaching is not mine! In the same vein, I have been crucified for no one, Saint Paul [1 Cor. 3:4] would not allow it that the Christians would be called Pauline or Petrine, but just Christians. How did it happen to me that I, a poor, stinking sack of maggots, should have someone call the children of Christ after my unworthy name? Not so, beloved friends! Let us eliminate the names that identify various parties and just call ourselves Christians, because of Christ, whose teaching we have... I am and wish to be master of no man. I have, along with the community, the one, universal teaching of Christ, who alone is our master [Mt 23:8].[68]

The insights of modern hermeneutic and linguistic theories have shown that reading is a process that includes the cooperation of the reader. Therefore, reading is not only the reception of the meaning a text proposes, but reading is an action of the reader who is constructing the significance of the text in cooperation with the text.[69] Indeed, thinking about hermeneutics means thinking about human actions and this includes an ethical dimension. Based on his semiotic approach, Stefan Alkier understands interpreting as acting with signs. He formulates three rules for ethics of biblical interpretation.

---

[68] *WA* 8, 685, 4–16 The English translation is cited from Bayer, op. cit. (note 9), 8.

[69] Cf. Müller, op. cit. (note 38), 120–60; Stefan Alkier, "Ethik der Interpretation," in Markus Witte (ed.), *Der eine Gott und die Welt der Religionen* (Würzburg: Religion-&-Kultur-Verlag, 2003), 21–41, here 22f.; The relevance of Martin Luther's hermeneutics in the context of modern hermeneutics starting with the text analyses, cf. Asendorf, op. cit. (note 9), 51–67.

The first criterion he calls the principle of reality, which means that the text is a counterpart to the reader.[70] Each reading or interpretation must be reviewed with the question if a reader accepts a biblical text as something different, without trying either to use the text to legitimate their own preconceived ideas or blindly to accept everything the text proposes. Interpreters should attempt to explicate aspects of the text considering that an interpretation is never identical with its basis. In Gadamer's words, the biblical text has its own historical horizon which cannot be grasped totally by means of interpretation. Even if a reader reads a text or a book in a different biographical situation, they can gain the experience that different aspects of the same text become important for them according to their personal circumstances. In hermeneutical terms, the text can be regarded as autonomous in reference to its readers.

The second criterion for Alkier, that here is translated as the principle of joint practice, takes into account that there are different people who read and interpret the Bible with different results.[71] Interpretations that propose being the one and only true interpretation of Scripture are to be criticized. This criterion should not lead to disinterest and casual thinking that each reader can make their own path to heaven. Different interpreters of the Bible should work together in trying to discover the significance of a text for today. Interpretations that differ from my own can be consulted in trying to find an important aspect of the text I did not recognize during my own reading process. But all interpretations are to be respected because of the contingency of each interpretation, since, spoken with Luther, it is the Spirit who reveals individually the inner clarity of the word to the heart of each reader or, in terms of modern hermeneutical theories, because of the contingency of human thought. If, however, the fruits of interpreting a biblical text are in contradiction to that which drives Christ home, then the content of an interpretation is to be criticized.

Alkier's third criterion is the principle of context.[72] A good interpretation is aware of its own cultural or political situation. Gadamer has pointed out that the reader's horizon influences the reading and interpretation of a text. Therefore, it is reasonable to explicate one's own position and personal interests combined with the reading. The idea of an objective interpretation—even in a scientific context—can no longer be sought for in the light of the given hermeneutical and linguistic insights.

---

[70] Cf. Alkier, op. cit. (note 69), 32–36.

[71] Ibid., 36–38.

[72] Cf. Alkier, op. cit. (note 69), 38f.

This third criterion has also to be borne in mind when assessing the relevance of Martin Luther's understanding and interpretation of Scripture for modern biblical hermeneutics. He, too, interpreted the Bible and wrote his voluminous works in a specific historical situation that influenced his reading of Scripture. Thus, both his interpretations and the effects of his interpretations must be thought about carefully in order to see if they are in accordance with the story of Christ. Surely our evaluation of Martin Luther's teaching and its effects will lead us to a differentiated approach recognizing assets and drawbacks of his work and influence.

An Introduction to the Gospel of John and Questions of Lutheran Hermeneutics

Craig R. Koester

My task is to introduce the Gospel of John in a way that can contribute to the discussion of Lutheran hermeneutics. There are three main dimensions for us to consider: First, the Gospel of John itself, second, the Lutheran theological heritage and third, the contexts in which the members of the Lutheran communities live and work. In this introduction, I would like to make some observations about the literary shape of the Gospel, and to do so theologically in light of Luther's provocative comments about John's message. After that, I will turn to the context in which this Gospel was written and first read. My hope is that these comments about the literary and theological dimensions of the Gospel, along with a sense of its ancient context, can contribute to the conversation about its significance for modern contexts.

When I refer to Luther's provocative comments about John's Gospel, I am thinking of his "Preface to the New Testament" of 1522. This is where he says that "John's gospel is the one, fine, true, and chief gospel, and is far, far to be preferred over the other three and placed high above them."[1] The reasons Luther gives for recommending John so highly include both a literary observation and a theological claim. The literary observation is that John gives more attention to Jesus' words than to his miracles and other works. The theological claim is that "the works do not help me, but his words give life." His comment recalls John 6:63, where Jesus says, "The words that I have spoken to you are spirit and life." These comments give us a starting point. They invite us to consider how John's Gospel relates "words" and "life," and how these in turn are related to the miracles or signs in Jesus' public ministry, as well as to his crucifixion and resurrection.

---

[1] Martin Luther, "Preface to the New Testament," in *LW* 35, 357–62, esp. 362; cf. *D. Martin Luthers Werk: Kritische Gesamtausgabe. Die Deutsche Bibel* 6 (Weimar: Hermann Böhlaus, 1929), 10.

The Word

The opening words of John's Gospel focus on a singular word. The text says, "In the beginning was the Word, and the Word was with God, and the Word was God" (Jn 1:1). Interpreters have often noted that the Greek term *logos* has a rich and evocative range of meanings. It resonates with Jewish traditions about God's power and wisdom, as well as with philosophical teachings about the energy that shapes the universe.[2] But it is helpful to keep in mind that the term "word" or *logos* is often used for the spoken word (e.g., Jn 2:22; 4:37; 5:24). In a basic sense, a word is an act of communication. A word is a form of address, a means of engagement. To say that "in the beginning was the Word" is to say that in the beginning is God's act of communication.[3]

The Gospel assumes that God can communicate with the world because God's Word created it. John says that through the Word "all things came into being" (Jn 1:3). The scope of this activity is cosmic. John sets the story of Jesus in the context of God's relationship to the whole world, and he indicates that the goal of God's activity is "life" (*zōē*). The Gospel says that in the Word "was life, and the life was the light for human beings" (1:4). It is important to note that in this Gospel "life" has multiple dimensions. At one level, it is physical. People are alive when their hearts are beating and their lungs are breathing. At this level, death occurs when the heart stops and the body ceases to function. But, at another level, life has wider theological dimensions. People were created by God for relationship with God, and they are truly alive when they relate rightly to the God who made them.[4]

But here is where the complexity comes in. The Gospel assumes that there are major barriers to life in this full theological sense. The opening lines picture the Word offering light to a world that is permeated by darkness. If light signifies a positive relationship with God, then darkness shows alienation

---

[2] On some of the proposed connotations of the logos idea, see Raymond E. Brown, *The Gospel According to John*, 2 vols, Anchor Bible 29-29A (Garden City, NY: Doubleday, 1966, 1970), vol. 1, 519–24; Peter M. Phillips, *The Prologue of the Fourth Gospel: A Sequential Reading*, Library of New Testament Studies 294 (London: T. & T. Clark, 2006), 71–141; Daniel Rathnakara Sadananda, *The Johannine Exegesis of God: An Exploration into the Johannine Understanding of God*, Beihefte zur Zeitschrift für die neutestamentliche Wissenschaft und die Kunde der älteren Kirche 121 (Berlin and New York: Walter de Gruyter, 2004), 151–72.

[3] The theme of communication is reflected in the way that the Word (*logos*) who is God according to John 1:1 is the one who is said to make God "known" (*exēgēsato*) according to 1:18. Interpreters sometimes use the term "revelation" for this central action of communication in John's Gospel. See D. Moody Smith, *The Theology of the Gospel of John* (Cambridge: Cambridge University, 1995), 75.

[4] On "life," see Craig R. Koester, *The Word of Life: A Theology of John's Gospel* (Grand Rapids: Eerdmans, 2008), 30–32, 44–47, Brown, op. cit. (note 2), vol. 1, 505–8.

from God. Where light indicates goodness, darkness depicts evil. Since light means life, then darkness signifies death.[5] In the Gospel, the world (*kosmos*) is God's creation, and yet it is a world whose people have become alienated from their Maker. The prologue can say that the Word that is true light "was in the world, and the world came into being through him; yet the world did not know him. He came to what was his own, and his own people did not accept him" (Jn 1:10–11).

Alienation from God is a fundamental problem that must be overcome if people are to have the life for which God created them. Here, again, the notion of "Word" as communication is helpful. At an ordinary level, people build relationships through communication. They speak words that can be heard with the ear in order to overcome the barrier of silence and facilitate understanding. But people often find that spoken words are not enough, so they also send messages or "words" in other ways. People communicate through gestures that can be seen with the eyes. They might smile or frown or use their fingers to point at something. And they will also use touch, by shaking someone's hand. At a human level, things that can be heard, seen and touched are all forms of communication that can build relationship.

God communicates with human beings in a human way when God sends God's Word in the flesh (*sarx*, Jn 1:14). God communicates by the words Jesus speaks, by the actions Jesus does, and by the death Jesus dies. In all of this, God addresses the world that has become alienated from God with the goal of restoring the relationships that give life. The Gospel refers to this renewed relationship as believing or trusting (*pisteuō*), which is a major theme.[6] When the Word of God evokes faith, it overcomes the world's alienation from God by creating a relationship of trust, which is true life (1:12).

By introducing the Gospel as the story of the Word made flesh, these opening lines invite readers to consider each episode that follows from the perspective of communication.[7] Whether the text narrates a dialogue, recounts a sign, or

---

[5] On sin in John's Gospel, see Smith, op. cit. (note 3), 81–82; Rainer Metzner, *Das Verständnis der Sünde im Johannesevangelium*, Wissenschaftliche Untersuchungen zum Neuen Testament 122 (Tübingen: Mohr Siebeck, 2000). On sin, evil, and the image of darkness, see Craig R. Koester, *Symbolism in the Fourth Gospel: Meaning, Mystery, Community*, 2nd ed. (Minneapolis: Fortress, 2003), 141–50.

[6] References to believing (*pisteuō*) appear throughout the Gospel. Believing in its basic sense is trusting, though faith also has cognitive content. For example, the statement of purpose in Jn 20:30–31 refers to believing that Jesus is the Christ and the Son of God, which involves some degree of comprehension. Words for believing are related to knowing, receiving and coming to God and Jesus. On John's vocabulary of faith, see John Painter, *The Quest for the Messiah: The History, Literature and Theology of the Johannine Community* (Edinburgh: T. & T. Clark, 1991), 327–33. The connection between believing and having life is a regular feature in John (Jn 3:15, 16, 36; 5:24; 6:40, 47; 11:25; 20:31).

[7] The term *logos* is not used as a Christological title outside the prologue, but its prominence in the opening lines gives a perspective on the narrative that follows.

tells the story of Jesus' crucifixion and resurrection, the central point is how the Word addresses the world in a manner than can create faith and bring life.

Words and actions or "signs"

The Gospel's opening portrayal of the Word of God generally fits well with the emphasis of Luther's *Preface*, which I noted earlier. A more complex question is how Jesus' words relate to his actions in the Gospel as a whole. Luther claimed that, in comparison to the other gospels, John gave great attention to what Jesus said and much less attention to what Jesus did during his ministry. For Luther, this was just fine since the words are what gives life.[8] But other readers of John's Gospel would argue that the miracles or "signs" that Jesus performed are essential to the message. Instead of downplaying the miracles, they give them a central part in the story. And this difference in perception gives us an opportunity to explore some of the key features of the narrative.

John's account of Jesus' public ministry is structured around seven miracles or "signs" (*sēmeia*). The first is turning water into wine (Jn 2:1–11). Then there are several healings (Jn 4:45–5:18; 9:1–41), along with feeding the five thousand and walking on the sea (Jn 6:1–21). The seventh sign is raising Lazarus from the dead (Jn 11:1–44). After the resurrection, there is an eighth miracle, which is the great catch of fish (Jn 21:1–14).[9]

The signs are revelatory. They convey the "glory" (*doxa*) of God and Jesus in a manner that is accessible to the senses (Jn 2:11; 11:40). Signs manifest the power and presence of God in ways that can be seen and tasted and felt. Their importance seems clear in the Gospel's concluding statement of purpose, which says

> Now Jesus did many other signs in the presence of his disciples, which are not written in this book. But these are written so that you may come to believe that Jesus is the Messiah, the Son of God, and that through believing you may have life in his name (Jn 20:30–31).

In many ways, John's attitude toward the signs seems to be quite positive.[10]

---

[8] Luther, op cit. (note 1), 362.

[9] Some interpreters have argued that one of the sources for John's Gospel was a collection of Jesus' signs that had been put together as an aid to proclamation. On the proposals, see Gilbert van Belle, *The Signs Source: Historical Survey and Critical Evaluation of the Semeia Hypothesis* (Leuven: Leuven University, 1994).

[10] Udo Schnelle, *Antidocetic Christology in the Gospel of John* (Minneapolis: Fortress, 1992), 173–75; Mari-

Yet, the Gospel also reflects ambivalence about the signs. The narrative shows that the signs are ambiguous and that people can interpret them in completely different ways, depending on their prior assumptions and perspectives. Signs evoke hostility and unbelief as often as they evoke faith. For example, Jesus healed a blind man on the Sabbath (Jn 9:14). We might expect the meaning of this action to be clear, but it was not. For the man who received the healing, the power to heal showed that Jesus was from God (Jn 9:32–33). But, for the Pharisees, this same sign showed that Jesus was a sinner. They reasoned that Jesus had violated the command to refrain from work on the Sabbath because he had made mud and performed a healing, even though the blind man's life was not in any danger (Jn 9:16). The Gospel shows us how the same sign could be perceived in diametrically opposed ways.

The same problem of interpretation occurs in connection with other signs.[11] When Jesus feeds the five thousand with bread and fish, the crowd thinks he is running a campaign for public office, and they want to make him their king. So because of their misunderstanding, Jesus has to escape from them (Jn 6:14–15). The crowd keeps looking for him, hoping for another sign in the form of more free food (Jn 6:22–30), and when Jesus calls himself the bread of life, they turn away in unbelief (Jn 6:41, 66). The writer of the Gospel understands all too well that signs can generate confusion and hostility rather than faith. Therefore, at the close of Jesus' public ministry, the writer comments, "Although he had performed so many signs in their presence, they did not believe in him" (Jn 12:37).

Because the signs are ambiguous, the Gospel must shape the readers' perspectives through words. Hermeneutically, this is important. The signs do not stand alone. People respond properly to the signs that they see when their perspectives are shaped by the words that they hear. Let me show you what I mean by turning to the beginning of Jesus' public ministry, where discipleship begins with the spoken word, not with a sign, and the disciples' initial faith perception is later confirmed by the miracle that Jesus performs at Cana.

Things begin when John the Baptist says, "Behold the Lamb of God" and this spoken message moves two of his own disciples to follow Jesus (Jn 1:35–37). It seems odd to find Jesus being called the Lamb of God at this early point in the Gospel. After all, this is the moment when his public ministry begins. It is the first time Jesus appears in the narrative portion of the text. Readers who already know the story of Jesus can see that introducing him as the Lamb of God anticipates his crucifixion.[12] It points to his coming self-sacrifice for the sake of

anne Meye Thompson, *The Humanity of Jesus in the Fourth Gospel* (Philadelphia: Fortress, 1988), 63–64.

[11] See Koester, op. cit. (note 5), 79–140.

[12] Some downplay the sacrificial dimension, e.g., John Ashton, *Understanding the Fourth Gospel* (Oxford: Clarendon, 1991), 491; cf. Esther Straub, *Kritische Theologie ohne ein Wort vom Kreuz*, Forschungen zur

the world. And in John's Gospel it is this message that generates a willingness to follow, even though the implications of what this means are not yet clear. The disciples who hear and then accompany Jesus soon learn that the sacrificial Lamb is also the Messiah, who was promised in the Scriptures of Israel (Jn 1:41, 45). What generates faith (*pisteueis*, Jn 1:50) and a sense of Jesus' identity among this early circle of disciples are the words that are spoken and heard.

When Jesus performs a sign in the next chapter, it confirms and deepens what the disciples have already come to believe. John says that Jesus attended a wedding, where he turned the water in six stone jars into a lavish gift of wine (Jn 2:1–10). On its own, the wine miracle could be interpreted in very different ways. For example, people with a traditional Greek or Roman background might think that anyone who provided this much to drink must be a new Dionysus or Bacchus, the god of wine and festivity.[13] So here the Gospel's literary context is crucial. The writer says, "Jesus did this, the first of his signs, in Cana of Galilee, and revealed his glory; and his disciples believed in him" (Jn 2:11). John has shown that the disciples accompany Jesus to Cana because they already believe that he is the Messiah promised in the Scriptures (Jn 1:41, 45). From this biblical perspective, the wine probably recalls biblical passages where abundant wine is associated with messianic kingship (Gen 49:10–11; Amos 9:11–13), so that the sign confirms the belief that Jesus fulfills Scripture.[14] The sign is a form of communication, but it does not stand alone. The verbal encounters that precede it shape the perspectives needed to discern its meaning.

The pattern continues in the second sign, in a royal official's son is seriously ill at Capernaum. The official quickly travels halfway across Galilee, so that he can ask Jesus to come down and heal the boy (Jn 4:46–47). But instead of following the man to his home, Jesus gives the man a word: "Go, your son will live" (Jn 4:50a). This word creates a new kind of crisis. The man had expected Jesus to come along with him, but Jesus does not. Instead, Jesus wants the man to believe the promise of life before he has seen any signs. The official is being asked to travel back home, halfway across Galilee, without knowing for sure

---

Religion und Literatur des Alten und Neuen Testaments 203 (Göttingen: Vandenhoeck & Ruprecht, 2003). But most interpreters recognize that the Lamb imagery has sacrificial connotations and that it anticipates the crucifixion. See Thomas Köppler, *Die theologia cruces des Johannesevangeliums*, Wissenschaftliche Monographien zum Alten und Neuen Testament 69 (Neukirchen-Vluyn, Neukirchener, 1994), 67–101; Jörg Frey, "Die '*theologia crucifixi*' des Johannesevangeliums," in Andreas Dettwiler and Jean Zumstein (eds), *Kreuzestheologie im Neuen Testament*, Wissenschaftliche Untersuchungen zum Neuen Testament 151 (Tübingen: Mohr Siebeck, 2002), 169–238, esp. 200–219; Sadananda, op. cit. (note 2), 21–30.

[13] See C. H. Dodd, *Historical Tradition in the Fourth Gospel* (Cambridge: Cambridge University, 1963), 224–25; C. Kingsley Barrett, *The Gospel According to St. John* (Philadelphia: Westminster, 2nd ed. 1978), 151–55, 188–89.

[14] See Brown, op. cit. (note 2), vol. 1, 104–105.

whether the boy is alive or dead. All the official has to go on is Jesus' word, and yet he believes (Jn 4:50b). This is what faith looks like from a Johannine perspective. It means trusting in the promise before one sees its fulfillment.[15] So when the man gets home and learns that the boy is alive, the sign confirms the faith that began with Jesus' word.

The third sign involves the healing of a man by the pool of Bethzatha, and it highlights the problem of interpretation (Jn 5:1–9). This sign generates opposition since it was done on the Sabbath, and the Jewish authorities persecute Jesus (Jn 5:10–16). So the Gospel must shape the perceptions of the readers by the words Jesus speaks.[16] From the perspective of the Jewish leaders, the sign shows that Jesus opposes the will of God because he seems to violate the command to refrain from work on the Sabbath. In response, the discourse argues that Jesus is actually carrying out the will of God. It makes the point that the work of God is to give life, and God gives life each day of the week. When Jesus heals, he is doing the same thing; he carries out the will of God by giving life. Whether healing occurs on the Sabbath or any other day of the week, it is deeply consistent with the creative will of God (Jn 5:17–22).

Words also shape the way in which readers are to see the other signs. For the sake of brevity, I shall move to the seventh sign, which is the raising of Lazarus. The sign itself takes only two verses, as Jesus calls the dead man out from the grave (Jn 11:43–44). Yet it is introduced by a long series of verbal encounters (Jn 11:1–42). The words that define the action appear in the middle of the story where Jesus says, "I am the resurrection and the life" (Jn 11:25). Jesus could have said this at the end, after he had called Lazarus out of the tomb and everyone could see that the dead man was alive again. But this is not what Jesus does. Instead, he calls himself the resurrection and the life in the middle of things, where death is still real. His words call Martha to believe even as her brother lies lifeless in the grave. She is not called to believe because of what she sees. She is called to believe in spite of what she sees. When she says, "Yes, Lord, I believe," her faith is tied to the word Jesus has spoken (Jn 11:27). Only later will the sign confirm her faith in his word.

The words are important because even Lazarus's resurrection is easily misunderstood. Some people may have celebrated Jesus' power to give life (Jn 11:41–45), but the Jewish authorities did not. They saw the sign as a threat. In their eyes, Jesus, the miracle worker, was starting a popular movement that endangered

---

[15] Hartwig Thyen, *Das Johannesevangelium*, Handbuch zum Neuen Testament 6 (Tübingen: Mohr Siebeck, 2005), 292.

[16] Martin Asiedu-Peprah, *Johannine Sabbath Conflicts as Juridical Controversy*, Wissenschaftliche Untersuchungen zum Neuen Testament 2.132 (Tübingen: Mohr Siebeck, 2001), 52–116.

social stability. They assumed that if the Romans got nervous about it, they would intervene and destroy the Jewish holy place and their nation. So, in order to prevent this from occurring, they decided that Jesus, the giver of life, had to be put to death (Jn 11:46–50). This is a major irony in the Gospel. The sign that shows Jesus' ability to give life is what prompts his adversaries to put him to death. Because the signs are ambiguous, the Gospel must shape the readers' understanding of them through the words of the surrounding literary context.

At this point, we might pause and reflect on the hermeneutical implications of John's account of Jesus' ministry. I find that Luther's emphasis on the word is actually quite helpful. The Gospel introduces Jesus as the Word of God made flesh, and throughout the narrative the spoken words play a key role in generating faith and shaping the readers' perspectives on Jesus' actions. We can also nuance and develop Luther's approach by linking Jesus' signs more closely to his words. After all, the signs are vehicles for communication. Jesus "speaks" through his actions as well as through his words. The signs confirm what the spoken words proclaim, and the spoken words create a framework within which the signs can be understood.

The crucifixion and resurrection

Another dimension that is important for our work is that, in John's Gospel, Jesus' signs and words are interpreted in light of his crucifixion and resurrection. From a literary perspective, we can see this pattern in the opening chapter, where Jesus is identified as the sacrificial Lamb of God (Jn 1:29; 36). Then, at the end of his public ministry, Jesus tells the crowd, "'And I, when I am lifted up from the earth, will draw all people to myself.' He said this to indicate the kind of death he was to die" (Jn 12:32–33). The crowd is incredulous, so Jesus hides himself from them, and the writer comments that in spite of all the signs, people still did not believe (Jn 12:34–37). For Jesus' work to reach fruition—and for us as readers to understand its significance—the crucifixion and resurrection must take place. This is also integral to Luther's perspective. He insists that the entire book is to be read in light of the central gospel message about Jesus overcoming sin and death through his own death and resurrection.[17]

---

[17] Luther, op. cit. (note 1), 360–62. Luther's *Heidelberg Disputation* of 1518 argued that a person who tries to understand the invisible things of God by contemplating what is visible is not worthy of being called a theologian. Rather, true theology requires discerning what is visible of God through Christ's sufferings and the cross. Luther thought that this was true of John's Gospel. See "Heidelberg Disputation," in *LW* 31, 52–53; cf. *D. Martin Luthers Werke*, op. cit. (note 1), vol. 1, 361–62.

As we turn from Jesus' ministry of signs to his passion and resurrection, it might be helpful to summarize the relationship. There where the signs show the character of divine power, the cross shows the depth of divine love.[18] In the signs, the power of God is revealed by healing people, feeding them and raising them from the dead. It is a power that gives life. In the cross, the love of God is revealed in its most radical form, when Jesus lays down his life for others (Jn 3:14–16; 15:13).[19] Through Jesus' death, the love of God is communicated to the world. When this gift of love evokes faith, it brings people into the relationship that is true life. This is the paradox at the heart of the Gospel's message: Jesus gives life to others by suffering death himself, because his death communicates the divine love that evokes faith and brings life. And this faith relationship has a future to it through the promise of resurrection.[20]

The theme of love is clear in the narrative introduction to the second half of the Gospel. The writer says that Jesus, having "loved his own who were in the world, loved them to the end" (Jn 13:1). This language is suggestive.[21] In Greek, the expression "to the end" is *eis telos*. In one sense, a *telos* is an end or goal. It indicates that Jesus will show love to the end of his life, so that love culminates in crucifixion. On the cross, his ministry comes to its end or goal, and he recalls the *telos* idea when he says *tetelestai*, "It is finished" (Jn 19:30). In another sense, this expression shows the quality of his love. By dying, he gives his love completely, not partially. To say that he loves *eis telos* is also to say that he loves "to the utmost."

The love that is fully given in crucifixion is foreshadowed by the foot washing that introduces the passion. The action occurs during the last supper, and John gives emphasis to the theme of divine power. He says Jesus "knew that the Father had put all things into his hands, and that he had come from God and was going to God" (Jn 13:3). It is clear that Jesus is operating from a position of strength. Yet now that God has put all things into his hands, Jesus lays

---

[18] C. H. Dodd, *The Interpretation of the Fourth Gospel* (Cambridge: Cambridge University, 1953) 207–208.

[19] For recent discussion of the meaning of Jesus' death in John, see the essays in Gilbert Van Belle (ed.), *The Death of Jesus in the Fourth Gospel*, Bibliotheca Ephemeridum Theologicarum Lovaniensium 200 (Leuven: Leuven University and Peeters, 2007); Koester, op. cit. (note 4), 108–23.

[20] For recent discussions on the theme of resurrection in John, see the essays in Craig R. Koester and Reimund Bieringer (eds), *The Resurrection of Jesus in the Gospel of John*, Wissenschaftliche Untersuchungen zum Neuen Testament 222 (Tübingen: Mohr Siebeck, 2008); Sandra M. Schneiders, "The Resurrection (of the Body) in the Fourth Gospel: A Key to Johannine Spirituality," in John R. Donahue (ed.), *Life in Abundance: Studies of John's Gospel in Tribute to Raymond E. Brown* (Collegeville: Liturgical, 2005), 168–98.

[21] On *eis telos*, see Gail R. O'Day, *The Gospel of John*, New Interpreter's Bible 9 (Nashville: Abingdon, 1995), 721. The double meaning is evident in the differences between English translations. For example, the New Revised Standard Version has "to the end." The New International Version reads "the full extent."

down his outer robe and uses his hands to wash feet (Jn 13:4–5). The movement shows that his power comes to expression in loving service for his disciples.

Foot washing is an effective way of showing the character of divine love. In the ancient world, the usual practice was that guests would wash their own feet or in some cases a slave might wash their feet. But no free person could be expected to wash the feet of another person. To do so would be to assume the position of a slave.[22] When someone willingly took on the role of a slave by washing feet, it was an act of complete devotion. This is what Jesus does. By washing the feet of the disciples, he assumes the position of a slave in order to communicate the fullness of his love. This action at the supper anticipates the complete act of self-giving that will follow in his death.

The love Jesus communicates through foot washing and crucifixion becomes the source and norm for Christian discipleship. Jesus summarizes this by his new commandment: the disciples are to love one another as he has loved them (Jn 13:34; 15:12). The new commandment includes an element of mutuality. The disciples are to love and serve one another, and this is what builds community. The Gospel assumes that people need to receive love as well as to give it, and it is in community that the love of Jesus comes to its expression. The Gospel recognizes that such love cannot be an end in itself. Rather, the way love takes shape in community is an essential form of Christian witness to the world. In Jesus' final prayer at the supper, he will make this clear. He prays that the community might be one in order that the world might come to know what the love of God is (Jn 17:22–23). This makes the community-forming power of divine love an essential part of Christian witness. According to Luther's "Preface," obedience to the love command is the way faith is lived out.[23]

An essential feature of Lutheran hermeneutics is the distinction between law and gospel.[24] Luther emphasizes that the "gospel" is the message of what Christ has done to bring salvation. By way of contrast, one of the functions of "law" is to expose human sin in order to show us the need for the gospel. As we read John's Gospel these categories are helpful. The categories help us to see how the account of Jesus' arrest, trial and crucifixion discloses the depth of the world's alienation from God, as well as the depth of divine love for that world.

---

[22] John Christopher Thomas, *Footwashing in the John 13 and the Johannine Community* (Sheffield: JSOT, 1991). Details in the foot washing story enhance the connection with the crucifixion. Note the theme of *telos/tetelestai* (Jn 13:1; 19:30), the mention of the betrayer (Jn 13:2), Jesus' departure to God (Jn 13:1, 3), and the way he lays down and takes up his garments, as he would "lay down" and "take up" his life (Jn 13:4, 12; cf. 10:17–18).

[23] Luther, op. cit. (note 1), 361.

[24] See Bernard Lohse, *Martin Luther's Theology: Its Historical and Systematic Development* (Minneapolis: Fortress, 1999), 267–76.

We turn first to the aspect of "law" by noting how the people who appear in the passion narrative regularly have their sin exposed.[25] At the time of the arrest, Peter appears to be a loyal disciple, who attempts to defend Jesus. But Peter's sin is brought to light at the high priest's house, where he denies that he has any connection to Jesus at all (Jn 18:10–27). Similarly, the Jewish authorities insist that Jesus is guilty of rebellion against Rome, yet they themselves prove to be guilty of the charge since they seek the release of Barabbas, a genuine rebel against Rome (Jn 18:40; 19:12). They also argue that Jesus' claim to be the Son of God makes him an opponent of Israel's God (Jn 19:7), yet they are the ones who say they have no king except Caesar, who was widely called "son of god," and whose claims stood in opposition to those of Israel's God (Jn 19:15).[26] Finally, Pilate is a Gentile, who has illusions of power (Jn 19:10). But even though Pilate knows Jesus is innocent, he has him crucified anyway, showing that Pilate is truly powerless to do what he knows to be true (Jn 18:38; 19:4, 6, 16). The trial narrative functions as "law" in the Lutheran sense by exposing the world's sin and showing how bondage to untruth leads to the death of Jesus.

Yet, the law functions for the sake of the Gospel. It shows us the character of the world, whose sin the Lamb of God came to take away (Jn 1:29). The "Gospel" or message of salvation that is narrated in the final chapters of the book is summarized in John 3:16, "God so loved the world that he gave his only Son." Note that in the context of John's Gospel, this means that God gives his love to the world that has rejected God. God gives his love to the world that is alienated from God. The crucifixion conveys the love of God in this radical form in order to overcome the world's alienation from its Creator so that relationship with God can be restored. When the Gospel message of divine love, which is conveyed through the crucifixion of Jesus, evokes faith, it overcomes the sin that alienates people from God and brings them into the relationship with God that is true life (Jn 3:14–15). When law and gospel work together in this way, by exposing sin and extending the promise of love, then John's text has the effect for which it was written, namely, that the readers may believe and have life (Jn 20:31).

---

[25] See Paul D. Duke, *Irony in the Fourth Gospel* (Atlanta: John Knox, 1985), 126–37; Andrew T. Lincoln, *Truth on Trial: The Lawsuit Motif in the Fourth Gospel* (Peabody, Mass.: Hendrickson, 2000), 123–38.

[26] The conflict with imperial claims has often been noted. See David Rensberger, *Johannine Faith and Liberating Community* (Philadelphia: Westminster, 1988), 87–106; Lance Byron Richey, *Roman Imperial Ideology and the Gospel of John,* Catholic Biblical Quarterly Monograph Series 43 (Washington, DC: Catholic Biblical Association of America, 2007); Tom Thatcher, *Greater than Caesar: Christology and Empire in the Fourth Gospel* (Minneapolis: Fortress, 2009); Warren Carter, *John and Empire: Initial Explorations* (New York and London: T. & T. Clark, 2008), 194–95.

The Spirit

John's Gospel is written with the needs of the post-Easter community in mind. For them, the events of Jesus' life, death and resurrection occurred in the past, and time has steadily widened the distance between the readers' context and that of the early disciples. What readers living after the first Easter have are the words of testimony handed on through the community of faith. The Gospel presents this testimony in written form so that those of later generations might believe and have life (Jn 20:30–31). The Gospel also recognizes that words do not create and strengthen faith on their own and that it is the Spirit that continues to make the words effective.

The Gospel introduces the crucial role of the Spirit in the opening chapter where John the Baptist acknowledges that, on his own, he would have had no means of recognizing the Christ whom God was sending (Jn 1:31, 33). John the Baptist received a word from God, telling him that the one on whom the Spirit descended and remained was the one who would baptize with the Holy Spirit. The descent of the Spirit on Jesus bore out the truth of the word the Baptist had received, making it possible for him to recognize Jesus as the Son of God and Lamb of God (Jn 1:33–34). Apart from the word and the Spirit together, John the Baptist would not have been able to recognize or bear witness to Christ. The same would be true for subsequent generations.

Jesus' conversations with the disciples at the last supper anticipate the role that the Spirit will play in making the community's witness effective after Easter. The Spirit will continually call the community to remember what Jesus had said to his first disciples, and the Spirit will also teach or disclose the significance of that message for the generations to come (Jn 14:26). The first disciples are charged with the task of bearing witness to Christ and yet they do not do so alone: the Spirit bears witness in and through them (Jn 15:26–27). On Easter evening, Jesus says "As the Father has sent me, so I send you" and he breathes the Holy Spirit into them (Jn 20:21–22). Without the Spirit, the words that the disciples will speak would remain only words; it is the Spirit that will use them to evoke faith. And, without the early community's witness to the life, death and resurrection of Jesus, the Spirit's work would seem vague and unfocused; it is the message of the disciples that gives content and focus to the faith that the Spirit will bring.[27]

---

[27] Koester, op. cit. (note 4), 133–60.

The context

Our work here involves reading John's Gospel in light of the Lutheran tradition and the many contexts now represented by Lutheran communities around the world. Let me contribute to this discussion of the role of context by considering the context in which the Gospel was composed and first read. The concluding verses of the Gospel say that the text is based on the testimony of the disciple whom Jesus loved (Jn 21:24). Although many interpreters have assumed that the beloved disciple was the apostle John, many modern scholars have moved away from this idea. The most important reason is that the Gospel never gives the author's name, and they find it unhelpful to speculate about it.[28] For our discussion, the Gospel's refusal to name its author has theological significance. In one of his "Prefaces," Luther commented that the apostolic quality of a text depends on what is said, not on who says it. He argued that whatever "does not teach Christ is not apostolic, even though St Peter or St Paul does the teaching. Again, whatever preaches Christ would be apostolic, even if Judas, Annas, Pilate and Herod were doing it."[29] The implication is that the value of a book really centers on the Christ to whom it bears witness and not on the identity of the author.

The Gospel probably was brought to its final form over a period of time in the context of an early Christian community. Rather than discussing the theories about the stages in which the text was composed, it might be more helpful to explore the theological and social factors at work in the context.[30]

First, the tradition on which John's Gospel was based was shaped in a community in which some members knew Scripture and Jewish tradition. The Gospel says that the earliest disciples identified Jesus as the fulfillment of the law and the prophets (Jn 1:45). For the discussion on hermeneutics, it is significant that the process of exploring Jesus' identity in light of Scripture as a whole continued in the community in which John's Gospel was written. The

---

[28] For discussion of authorship by those who do not think that the Gospel was written by John the apostle, see Raymond E. Brown, *An Introduction to the Gospel of John*, ed. Francis J. Moloney (New York: Random House, 2003), 189–99; Andrew T. Lincoln, *The Gospel According to Saint John*, Black's New Testament Commentaries (London: Continuum 2005), 17–26. Some scholars continue arguing in favor of the apostle as the author. See Craig S. Keener, *The Gospel of John: A Commentary*, 2 vols (Peabody, Mass: Hendrickson, 2003), vol. 1, 81–115.

[29] Martin Luther, "Preface to the Epistles of St. James and St. Jude," in *LW* 35, 396. Cf. *D. Martin Luthers Werke*, op. cit. (note 1), 384. Beginning in 1530, the Preface added the word "yet" ("noch") so that it read that whatever "does not teach Christ is not *yet* apostolic."

[30] For discussion of theories concerning the stages in which the Gospel was written, see Brown, op. cit. (note 28), 40–89; Paul N. Anderson, *The Riddles of the Fourth Gospel: An Introduction to John* (Minneapolis: Fortress, 2011), 125–55.

phenomenon of post-Easter reflection in light of Scripture is explicit in the accounts of the temple cleansing (Jn 2:17–22) and approach to Jerusalem (Jn 12:14–15) and is implied in the account of the crucifixion (Jn 19:24, 36–37). The Gospel also relates Jesus' ministry to the Jewish festivals, including the Sabbath (Jn 5:9; 9:14), Passover (Jn 2:13; 6:4; 19:14), Booths (Jn 7:2), and Dedication or Hanukkah (Jn 10:22). The assumption is that at least some readers will find these connections meaningful.

Second, the Gospel includes debates over Jesus' relationship to the Jewish tradition. The debates may have originated in the ministry of Jesus, but they continued to play a role in the experience of the early Christian community, which had to respond to questions about Jesus' identity and work in the decades after Easter.[31] At points the conflict seems negative. Jesus' opponents charge that his teachings lack credibility (Jn 7:12), that he is violating the will of God by healing on the Sabbath (Jn 5:16; 9:16) and that he is a blasphemer for claiming to be one with God (Jn 5:18; 8:58–59; 10:33). There is evidence that at least some of Jesus' followers felt pressure to deny their relationship with him in order to remain in good standing with the wider Jewish community (Jn 9:22; 12:42–43). Yet, rather than ignoring these issues, the Gospel weaves the debates into the account of Jesus' life.[32] The result is that allowing readers to hear the questions and the responses gives greater clarity to the Gospel's central message.

Third, the Gospel envisions a wider circle of readers, who are not of Jewish background. The narrative shows Jesus being "sent" into the world, where he forms a community of people from different backgrounds. This in turn anticipates the experience of his followers after Easter, as they are "sent" into the world to continue his work. John takes seriously the mission of Jesus and his followers into a multi-ethnic world.[33] The Gospel tells of Jesus reaching out to the people of Samaria, where the woman at the well brings the Samaritan townspeople

---

[31] The idea that John's account of Jesus' ministry reflects the experience of the later Christian community has had an important place in Johannine studies. Among the classic studies are, J. Louis Martyn, *History and Theology in the Fourth Gospel*, 3rd ed. (Louisville: Westminster John Knox, 2003); Raymond E. Brown, *The Community of the Beloved Disciple*. (New York: Paulist, 1979). Interpreters have debated about the extent to which the history of the later community can be reconstructed from the Gospel, but even if the details remain unclear, it seems likely that the issues addressed by the Gospel were significant in the experience of the post-Easter church.

[32] Asiedu-Peprah, op. cit (note 16), 184–232.

[33] The Gospel identifies Jesus as the one whom God "sent" (*apostellō, pempo*) into the world, and Jesus in turn sends his disciples. On the theme, see Teresa Okure, *The Johannine Approach to Mission: A Contextual Study of John 4:1–42*, Wissenschaftliche Untersuchungen zum Neuen Testament 31 (Tübingen: Mohr Siebeck, 1988); Edward W. Klink III, *The Sheep of the Fold: The Audience and Origin of the Gospel of John*, Society for New Testament Studies Monograph Series 141 (Cambridge: Cambridge University, 2007), 220–38.

to meet him (4:28-30, 39-42), and the disciples are expected to continue this kind of outreach (Jn 4:36–38). Later, some Greeks want to see Jesus and their arrival foreshadows the way in which the crucified and risen Jesus will "draw" people of all sorts to himself through the work of his disciples (12:20–23, 32). As the Good Shepherd, Jesus envisions a community that includes people of Jewish background as well as those who are not of the Jewish "fold" but come from other ethnic groups (Jn 10:16). That is why his final prayer at the last supper and his words to the disciples after Easter emphasize that his followers are being sent into the world, where they will create a growing community of faith (Jn 17:18–20; 20:21).

In light of this increasingly diverse social context, John's Gospel conveyed its message in ways that were accessible to a wide spectrum of readers from different backgrounds.[34] Above I noted that sometimes the text assumes that readers will catch subtle allusions to passages from the Scriptures, but there are also places where it gives basic points of information to those who did not know that tradition. For example, the Gospel explains what words like "rabbi" and "Messiah" mean (Jn 1:38, 41), that stone jars were used for Jewish purification rites (Jn 2:6) and that Jews did not share things with Samaritans (Jn 4:9). These explanations give readers from this wider circle the perspectives they need to understand the story.

It is also significant that the imagery in the Gospel would have been broadly appealing to people of various backgrounds. For example, the Gospel identifies Jesus as "the bread of life" (Jn 6:35) and "the light of the world" (Jn 8:12; 9:5) in contexts that evoke connotations from Scripture and Jewish tradition. But these same images of bread and light were broadly accessible to people throughout the Mediterranean world. Even if some of the early readers missed the traditional biblical overtones in these images, their own life experience would allow them to make basic connections between bread and light and fullness of life. Other images, such as water, a vine, shepherding and foot washing would also have been widely accessible to ancient readers, even as they invited people into a process of ongoing reflection as the Gospel was read within the community of faith.

In closing, it is helpful to note that the sign above Jesus' cross proclaims the kingship of the crucified Jesus to those who speak Hebrew, as well as those

---

[34] There have been many proposals on the character of the readers presupposed by the Gospel. From a literary perspective, R. Alan Culpepper noted that some aspects of the Gospel presuppose a highly informed audience, while others assume a less informed audience. The result is that the Gospel suggests a mixed group. See R. Alan Culpepper, *Anatomy of the Fourth Gospel: A Study in Literary Design* (Philadelphia: Fortress, 1983), 221, 225. Some historical studies also discern an increasingly mixed community. See Brown, op. cit. (note 31); Anderson, op. cit. (note 30), 134–41.

who know Latin and Greek (Jn 19:19–20). The Gospel's message is designed to cross the boundaries of language and culture. These observations invite us to consider how this Gospel might continue speaking to a spectrum of modern readers. The churches that belong to the Lutheran World Federation also represent a spectrum of readers, who have differing perspectives that are shaped by their unique cultural backgrounds. Our churches include members who speak a wide range of languages and face distinctive challenges in the contexts where they live and work.

The Gospel of John speaks of a unity or oneness that centers on a shared faith, which brings people of different backgrounds together in the crucified and living Christ. The Gospel does not consider such oneness to be an end in itself, but speaks of oneness as an integral part of Christian witness. When Jesus prays that "they may all be one," he goes on to say that the reason is "that the world may believe" in the God revealed in Jesus Christ and "that the world may know" what the love of God means (Jn 17:21, 23). According to John, the community of faith is where the love of God is shared and proclaimed. Discerning ways in which members of the global Lutheran community, with its many distinctive languages and cultural contexts, can be enriched by a common faith tradition and can support one another in our common call to bear witness to Christ is both the opportunity and challenge that lie before us.

Law and Gospel (With a Little Help from St John)[1]

Sarah Hinlicky Wilson

Law and gospel—more precisely, the distinction between law and gospel—is one of the nearest and dearest characteristics of Lutheran theology. It is not one piece of the puzzle among others, but the hermeneutical expression of justification by faith. However, being so pervasive in Lutheran thought, the distinction between law and gospel tends to get distorted with use. This is not automatically a disaster: a living, meaningful piece of tradition is always being handled, weighed and sifted, and some wrong turns are part of the process of getting to the right destination. Better to be used, abused and then corrected, than to sit primly on the shelf with no attention paid to it at all.

There are, in particular, five typical misreadings of law and gospel across Lutheran history. The distinction between law and gospel is **not** the distinction between:

1. The Old Testament and the New Testament
2. That which makes me feel bad (guilty, inadequate) and that which makes me feel good (righteous, loved)
3. The natural and the supernatural
4. The pre-Christian and the Christian life
5. God's wrath and God's love

Such misinterpretations are only compelling because they have some grain of truth in them, and so it is with these. They are a little bit right but not right enough.

To get the right read on law and gospel, it is best to let Luther do the talking; herewith three selections from early in his career. First, at some length, he expounds on the matter in his "Brief Instruction on What to Look for and Expect in the Gospels" of 1521.

> [Y]ou should grasp Christ, his words, works, and sufferings, in a twofold manner.
> First as an example that is presented to you, which you should follow and imitate.
> As St. Peter says in I Peter 4, "Christ suffered for us, thereby leaving us an example."

---

[1] Editor's note: While it is LWF policy and practice to use gender neutral language when referring to God, the male language for God has been retained in this article upon the author's specific request.

Thus, when you see how he prays, fasts, helps people, and shows them love, so also you should do, both for yourself and for your neighbor. However, this is the smallest part of the gospel, on the basis of which it cannot yet even be called gospel. For on this level Christ is of no more help to you than some other saint. His life remains his own and does not as yet contribute anything to you. In short this mode [of understanding Christ as an example] does not make Christians but only hypocrites. You must grasp Christ at a much higher level. Even though this higher level has for a long time been the very best, the preaching of it has been something rare. The chief article and foundation of the gospel is that before you take Christ as an example, you accept and recognize him as a gift, as a present that God has given you and that is your own. This means that when you see or hear of Christ doing or suffering something, you do not doubt that Christ himself, with his deeds and suffering, belongs to you. On this you may depend as surely as if you had done it yourself; indeed as if you were Christ himself. See, this is what it means to have a proper grasp of the gospel, that is, of the overwhelming goodness of God, which neither prophet, nor apostle, nor angel was ever able fully to express, and which no heart could adequately fathom or marvel at. This is the great fire of the love of God for us, whereby the heart and conscience become happy, secure, and content...[2]

Now when you have Christ as the foundation and chief blessing of your salvation, then the other part follows: that you take him as your example, giving yourself in service to your neighbor just as you see that Christ has given himself for you. See, there faith and love move forward, God's commandment is fulfilled, and a person is happy and fearless to do and suffer all things. Therefore make note of this, that Christ as a gift nourishes your faith and makes you a Christian. But Christ as an example exercises your works. These do not make you a Christian. Actually they come forth from you because you have already been made a Christian. As widely as a gift differs from an example, so widely does faith differ from works, for faith possesses nothing of its own, only the deeds and life of Christ. Works have something of your own in them, yet they should not belong to you but to your neighbor. So you see that the gospel is really not a book of laws and commandments which requires deeds of us, but a book of divine promises in which God promises, offers, and gives us all his possessions and benefits in Christ. The fact that Christ and the apostles provide much good teaching and explain the law is to be counted a benefit just like any other work of Christ. For to teach aright is not the least sort of benefit... He simply tells us what we are to do and what to avoid, what will happen to those who do evil

---

[2] *LW* 35, 119.

and to those who do well. Christ drives and compels no one. Indeed he teaches so gently that he entices rather than commands.[3]

How this relates to the Old Testament is a matter on which Lutherans have fallen down too many times to count. Even though Luther was an Old Testament professor, he did not have a dispensationalist first-law-then-gospel division of the ages. All people at all times live under the law of God and by the gift of God. His "Preface to the Old Testament" from 1523 explains:

> Know, then, that the Old Testament is a book of laws, which teaches what [people] are to do and not to do—and in addition gives examples and stories of how these laws are kept or broken—just as the New Testament is gospel or book of grace and teaches where one is to get the power to fulfill the law. Now in the New Testament there are also given, along with the teaching about grace, many other teachings that are laws and commandments for the control of the flesh—since in this life the Spirit is not perfected and grace alone cannot rule. Similarly in the Old Testament too there are, beside the laws, certain promises and words of grace, by which the holy fathers and prophets under the law were kept, like us, in the faith of Christ.[4]

The Old Testament saints lived by the promise (another word for gospel in Luther's parlance), just as we do today. And just as they needed the law to regulate their bodies, souls and societies back then, so we need it now, not yet having achieved the perfection of the life to come.

Luther takes up the question of "How Christians Should Regard Moses" in 1525, in part because of certain repristinating movements that wanted to impose Levitical law on Christians. Luther quite often liked Levitical law, but only when it was a sensible way of implementing the principles of natural law—which itself is the divine law written on every human heart, as in Romans 1. The law is good, after all; it is not just the gospel that is good. The only problem with the law is that it cannot give what it demands. Luther captures the distinction very nicely in his discussion of God's two public sermons, the one on Mt Sinai and the other at Pentecost.

> Now the first sermon and doctrine is the law of God. The second is the gospel. These two sermons are not the same. Therefore we must have a good grasp of the matter in order to know how to differentiate between them. We must know

---

[3] Ibid., 120–21.

[4] Ibid., 236–37.

what the law is, and what the gospel is. The law commands and requires us to do certain things. The law is thus directed solely to our behavior and consists in making requirements. For God speaks through the law, saying, "Do this, avoid that, this is what I expect of you." The gospel, however, does not preach what we are to do or to avoid. It sets up no requirements but reverses the approach of the law, does the very opposite, and says, "This is what God has done for you; he has let his Son be made flesh for you, has let him be put to death for your sake." So, then, there are two kinds of doctrine and two kinds of works, those of God and those of men. Just as we and God are separated from one another, so also these two doctrines are widely separated from one another. For the gospel teaches exclusively what has been given us by God, and not—as in the case of the law—what we are to do and give to God.[5]

To say pithily what Luther explains at length: the law is what God requires while the gospel is what God gives.

The difficulty for Lutherans is bearing in mind that law and gospel are **both** words of God. They are equally eternal; neither is to be eliminated by the other. The antinomian tendency wants to see the law overcome, as if the law were not "holy and righteous and good" (Rom 7:12), as if it were not the very expression of God's unassailable goodness and trustworthiness. The legalist tendency wants to see the gospel overcome, as if we got grace to vault us over our initial resistance to the law but then could carry on, by our own powers, the eminently achievable task of being holy. But both law and gospel persist now and always, and neither can be defined without reference to God. The law is what God demands. The gospel is what God gives. God is the subject in each case, law and gospel are the direct objects, and we are simply the indirect objects.

Because of our awkward situation as sinful images of God, our human reactions to the law and gospel are manifold and various. There is no *ordo salutis* in the sense of a mandatory set of experiences to be passed through; people are much too complicated for that. The human response to God's law and God's gospel is always secondary and derivative, which is why law and gospel should never be defined on the basis of the human reaction (cf. error #2 above). In fact, the very same passage of Scripture might be received as law or as gospel: think of the scriptural exhortations to faith, which to one person might be an accusing demand that cannot be fulfilled because the God-given desire to fill it is lacking, while to another it is the breakthrough from darkness to dazzling light because it actually gives what it demands.

---

[5] Ibid., 162.

It might help, though, to map out some possible human reactions to law and gospel. The law, for instance, might provoke joy and rapture. How often we forget this. But we cannot make any sense of the Old Testament without understanding the joy of the law. Psalm 1 praises the one whose "delight is in the law of the Lord, and on His law he meditates day and night." It is good to know what God requires: the law both reveals God's character and cultivates human flourishing. Especially if a false god, like an abusive ruler or the society's Zeitgeist, demands adherence to its own false notions about human flourishing, God's true demands are a joyful alternative, liberation from idolatry and tyranny. But the opposite reaction is possible, too. The law can provoke hatred and revolt, especially when sinners love their sins more than God's just demands, for the law exposes those who do not want to be exposed. Yet, a third reaction lies somewhere between the two: this is repentance. It can be a genuine relief to be nailed by God's requirements when they expose our self-destructive behaviors or reveal how we have been living a lie.

The gospel can provoke the same three types of human reaction. We hope, naturally, that joy will be the dominant one. But the New Testament gives us little reason to think it will be the only one. For some, the fact that God has already given us everything that we call our own, that our salvation and righteousness are out of our hands, that we are supplicants and receivers rather than heroic actors—this can be perceived as offensive and insulting. And the gospel can provoke repentance, too, for instance from Christian hearts grown cold, or previously little moved to give in gratitude for how much they have been given.

A cautionary note from the history of doctrine is needed at this point. Luther's close attention to the doctrine of justification was caused, in no small part, by the medieval scholastic Gabriel Biel's treatment of the subject. In fact, in most of Luther's teaching on justification, his profound disagreement with Biel is near at hand. Biel had something like a distinction between law and gospel, but in his thought the two played out very differently. Biel said, do as much as you can by your own powers of what God requires, and then God will give you credit for all the rest. There you go: law, gospel. Does that work? No, it does not: it is barely disguised Pelagianism, and the only way Biel could justify it as not being Pelagian was by stressing how gracious it was of God to give all that we could not supply on our own, not to mention accepting our best efforts that always fall short of His expectations.

But for Luther, both God's demands and God's gifts are absolute, total. God demands the total keeping of His law, not just our best efforts (as in Jesus' dictum, "You therefore must be perfect, as your heavenly Father is perfect," Mt 5:48). And God also gives all of His righteousness to us to make us righteous, quite apart from the demands of His law, on account of His Son (for example, "not having a righteousness of my own that comes from the law, but that which comes through faith in Christ," Phil 3:9). Justification is not, as per Biel, a result of us and God meeting as partners somewhere in the space between us (cf. error #3 above). It is by God's coming all the way to us, demanding all and giving all. Augustine's famous prayer expresses it beautifully: "Give what You command, and command what You will." Luther would probably reverse the order of the clauses.

So here lies the danger: there is a great temptation to mislabel law as gospel, by saying that God gives the ability to keep the law and thus our doing so is, in fact, what justifies and saves us. Under this disguise, the primacy of God's mercy is lost entirely, and the whole obligation is thrown back on us. Luther was no enemy of sanctification, as later Lutherans have sometimes been, but sanctification is not the **basis** of our relationship with God: it is the **consequence**. And it is generally modest. The law-gospel distinction presumes a strong emphasis on the forgiveness of sins and a firm grasp of the depths of human sin that cannot be lightly sloughed off in this life. Optimism about sanctification, practically speaking, usually leads to lying about ourselves. Sanctified people are not supposed to screw up—so instead they cover up.

Because of the centrality of the law-gospel distinction, Luther insisted that all the church's practices should be subject to the law-gospel critique. Violations of the law are those that require what God does **not** require or do not require what God **does** require. These are fairly easy to spot, though not necessarily easy to deal with. In the sixteenth century, typical errors of the former kind were to require fasting on certain days and celibacy for priests while those of the latter denied the Christian obligation to lead a holy life and do good works. Violations of the gospel are usually more subtle: on the one hand withholding what God gives, on the other hand, claiming to give what God does not in fact give. The former category, in Luther's day, came to expression in such ways as distributing only the consecrated bread and not the wine, or making absolution conditional on perfect human repentance. The latter category included promising perfection in this life rather than the forgiveness of sins, or inventing church rituals that claimed to bestow a divine blessing but carried no scripturally-sanctioned promise. It is probably all too easy to think of violations of both law and gospel in our churches today.

The law-gospel distinction arose out of Luther's reading of the Scripture; in turn, it became a key for the interpretation of the Scripture. It is no accident that his above-cited descriptions of the distinction come out of his introductions to the Bible. The Gospel of John is a good place to practice the law-gospel distinction today since it is particularly resistant to the usual

Lutheran misreadings. If anything, it is a corrective to them, reorienting us toward Luther's original sense. After all, John was Luther's favorite gospel, for the clarity of its christology.

For instance, it is very difficult to create a competition between the testaments with John (cf. error #1 above): he regularly invokes Scripture, which of course for him was our Old Testament (and possibly some of the Apocrypha), assuming that Jesus is the confirmation rather than the abrogation of Moses' teaching. There is no negative contrast in the prologue's statement, "For the law was given through Moses; grace and truth came through Jesus Christ" (1:17)—they are simply set side by side. Jesus' resurrection from the dead makes the disciples believe the Scripture (2:22), and Jesus teaches that the eternal life promised in the Scriptures is found in himself (5:39). In fact, it is not possible to believe in Jesus without first believing Moses: "For if you believed Moses, you would believe me; for he wrote of me. But if you do not believe his writings, how will you believe my words?" (5:46–47). For "Scripture cannot be broken" (10:35).

There is also no way you can squeeze out of John the idea that obedience to the law is irrelevant to the Christian life (cf. error #4 above). One of Jesus' most incisive criticisms of his compatriots was their disdain for what God demands. "Has not Moses given you the law? Yet none of you keeps the law" (7:19). By contrast, Jesus' disciples should be recognizable to the community at large as those who do exactly what he commands, namely "that you love one another: just as I have loved you, you also are to love one another" (13:34). Here we see that, in fact, the gospel enables the keeping of the law, without collapsing the distinction between the two. Love is at the heart of the law as much as it is at the heart of the gospel (cf. error #5 above). Only a false disciple could claim to rejoice in what God gives and yet have no regard for what God demands, for "if you love me, you will keep my commandments" (14:15).

But when this Gospel is examined through the law-gospel lenses, John's most recurrent theme becomes clear: the whole drama is about what God gives and whether we do, or do not, receive that gift. Already in the prologue there is the mournful/joyful observation:

> He came to his own, and his own people did not receive him. But to all who did receive him, who believed in his name, he gave the right to become children of God, who were born, not of blood nor of the will of the flesh nor of the will of man, but of God (Jn 1:11–13).

Throughout the whole Gospel, Jesus and others bear witness to him, but again and again "you do not receive our testimony" (3:11). "God so loved the world, that He gave His only Son" (3:16), yet even the receiving of this Son is a gift: "A person cannot receive even one thing unless it is given him from heaven" (3:27; see also 6:44). The divine habit of giving is at root an extension of the trinitarian divine nature: "For he whom God has sent utters the words of God, for he gives the Spirit without measure. The Father loves the Son and has given all things into his hand" (3:34–35; see also 14:16–17 on the gift of the Spirit "Whom the world cannot receive"). The Samaritan woman at the well learns of and asks for living water; she receives life-giving faith. But those who learn of the bread from heaven and ask for it eventually find that they do not want it after all: "After this many of his disciples turned back and no longer walked with him" (6:66). What God gives does not inspire joy in everyone, and some refuse to accept it: "I have come in my Father's name, and you do not receive me" (5:43). Even Peter proves to be reluctant to receive God's gift, declaring, "You shall never wash my feet," but Jesus answers, "If I do not wash you, you have no share with me" (13:8). Jesus' gifts are not worldly gifts with strings of fair play and recompense attached: "Peace I leave with you; my peace I give to you. Not as the world gives do I give to you" (14:27). The whole interplay of law and gospel, command and gift, is summed up in words from Jesus' final discourse with his disciples: "You did not choose me, but I chose you and appointed you that you should go and bear fruit and that your fruit should abide, so that whatever you ask the Father in my name, He may give it to you" (15:16). And John's closing lines suggest with whimsical charm, in a final hopeful antidote to the severity of much of the book, the sheer infinity of God's gifts: "Now there are also many other things that Jesus did. Were every one of them to be written, I suppose that the world itself could not contain the books that would be written" (21:25).

The cumulative effect of revisiting the law-gospel distinction with Luther and John the Evangelist is to remember that what we preach is **God**. We preach all of God, His righteous will and what He justly demands, His mighty deeds and what He graciously gives. We preach in confidence that both of these words of God, law and gospel, are good and worthy for His people to hear, and the Holy Spirit (not the preacher!) will apply them as needed in each individual. We do not need schemes or strategies to achieve a calculated effect because the array of human reaction to God's words is so broad. It is our prayer that the law will evoke repentance and obedience, and that the gospel will evoke joy and generosity, but ultimately the matter is out of our hands and in God's instead.

Political Love: Why John's Gospel is not as Barren for Contemporary Ethics as it Might Appear

Bernd Wannenwetsch

The Fourth Gospel and modern ethics

Compared to the synoptic gospels and most apostolic writings, the Gospel of John appears one of the least "ethical" books in the New Testament. Not only does it lack the finesse of ethical casuistry that, say, the letters of Paul display, many of which were occasioned through concerns which we label "moral"; the Fourth Gospel also appears to lack much of the literary charm by which the Synoptic Gospels narrate the story of Jesus so as to shape the reader's moral imagination through the invitation of the reader to identify with the protagonists or to learn from what is happening to them.[1] Also, in comparison with the other gospels, John portrays Jesus as stressing more his distance from the world than his caring for its needs. The Fourth Gospel seems to be more interested in sovereignty than solidarity. As a consequence, the Jesus in John appears a less inviting moral exemplar to emulate, and in his teaching there is apparently less that can be gleaned for a Christian ethics than, say, for the purposes of speculative theology.

No wonder then that we find the Fourth Gospel not featuring much in biblical indexes of contemporary textbooks on moral theology. It is interesting to note that Christian writers in the Patristic period held this gospel in particularly high regard, not least because of its inspirational quality for the conduct of the Christian life—a quality that was often ascertained through allegorical interpretation, a prominent feature in St Augustine's 124 Homilies on St John.[2] This

---

[1] On the role of narratives for the formation of moral convictions and sensitivities, see Stanley Hauerwas and L. Gregory Jones (eds), *Why Narrative? Readings in Narrative Theology* (Grand Rapids: Eerdmans, 1989); cf. also Bernd Wannenwetsch, "Leben im Leben der Anderen. Zur theologischen Situierung und Pointierung der narrativen Dimension der Ethik in der angelsächsischen Diskussion," in Marco Hofheinz, Franz Mathwig, Matthias Zeindler (eds), *Ethik und Erzählung. Theologische und philosophische Beiträge zur narrativen Ethik* (Zürich: Theologischer Verlag Zürich, 2009), 93–112.

[2] Cf. Mark Edwards, *John*; *Blackwell Bible Commentaries* (Oxford: Blackwell, 2004), with a strong focus

finding should alert us to the possibility that the lack of interest in the Fourth Gospel for the construal of Christian moral thought today may have something to do with the way in which we conceive of "ethics" as a separate discipline and of its tasks and purposes in specifically modern terms.[3] There are powerful and specifically modern biases that trigger the suspicion that with John we cannot do the sort of ethics we think we should be doing today.

A threefold suspicion comes to mind by which the Gospel of John is ascribed a certain ethereal, nomistic and exclusivist character. **Ethereal**: Is there a certain speculative air in this gospel, a preoccupation with a quest for knowledge that distances it from the need for every ethics to be grounded in the concreteness of the realities of this world? **Nomistic**: Must the strong emphasis in Jesus' sayings on the "keeping of my commandments" not make us feel uneasy precisely as we sense how much the stressing of "obedience" is at odds with modern sensitivities? And, finally, do we perceive an air of **exclusivism**, if not tribalism, in this gospel's stressing of love amongst fellow disciples? It is not prescribing a type of love that is less than the neighborly love that we have learned to acknowledge as the core principle of every Christian ethics and a necessary feature of any such ethics that acknowledges universal responsibility? For these reasons, when it comes to the value of the Fourth Gospel for the construal of a Christian ethics today, we tend to agree with the sentiment of Jesus' disciples already then.

"This is a hard teaching. Who can accept it?" (Jn 6:60)[4]

In what follows, I hope to demonstrate that this gospel is not like the threefold suspicion assumes it must be and that it does, in fact, possess qualities that commend it for Christian moral reasoning. Yet, my point is not to soften the blow of the suspicions we named by demonstrating that this gospel is, after all, somewhat less nomistic, ethereal or exclusivist, and hence not completely irreconcilable with modern sensitivities. Rather, what I wish to suggest is based on a principled hermeneutic conviction. In order to be able to read Scripture imaginatively, we are to embrace a canonical approach that assumes the authoritative role for Christian discourses of Scripture as a whole, which implies the challenge to withstand the impulse to flee from or ignore the apparently difficult, non-congenial or scandalous passages in the canon. Without the courage to resist the urge for censorship, there would not be much

---

on the reception history of the text through the ages.

[3] For the specifically modern biases, as they appear in comparison with earlier (as well as with postmodern) accounts, see Alasdair MacIntyre, *Three Rival Versions of Moral Inquiry: Encyclopedia, Genealogy and Tradition* (New Haven: Notre Dame Press, 1992).

[4] Editor's note: In this essay, biblical quotations are taken from the New International Version UK.

of "relevance" left in the Bible. After all, every generation inevitably brings their own and very different biases to the reading of Scripture, which, at any given point of time in the history of interpretation, will single out different aspects or passages as candidates to be at odds with. What I suggest as a hermeneutic base rule in approaching our own contemporary reading of Scripture is that we allow for and honestly register our sense of unease about certain texts in the Bible but take this precisely as a challenge simultaneously to explore both the text afresh, and the reasons why we tend to shy away from it. Imaginative reading of Scripture will have to give prominence to a self-critical inquiry into the sources of our perception: whether our perception is driven, for example, by our understanding of the overall tendency we encounter in other biblical traditions as to what "is driving Christ" (Luther), or rather driven by our desire snugly to "fit" into contemporary discourses and appear "relevant" to the modern world and their agendas. Neither of these alternatives is wholly unproblematic or wholly wrongheaded, and there might be other desires, circumstances or objects that contribute to the patterns of our perception of the biblical text.

Scripture as interlocutor of tradition: A fresh reading of both

One basis of our instant perception of biblical passages with regard to their usefulness or lack thereof for contemporary moral reasoning is, of course, the distinct tradition of thought and practices to which we belong. Facing our sense of unease (or instant enthusiasm) with regard to biblical passages or books may therefore also tell us something about our respective tradition, certain strands, emphases or blind spots within it, which have contributed to the shaping of our reaction to those passages, when we encounter them. In keeping with the Reformation slogan of relating Scripture and Tradition as *norma normans* to *norma normata*, I suggest reading Scripture as a sort of critical interlocutor of our tradition, so as eventually to trigger a fresh reading of both.[5]

Even if it can be done in only a sketchy and tentative way in the context of this contribution, I will try to demonstrate what a fresh reading of John could bring to the ongoing task of writing forth the tradition of Lutheran moral theology. As the Lutheran heritage has been particularly fond of the claim to have been shaped by the rediscovery of Scripture as its prime inspiration and defining norm, it would be a sort of hermeneutical "deism," were we to reduce the impact of the Word to

---

[5] On the positive role that tradition plays for the reading of Scripture, see Bernd Wannenwetsch, "Conversing with the Saints as they Converse with Scripture," in *European Journal of Theology* 18:2 (2009), 125–35.

the role it **once** played in the formative period of our tradition. If the character-izing of Scripture as the *externum verbum* is to be of lasting significance, it needs to be sought over and over again as critical interlocutor so that we read Scripture against our tradition, just as individually we need to be prepared to read it against our own private perceptions, opinions, or chosen lifestyles. To read Scripture as a critical interlocutor of our tradition does not, however, mean principally to call into question all former judgments, propositions and consensus that have formed the tradition, although it cannot be ruled out that, in exceptional cases, an investigative reading of Scripture may challenge the churches towards a major shift of perception and transformation of practice. A tradition does not represent a monolithic block of meaning but, rather, a coherent discourse, invested with a sense of direction but also with a plurality of threats woven into it. Hence the challenge that a fresh reading of Scripture will pose to a tradition could well be one to rediscover the significance of suppressed or marginalized threats within the fabric of that tradi-tion, which need to be brought to new prominence; alternatively, a fresh reading of Scripture may help us discover how a particular threat of interpretation has become sterile or overly influenced by alien factors.

Before we turn to the task of exploring the moments of suspicion against the Fourth Gospel as for its perceived futility for contemporary ethics, it would seem useful to pause for a moment, take a step back and consider the very *gestus* in which this gospel describes Christian life. It would be impossible not to characterize this account as deeply drenched in the language of love. *Agape* certainly abounds in the Fourth Gospel, more than in any other writing of the New Testament. But, rather than rushing into an immediate attempt at describing what this love entails (whether in the form of Anders Nygren's famous distinction between *eros* and *apape* or in the form of other definitions that his account triggered in response), I suggest we begin by observing the overall type of "gesturing" within which John invokes *agape*.

The narrative of the washing of the disciples' feet in chapter 13, which the Fourth Gospel employs as a paradigmatic portrayal of Christ's love, begins by stating,

> … Jesus knew that the hour had come for him to leave this world and go to the Father. Having loved his own who were in the world, he loved them to the end.[6]

---

[6] *Eis telos egapesen autous*, [loved them until the end], is a formulation that hints at his sacrificial death on the cross, but the aorist tense seems to suggest a more immediate reading that understands the foot washing as indicating the utmost, the "extent" of Jesus' love, which certainly foreshadowed his passion as a whole.

"Remaining in God's love": An ethic of belonging

The stress on the "extent" of love leads to a different conceptualization of its moral significance. We tend to identify love either with emotion or action, or a combination of both; though neither of these dimensions is ruled out in John (when, for example, we see Jesus "deeply moved" and "weeping" at the death of Lazarus in chapter 11), the emphasis is on a more spatial account of love, on love as something to "remain" within.

> As the Father has loved me, so have I loved you. Now remain in my love. If you keep my commands, you will remain in my love, just as I have kept my Father's commands and remain in his love (Jn 15:9–10).

The vision of Christian life—and hence the life of the church—as one that does not have (nor should aspire) to be more or anything other than a remaining in God's love could be refreshingly different and liberating if taken seriously. It conveys a healthy challenge to specifically modern traditions of moral thought that center around metaphors of achievement or realization, if not of production, of a more engaged life, a "better world," a more successful church, and so forth. The irony of this immediacy, in which these modern accounts of the moral life tend to link human action with notions of "realization," "making happen" or "outcome," is that they so often only render such activity sterile and fruitless by subjecting it to the dictate of a meliorist account of reality, where nothing can be (assumed to be) good unless it is in the process of constantly being bettered.

> I am the vine; you are the branches. If you remain in me and I in you, you will bear much fruit; apart from me you can do nothing. … This is to my Father's glory, that you bear much fruit, showing yourselves to be my disciples. As the Father has loved me, so have I loved you. Now remain in my love (Jn 15:5; 8–9).

The Gospel according to John is certainly interested in "bearing fruit," but the emphasis on "remaining" in Christ, in his love and words, should encourage us to be more seriously interested in what it takes to understand, embrace and celebrate the "belonging," which grounds this "remaining" in the first place.[7] "Whoever belongs to God hears what God says. The reason you do not hear is that you do not belong to God" (Jn 8:47). An ethics of "belonging" in this

---

[7] "The slave does not have a permanent place in the household; the son has a place there forever" (Jn 8:35).

sense would be good news for a world, in which it has become painfully unclear for an increasing number of people where they actually belong.

From this perspective, we can formulate a list of questions that throw into relief what would be at stake in a contemporary ethics of belonging. The following list was compiled bearing in mind what has been called the "grammar" of Lutheran ethics—with its focus on a "particular ethos that communicates what is constitutive for human life," reflective of "the spheres of human living which bear God's promises"[8] (what Luther called "stations" or "regiments," what Dietrich Bonhoeffer called "mandates," or Ernst Wolf called "institutions").

- Do we **belong** to God as God's redeemed creatures, or do we belong to whoever or whatever claims our allegiance in this world?

- Do we **belong** to a world that the Creator has structured through institutions that invite our participation (*oeconomia, politia, ecclesia*), or is everything in the world subjected to utilitarian calculi?

- (*Ecclesia*) Do we **belong** to God's people, or is the church but a religious service provider that we chose to engage if we feel that we need it?

- (*Oeconomia*) Do we **belong** to our family, our wife or husband, or are these relationships no more than contractual commitments that can be negotiated and renegotiated at will?

- Do we **belong** to the earth as "earthlings" who are made of the same material as our fellow creatures, or is the earth our "environment" that we have at our disposal?

- (*Politia*) Do we **belong** to the civic community where we make our home as an invitation to contribute to the common good, or is the civil community a mere provider of services which we have a right to? (For some, though, this question will read painfully differently: Do I belong to any

---

[8] Hans G. Ulrich, "On the Grammar of Lutheran Ethics," in Karen L. Bloomquist (ed.), *Lutheran Ethics at the Intersections of God's One World*, LWF Studies 2/2005 (Geneva: The Lutheran World Federation, 2005), 27–48, here 28, 29. Luther: "Firstly, the Bible speaks of and teaches about the works of God without any doubt; these are divided into three hierarchies: economics, politics and church" (*oeconomia, politia, ecclesia: WA* TR 5, 218, 14ff). In conceiving these estates as "fellow-creatures" of humankind ("*concreatae sint,*" *WA* 40 III, 222, 35f.), Luther emphasized their character as elementary and paradigmatic forms of social life appropriate to creaturely existence from the beginning.

civic community at all, or am I dispossessed even of the one right to have rights?)

To understand the Christian life according to the "belonging" that the Fourth Gospel emphasizes as central, and according to the task which arises from it as "remaining" in God's love, will also yield a distinctive understanding of sin. The opposite of "remaining" is what John calls "going astray." "All this I have told you so that you will not go astray" (Jn 16:1).

"Going astray" echoes the Hebrew word for sin, *pesha*: "transgression," "trespassing"; but the Fourth Gospel reminds us that the transgression that is "sin" is not (at least not in the first instance) a trespassing of rules, but rather a forgetting or denial of where we actually belong. What we violate when sinning is not a moral principle, but our very "belonging"—the love of the Triune God as the properly assigned place of dwelling for God's redeemed creatures.

By characterizing the Christian life as a matter of a proper (sense of) belonging, I do not mean to downplay the demand to live a life worthy of the gospel. To wander off the love of God is not a lesser, but rather a more serious predicament to be in, since it cuts off from the source of all life, truth and joy. It is from this perspective that we best understand the sometimes rather harsh linguistic surface, by which the Fourth Gospel portrays Jesus' teaching as emphasizing the categorical rift between belonging with God and his word on the one hand and belonging to the "world" on the other.

> If you belonged to the world, it would love you as its own. As it is, you do not belong to the world, but I have chosen you out of the world. That is why the world hates you (Jn 15:19).

"Ethics," as it has been construed in the modern era, often appears as the principled and infinite art of determining degrees of compatibility between distinct moral principles, or of weighing them up against each other according to circumstance; but if the basic question is about our belonging, the rivalry between various agencies and powers that claim our allegiance will be much more obvious, and hence the need to become clear about where we really belong. Our actions and overall conduct of life will then simply "tell the tale" of where we actually belong.

Perhaps, then, there is a good theological reason for the Gospel according to John to be less concerned with "ethics" in the way we know it and tend to think of it today—precisely as it is interested in an unambiguous and clear sense of belonging as the root of human action and conduct. What we described as this "sense" of belonging and remaining cannot, however, remain vague. Left underdetermined it might be attractive, but attractive for the wrong reason, as a basis for a morality that remained sufficiently general and flexible to accommodate all sorts of individualist and arbitrary interpretations.

For John, though, this belonging and remaining it is highly specific: the invitation and challenge that the Fourth Gospel conveys is precisely to remain in Christ, in his love, and in his words (commands) as a way of remaining in the love of the Father, and hence as a sharing in the works of the Triune God.

With this specification in mind, we now turn to a more detailed attempt at understanding what this "love" is that Jesus gives his disciples as "a new commandment." This is also the time to deal with the moments of suspicion that we described at the beginning of this paper with regard to ethereality, nomism and exclusivism that are easily perceived as present in the Fourth Gospel. What we need to investigate is, therefore, How is this love that John stresses related to the structure of commandment? Who are the addressees and beneficiaries of that love? What is its paradigmatic form of activity?

Sisterly and brotherly love: Less than neighborly?

As interpreters of the modern era in particular have observed, in the Fourth Gospel the love command is not only addressed to the disciples more specifically (rather than, say, to the "crowd"), but also appears to be confined to this inner circle.[9] The Johannine standard formulation is *agapate allelous,* "love one another." How narrow must this appear when compared with the way in which in Luke 10 Jesus explicitly presses against any reductive interpretation of the love of neighbor, not to mention his call to love one's enemies? The impression of an exclusivist ring of the love command in the Fourth Gospel is reinforced, if looking at it in the context of the wider Johannine corpus. 1 John, for example, specifies the meaning of *allelous* explicitly as toward the "brother or sister" (1 Jn 4:19–21). As there is no reason to presume a difference of semantic intention between the Fourth Gospel and 1 John (irrespective of the question of authorship), it is safe to say that we find in John a stressing of brotherly and sisterly rather than neighborly love. The question we need to explore, though, is what this distinct language game of sisterly and brotherly love actually entails, and whether there are alternatives to that *prima facie* reading, which associates brotherly and sisterly love with a closing of the ranks attitude.

---

[9] "Immer aber ist es nur die Bruder-, nicht aber die Nächstenliebe, zu der aufgefordert wird." Siegfried Schulz, *Das Evangelium nach Johannes,* NTD 4 (Göttingen: Vandenhoeck&Ruprecht, 1978), 181.

The key to answering this question is to become clearer about two sub-questions. What sort of person is the "brother or sister" that John designates as the proper object of love, and why can the summons to love him or her be called a "new commandment"? First of all, we need to come to terms with the all too obvious (and hence under-investigated) fact that "brother or sister" is not a natural, but an "artificial" designator for a fellow disciple. Christians are brothers and sisters to one another as "children born not of natural descent, nor of human decision or a husband's will" (Jn 1:13), but, as the Fourth Gospel never tires of stressing, by virtue of divine initiative, in which the Father adopts the friends of his Son as his children. It is only on account of this divine act of adoption that fellow-Christians understand themselves as brothers and sisters to one another.

The artificiality of the status "brothers and sisters" as per divine grace, as opposed to reflecting a natural tie of blood and genes, points to an crucial insight: the Christian brother or sister is not brother or sister immediately,[10] but first encounters us as other—as "them," not the natural "us." Hence, if Jesus stresses sisterly or brotherly love, he cannot simply mean to emphasize the well-known love command (as we would expect him to), only this time with a slightly less demanding scope. Rather, by stressing love as specifically brother or sisterly, Jesus really gives a "new commandment," one that actually differs from the inherited commandment to love the neighbor (Lev 19:18). We keep missing the novelty in Jesus' commandment, as long as we stick to the framework of asking as to whether this love must be narrower than neighborly love. The actual difference is not in quantity, but quality. What we need to realize in the first instance is that sister or brotherly love is different from neighborly love, not more or less than it. The two cannot be in direct competition with each other.

In order to grasp more fully the particular character and purpose of this love, we turn to the narrative of the foot washing in chapter 13, which the Fourth Gospel explicitly presents as a paradigm for the new commandment. The pericope begins by stating: "Having loved his own who were in the world, he loved them to the end" (v.1), and culminates in the summons to do likewise: "Now that I, your Lord and Teacher, have washed your feet, you also should wash one another's feet" (v. 14).

---

[10] The mediated nature of the Christian community is emphasized by Dietrich Bonhoeffer in his *Life Together* as a feature of genuine "spiritual" love, which he sees as categorically distinct from self-centered love: "Self-centered love loves the other for the sake of itself; spiritual love loves the other for the sake of Christ. That is why self-centered love seeks direct contact with other persons. ... Because spiritual love does not desire but rather serves, it loves an enemy as a brother or sister. It originates neither in the brother or sister nor in the enemy, but in Christ and his word. ... Because Christ stands between me and an other, I must not long for unmediated community with that person. ... However, this means that I must release others from all my attempts to control, coerce, and dominate them with my love." Dietrich Bonhoeffer, *Life Together and Prayerbook of the Bible*, DBW 5, transl. D. W. Bloesch and J. H. Burtness (Minneapolis: Fortress Press, 2005), 42–44.

Jesus performs on his disciples an act that a host in antiquity would usually delegate to a slave: of welcoming his guest, perhaps a sojourner, by untying his sandals, cleansing and refreshing his feet.[11] A number of liturgical traditions have attempted literally to follow Jesus' commandment by performing the ritual of foot washing (*ablutio*) in the context of Christian public worship, in particular on Maundy Thursday. Whoever has once partaken of this ecclesial practice, either on the giving or receiving side, will know that it tends to make people uncomfortable, almost without fail. Although the narrative in John dwells mainly on the aspect of status, as it is typically associated with this act, and the self-humiliation of the Lord when performing it on his disciples, one aspect of this ritual, which is particularly difficult to bear for us today, is its intimate bodily character. In Western societies at least, we are used and trained to keeping our distance from other bodies and, with the exception of family members or those in professional medical care, tend to live our social lives on a non-touch basis. In addition to the general reticence with regard to touching other bodies, we know that the particular parts of the human body that keep contact with the ground can be smelly when in need of cleaning, and the unease that accompanies sensual perception of this phenomenon is (hormonally) buffered only with regard to our genetic proxies: family members.

I suggest that sisterly or brotherly love is not a reductive version of the general love command, but one that makes it theologically more specific. To love another (whether initially a stranger, loose acquaintance, or peer) as a brother or sister, means to love with the unreserved, unconditional and faithful and lasting love that we associate with family relationships. The Gospel according to John both articulates and intensifies this characterization of the love of the fellow believer as brotherly or sisterly by linking it to the love of the Father as received through the Son in the work of the Spirit. The unconditional, faithful and true love that we associate with family relationships, but which we know is often compromised within families, is anchored in the one true source of this love, the Triune God.

Political love

But even when we are prepared to acknowledge that the point of the Johannine summons, "My command is this: love each other as I have loved you" (Jn 15:12), is one of specifying love rather than confining its scope, we still need

---

[11] In Israel the act was seen as so degrading to the one who performed it so that only Gentile slaves would be considered for it. Cf. Schulz, op. cit. (note 9), 173.

to address the critical question as to whether this emphasis on brotherly or sisterly love has not effectually undermined a wider, political paradigm, under which we configure human sociality.

This, so the great political philosopher Hannah Arendt sharply alleges, is the (in her opinion disastrous) political legacy of Christianity. Arendt believed that when Christianity enthroned "love" as the new overall organizing principle of human sociality, it replaced the older and more appropriate political ideal of respect/honor (in the sense of the Aristotelian *philia politike,* political friendship), and thus effectively privatized the public sphere. Love, Arendt suggests, is perfectly appropriate within the private world of the family, but could not but destroy political culture when it begun colonizing the public sphere with its inappropriate (in this context) code of affective alliances instead of rational ones.[12]

While Arendt certainly put her finger on a critical issue, illustrated, for example, by patterns of tribal loyalty that obstruct a political culture's need to be free for any sort of sensible coalescing, her blaming of Christianity was prone to overlook the critical insight we have gleaned from our exposition of John about the unnaturalness of sisterly or brotherly love: the summons to love the (potential) stranger and (perhaps very different) other as brother or sister, is already political in nature. It initiates an ethos that trains the members of such a community in what it takes peacefully to coexist with all others: with one another (fellow believers) at first, but then also in wider human societies and, eventually, between different societies, peoples and nations. We may be reminded in this context of Aristotle's claim that the family is the core and kernel of every larger human society because the family provides not only members for the wider society due to its reproductive purpose, but also prepares them to become citizens according to its educational purpose. In the Gospel of John, however, the political dimension of this "unnatural family" of disciples of Jesus is not a matter of Christian pedagogy, but in a most immediate sense a divine gift—the gift of reconciliation as the matrix in which this new form of human society has its very existence.

This is the conceptual gain of the intertwining *en* ("in") rhetoric that abounds in John. When the Fourth Gospel portrays Jesus as praying for unity amongst his disciples, "as the Father and I are one," we gather from it that unity must not to be understood as the immediate purpose of politics. Such an understanding would trigger all sorts of identity politics with their inherent moments of violence and exclusion. Rather, God bestows unity on the believers as a partaking

---

[12] Arendt calls love an "unworldly phenomenon" and "the most powerful of all antipolitical human forces." Hannah Arendt, *The Human Condition*, 2nd ed. (Chicago, London: University of Chicago Press, 1998), 242.

in the unity of the Trinity, which is a unity of love. When unity is no longer the purpose of politics, but its endowment, the love that it summons is already political in nature and hence should be free to act in such a vein.

The paradigm of that love that the Fourth Gospel sets before us in Jesus' washing the disciples' feet is of a serving but not condescending kind. It is a love that allows the other to "have a part" in us—like Jesus instructs Simon, when he is rebuking him for performing a slave's service, "Unless I wash you, you have no part with me" (Jn 13:8).[13] This participatory love engages the disciples with each other, as recipients at first, but then also as agents of that same love which they have received. Note that the form in which the disciples receive this love is already communal, in that Jesus takes turns in washing each individual's feet so as to turn each recipient of his love into a witness, as each observes at the same time what Jesus is doing to the other disciples. We speak of individual, yet not private reception of this high act of love, as it occurs, not in an intimate one-on-one setting, but in the semi-public of the Passover banquet. Correspondingly, when Jesus summons his friends to wash each other's feet, the purpose of these acts of love is not confinable to an in-group, but is to be a witness to the world: "By this everyone will know that you are my disciples, if you love one another" (Jn 13:35). Political love, as I would call it, is both participatory and proclamatory. In spite of the rather different rhetoric that the Fourth Gospel employs, we discern in its portrayal of love a highly interesting parallel with apostolic writings, where citizenship language is taken up explicitly, when Paul, for example, summons the believers "[w]hatever happens, conduct yourselves in a manner worthy of the gospel of Christ" (Phil 1:27), or when the Letter to the Ephesians addresses them as "members of his [God's] household" (Eph 2:19).[14]

It must be admitted that the church's political nature as the corporate witness of God's love has been severely underplayed in the churches of the Reformation, not least in liberal countries, where a highly individualized notion of faith has resulted in a perception of church as a mere expression of the natural desire of the religious consciousness to congregate.[15] This trend was certainly aided by

---

[13] Paul seems to echo this conjecture in Romans 12, when he describes the new kind of sociality that the *ekklesia tou theo* is in terms of individual believers being "members of each other." See Bernd Wannenwetsch, "Members of One Another. Charis, Ministry and Representation. A politico-ecclesial reading of Romans 12," in Craig G. Bartholomew et al. (eds), *A Royal Priesthood. The Use of the Bible Ethically and Politically* (Carlisle, Grand Rapids: Paternoster and Zondervan 2002), 196–220.

[14] For the wider context, see Bernd Wannenwetsch, *Political Worship. Ethics for Christian Citizens,* Oxford Studies in Theological Ethics (Oxford: Oxford University Press, 2004, paperback 2009).

[15] The assumption of the "necessarily social" character of religion was most famously expressed by Friedrich Schleiermacher in his "Speeches." "Ist die Religion einmal, so muß sie notwendig auch gesellig sein ... ihr müßt gestehen, daß es etwas Widernatürliches ist, wenn der Mensch dasjenige, was er

the coming to prominence of a simplistic (and very Luther-unlike) doctrine of the two kingdoms, which tied the notion of the political to the "worldly kingdom" and thus kept it separate from the church and its mission. Yet, to be reminded of political love (John) and, hence, of the exemplary role of the church as God's *polis* (Paul) should at the same time caution us about another stream of political thought in Protestantism, which in its well-grounded rejection of the separatism associated with the two kingdoms theology tended to stress the outward direction of "neighborly love" so immediately as to dissolve it into social activism. In either case, the crucial role of the church as an exemplary place and mediator of the politics of God was eclipsed.

For both these slips in the tradition of Lutheran political (and ecclesiastical) thought, the Johannine emphasis on a belonging and "remaining" has the capacity to provide a healthy corrective: based, as it is, on account of God's love as a space in which human love is empowered to transcend its natural bounds and become "political love," in which the other is treated as one would treat one's own brother or sister.

---

in sich erzeugt und ausgearbeitet hat, auch in sich verschließen will." Friedrich Schleiermacher, *Reden über die Religion. Kritische Ausgabe*, besorgt von G. C. B. Pünjer (Braunschweig, 1879), 4. Rede, 181.

Exploring Effective Context – Luther's Contextual Hermeneutics

Vítor Westhelle

Introduction

We theologians are weavers. We weave a special kind of tapestry called "theology" and each of our tapestries is distinct; it has a unique tint. Weaving is done by interconnecting warps and wefts; warps are the longitudinal threads and wefts are the transverse threads. In other words, it is the intersection of that which is thrown across, the warps, with that which is woven, the wefts. The result of this weaving is the tapestry. Our tapestries take shape depending on what we throw across. A tapestry has a context within the context in which it is being woven. I was given the topic, "Exploring Effective Context," and I cannot do that without providing a working definition of context. Can there be a better definition of contexts than the one I have just given?

Etymologically, context comes from the Latin *contextus,* the weaving together of words, from *contexere* to weave together, from *com- + texere* to weave. In the literary field, a text is the product of something that has been woven, the weaver being the writer, author, or composer of the text. What comes together are the surrounding circumstances that affect and allow for the weaving to take place; hence its importance for hermeneutics. In biblical exegesis, context referred first to the relationship of a pericope to the broader literary work into which it is inserted. It was then expanded to include also other, extra-biblical, literary works of the time of composition, and finally also to historical and cultural circumstances that might have influenced the composition, i.e., the sociopolitical and economic settings. In other words, contexts are made of a set of commonly shared experiences that offer lenses through which the reception of given information is filtered. This changes the interpretation that can be given to a text. This is the task of hermeneutics.

Context and hermeneutics

Since Friedrich Schleiermacher, at the beginning of the nineteenth century, modern hermeneutics has recognized the distinction between the grammatical sense of a text and that which Schleiermacher called the psychological sense, achieved by a reader's insight or divination into the meaning of a text. The psychological sense tried to establish the non-grammatical features accounting for peculiarities that allow for the understanding of a text. Texts bear the mark of the environment in which they were woven and which is required for the understanding of it; texts have an ecology, an environment with which they interact. Since the last century, after the work of Martin Heidegger, Hans-Georg Gadamer and, particularly, Paul Ricouer, it also became clear that it is not only the environment of the "weaver" of a text that matters for the understanding of a text but also the environment of the reader. This is so because the meaning of the text is not only in and behind the text, but always also ahead of the text itself, i.e., in the milieu of a future reader who encounters it with a pre-understanding that tints the understanding as colored spectacles do when looking at a texture.

In dealing with a text theologically, it is the context of the writer and that of the reader, in addition to the grammatical features, that need to be probed for meaning to be realized. The development of the historical critical method in biblical studies, to use an example of a hermeneutical technique, can be traced back to the fifteenth century, when the Italian humanist Lorenzo Valla demonstrated that the "Donation of Constantine" was a forgery, a discovery that was very important for Luther and the Reformation. But it really became a core concern in Protestantism when it was applied to biblical interpretation. Since the eighteenth century, starting with Hermann Samuel Reimarus and Gotthold Ephraim Lessing, rules for textual and exegetical studies taking its original context into consideration were established and continued to be developed over the next couple of centuries. Yet, it was mostly due to the emergence of liberation theologies in the second half of the last century that the context of the reader became decisive for determining the theological meaning of a text. The meaning of a text changes decisively depending on a series of factors: the author's setting, the circumstances under which a text is read, and also texts that are in- or excluded. In the following, I shall refer to some examples of contextual impact, followed by pointing to some of the critique of the contextual approaches in the hermeneutical endeavor and, finally, I shall use one of Luther's texts as a case study in contextual theology.

Setting of the author: First we shall consider an original context and how it has shaped the message and then look into the significance of the receiving context. Let us take the Gospel of John. Written late in the first century CE, when the Christian message made its inroad into the surrounding pagan culture, it adopted from the new enveloping environmen, a language and concepts used therein and was thus contextually relevant. One of the most influential popular philosophies of the day, shaping the language and culture encircling the Christian incursion into the pagan world, was Gnosticism. The Gospel of John was developed in such an environment that encased its message. Yet, even with the adoption of elements of a philosophical system that by the second half of the second century was deemed inimical to main claims of the Christian gospel, as Irenaeus fiercely argued,[1] John was able to be a witness to the gospel.[2]

Circumstances of the reader: Let us consider an example of the importance of the receiving context. For many liberation theologians, particularly from Latin America, the text of Exodus, from the deliverance from Egypt to the possession of the Promised Land in the Book of Joshua, became paradigmatic for a whole generation of theologians. But the same texts that promise a land for displaced people is read very differently by black South Africans, by Dravidians in India, or by Native Americans and Mexicans whose land has been taken by the Boers, Arians and the USA, respectively, who, not surprisingly, often appealed to the same biblical promise of land to be conquered in the name of God. Indeed, the receiving context matters.

Selective readings: Readings are always selected not only on the grounds that they are appropriate for certain circumstances, but also because they may and do serve ideological purposes. Howard Thurman, the dean of early black theology in US academia and mentor to Martin Luther King, Jr., remembers growing up on a farm. During his childhood, a preacher would regularly come for worship services and Thurman heard the Bible read and the sermons preached on them. And every day, at night, his mother would read him biblical stories. He grew up thinking that there were two Bibles because he never heard the same stories from the preacher and from his mother. Only later did he realize that the preacher only read to the black farm laborers from the letters of Paul, while his mother was always reading to him from the gospels. The ideological implications are quite suggestive, if not disturbing, but the decisive element in this memoir is to show that selection implies also exclusion. As in

---

[1] Irenaeus, *Against Heresy*, transl. Dominic J. Unger (New York, N.Y.: Paulist Press, 1992).

[2] Ernst Käsemann, "Ketzer und Zeuge: Zum johanneischen Verfasserproblem," in *Zeitschrift für Theologie und Kirche* 48(1951), 292–311.

a picture, what the camera captures is a scene intentionally abstracted from other surrounding features.

Critiques of contextual theologies

We should not forget that the contextuality of all theology has often been criticized. Three of these critiques are worth mentioning, the most notable among them being the fundamentalists. The fundamentalists would reject the importance of any sense of context: the grammar and placement within the work, the circumstances surrounding the author, and definitely the context of the receiving end were decried. The letter, the written word, is to be maintained in its assumed pristine purity. This theological posture has often been dismissed outright by academic theology with nonchalance. Yet, its relative sociological importance needs to be addressed for it is itself part of many a context.

Some theological and philosophical developments have, not without reason, led to the critique by the neo-orthodox movement in the twentieth century. With its stress on God's revelation as unfettered by any human circumstance, history and context are regarded only as pointers to a dogmatic content, as in the creedal expression "… under Pontius Pilate." The reference to Pilate in the creed is only to attest to the full humanity of Christ, but substantially the prefect's name is an accident in the philosophical sense of the term; essentially it does not bear any dogmatic weight. Yet, this stance shoulders the marks of a context in which forms of existentialism were a response to a situation in which the message of the gospel could not be distinguished from the context itself.

Still others point to a more complex issue that plagues contextual approaches to a text. In this third critique, context is too spongy a word. What are the limits of a context? When is something out of context? How porous are the boundaries of a context? How far can they be expanded, or how constrictive are they? Which are the social parameters that serve as a criterion to define a context? Here, issues such as race, gender, geographic location, economic stratum, nationality, language and so forth create unmanageable variables that defy a working definition. Contexts are made of shared experiences. But experiences are themselves an ensemble of stimuli in an individual that are not reproduced exactly the same way in any other. This means that if a strict definition were to be adopted the result would be a form of solipsism since my context, in a *reductio ad absurdum*, is only my own solipsistic self. And that is the end of communication because meaning, bound to context, can only be assessed by me and nobody else, because this alone is the "context" to decipher meaning, since no one else shares exactly the same experience as I. This is self-contradictory because meaning that cannot be communicated is no meaning at all, since it cannot be mediated.

The representation of context

Over against the impasse of the importance of context and its reduction to absurdity, postcolonial theory has offered some help.[3] Context as such is not the issue to be abstractly defined and transcendentally used. The point is to recognize how a context is produced and conveyed as such to others, and thus the importance of weaving. How does a context present itself as a context and who does this "presenting"?[4] In other words, the issue that concerns us is not the context as an abstract category, but the mechanisms through which a given context is represented and who does the representation. So this moves the discussion from the classical hermeneutical question of meaning to who defines what a context entails, what the variables are that define its contours, and to what end the definition is employed. Put differently, Who is the stool pigeon? Whose is the representation, and whose is the reading of the text? For postcolonial writers, the representation of a given context, when done from outside, independently of the moral intent of the one doing the representation, is already cast in the cultural presupposition of the context of the one who does the representation; and this, again, independent of the moral intent, is an act of violence, because violence is precisely to deprive the other of the possibility of self-expression, of having the other's representation recognized.[5]

However, this is not exactly an either/or logic. There is always an asymmetry between the representation of a context and the context itself. There is a difference, for example, between how a burka is represented by a Westerner and by an Afghan woman. For the Afghani it might be a liberating mode of self-representation while, for the Westerner, say a journalist or politician, it is turned into a symbol of oppression and gender discrimination. The difference between the two approaches on how to represent a context is the one that marks the dividing line between the hegemonic context and the subaltern one. The

---

[3] Vítor Westhelle, *After Heresy: Colonial Practices and Postcolonial Theologies* (Eugene, OR: Cascade Books, 2010)

[4] See for example the fascinating discussion of the sati ritual and how it was portrayed in colonial India in Gayatri C. Spivak, "Can the Subaltern Speak?" in Cary Nelson and L. Grossberg (eds), *Marxism and the Interpretation of Culture* (Chicago: Illinois University Press, 1988), 271–313.

[5] In the story of Cain and Abel, the first human act of violence recorded in the biblical narrative, this is well illustrated. Abel's offering was recognized and Cain's not, thus violence ensued.

former, the hegemonic context, enjoys the pretense of holding the accuracy of the representation, its "scientific" status because it also controls the regime of truth and the canons to which it is accountable. The other is denigrated insofar as it does not operate within the environment of the hegemonic epistemology or the reigning regime of truth.

The latter, the subaltern's self-representation, is either totally neglected for not meeting the hegemonic standards or by being inept in operating them; the subaltern in aiming at self-representation is always "contaminated" by elements imported from the external contexts that do the casting of the representation from the outside, or the hegemonic side. The reason for this is the following: The context that claims the right to represent itself does it in such a way as to intervene in the field controlled by the dominant context. For this it needs to use concepts and categories that are imported. This process in postcolonial theory is called hybridity. In postcolonial studies, hybridity is the ability to make incursions into other contextual and conceptual territories and employ, for its own purposes, notions familiar to the hegemonic context. This process is in play, for example, when Franz Fanon uses Freud, when Paulo Freire employs Hegel in his pedagogy, when Gayatri Chakravorty Spivak uses Jacques Derrida, when Edward Said employs Michel Foucault, or anyone of them uses Karl Marx. They employ critically progressive elements coming from the very context that has always defined them from outside and imposed on them an identity that is not proper. The postcolonial response is to represent the subaltern from inside out but always also making improper incursions into the hegemonic context. This is called resistance or counter-violence.

Luther: A case study

What is the point of this introduction to addressing "effective" context? The point is best laid out in a sermon that Luther delivered in August of the turbulent year 1525 as part of a series of seventy-seven sermons on Exodus.[6] Contemporary postcolonial theorists have explained the problem regarding the role of representation in interpretation or hermeneutics. However, Luther, much before these explanations/instructions, was practicing it in the midst of a tumultuous year in the life of the Reformer. The published essay titled

---

[6] The text of the sermon was reworked for a publication as a pamphlet a year later, and in 1527 was used as a fitting introduction to the publication of Luther's sermons. This translation is from the reworked pamphlet of 1526, as found in *WA* 16, 363–393.

"How Should Christians Regard Moses,"[7] is exemplary of this practice. Luther was struggling with the influence of some enthusiastic preachers who, not unlike fundamentalists today, would take the laws of the Pentateuch (then still attributed to Moses, and thus Moses becoming the metonymy for the law and promises in the Pentateuch) and impose them on the people under the admonition, "Dear people, this is the Word of God." Luther's response is a terse lesson in contextual hermeneutics, "That is true; we cannot deny it. But we are not the people." And further, "It is not enough to look and see whether this is God's word, whether God said it; rather we must look to whom it has been spoken, whether it fits us."[8]

Luther's sermon and the essay as published tell us three things about contextualization, or three criteria by which it should be normed. The first is about pertinence. A text is valid for one insofar as it addresses one's situation, one's context, and offers a language adequately giving expression to it. If it does not, it does not pertain to one. The law is helpful insofar as it addresses a particular condition. The second criterion is about innovation. Moses is of universal validity, not because of the particular laws addressed to a particular people, but because of "the promises and pledges of God about Christ."[9] This newness, this gospel, speaks to and delivers promises to Jews and Gentiles alike, and it is for all nations and addresses all, indeed, "also to angels, wood, fish, birds, and animals, and all creatures," but we are neither one of those.[10] Thirdly, Moses becomes an example, as many of the other prophets, to be emulated in one's own context, and serves as the hermeneutical *locus* to the task of transfiguration, of translating the figure of Moses from his context and his people to another context and another people. I shall briefly expound on these three criteria that Luther identified as the ruling task of hermeneutics. I will do it not to find a pristine Luther but to apply to Luther's own text the same contextual hermeneutic principles he applied to the biblical text.

Pertinence

The first task and criterion takes into consideration the germaneness of a text for a given people, how it resonates with the experience of a people. Here, Luther distinguishes between the universal ground "implanted in me by nature," or "natural law" and its codified form, positive law, that is contextually bound.

---

[7] *LW* 35, 161–174. The German title is, "Ein Unterrichtung, wie sich die Christen in Moses sollen schicken." *WA* 16, 363.

[8] Ibid., 170.

[9] Ibid., 168.

[10] Ibid., 171f.

The Decalogue, for example, is the codified form for a given people. We do not follow the Decalogue because God gave it to Moses and Moses gave it to us, but because "Moses agrees with nature."[11] But from natural law to its codification in positive law requires adaptation, even insofar as the Ten Commandments are concerned. On encounter with new and different circumstances/contexts, be it time, place, experience, they are renewed; "these [new] Decalogues are clearer than the Decalogue of Moses," boasted Luther on the basis of this hermeneutical principle.[12] "Clearer" (on other occasions he said also "better") is to be understood in the sense of being more suitable to the context different from the one of the Israelites camping by Mount Sinai.

Yet, we often long for an indisputable external word that we can rely upon independent of our own circumstances. Why? So we do not need to argue, and we do not need to think, just obey; we need only to be sure that the unquestionable word is maintained. We suffer from what Derrida called archive fever or the malady of the archive (*mal d'archive*), that is, to use the past to authenticate the present, to find a pristine origin, a pure and authentic source. But this always implies a disregard for the present and the places this present occupies (and the present always takes place, or it is not a present, a gift). This is what we do when we use other categories, ideas and concepts (biblical or not) that other contexts honor as crucial to their experience, and repeat them, parroting them, in complete abstraction of our present and where it is situated. What might have been good in one context will not necessarily be good in another. Luther uses examples of Old Testament ordinances—as the one of a widow being taken as a wife by the brother-in-law, or the practice of tithing, and the Jubilee year—as good practices. But they do not "pertain to the Gentiles, such as tithing and other equally fine" ordinances.[13] So how do other contexts become important for us in our context? They help us to devise strategies and tactics to enlighten the present. It is necessary to recognize how the Word of God is addressed to a given people so that we might also discern how it is relevant to our context. In the words of the Brazilian bishop Pedro Casaldáliga, "The universal Word speaks only dialect."

So this is the first task: to discover what resonates in the text. Resonance is a term that has long been used in physics and chemistry and has been applied by social psychology to describe the fact that our nervous system is not self-contained, but reacts to stimuli from the social environment in which an individual is

---

[11] Ibid., 168.

[12] *LW* 34, 112–13.

[13] Luther, op. cit. (note 7), 168.

inserted, i.e., their context. Resonance implies responsibility. In this sense, one can say that a text resonates not because one individual relates empathically to it, but because it feels right and responsibly fits the context offering vistas to move along. Resonance in socio-psychology is the opposite of dissonance, the experience of something not expected and disturbing assumptions.

An illustration that exemplifies the task of resonance is pertinent here. Flávio Koutzii is a Brazilian militant of the 1960s and 70s (today he is a politician). He went into exile in Argentina after the military coup d'état in Brazil in 1964. When the same happened in Argentina some ten years later (1975–76), he was arrested and jailed with other political prisoners. In prison they had no access to outside information and the conversation among them was monitored, and any mention of politics did not go unpunished. Yet, the military jailers allowed them to have a Bible. Instead of the political jargon, they were used to and that was off-limits, they started to have conversations using biblical stories and concepts to describe the political situation, and thus fooling the censors. Koutzii, himself a secular Jew, recounts in his memoires, entitled *Pieces of Death in the Heart*,[14] a surprising phenomenon. Biblical stories of exile, oppression, liberation, the healings of the New Testament, the Cross and Resurrection provided them with a language that amazingly was adroitly pertinent to describe the context and pointed to rays of hope in a way that the socio-political language they mastered so well was not able to do with the same incisiveness. This is a story that can also be heard from many annals documenting the early experience of Base Christian Communities as they morphed into an ecclesial context from outlawed political groupings in Latin America, which originally were not connected to the church or religion in general. This is resonance: the text speaks to my situation.

Now, the critical issue that emerges with this criterion of pertinence and the hermeneutical principle of resonance is the risk of acculturating Christian theology and proclamation. Inculturation, instead, has been the goal of the criterion of resonance, but when difference is hampered, inculturation turns into acculturation. Difference and otherness are dimmed by adjustment to a cultural ethos. This has been the warning issued in the twentieth century by neo-orthodoxy, particularly against Lutheranism's alleged tendency to acculturate the message of the gospel. But this is what Luther says in the same essay we have been discussing. "In this manner, therefore, I should accept Moses, and not sweep him under the rug: first because he provides fine examples of

---

[14] Flávio Koutzii, *Pedaços de Morte no Coração* (Porto Alegre: L&PM, 1984).

laws, from which excerpts may be taken. Second, in Moses there are promises of God which sustain faith."[15]

This brings us to the second criterion, and this is a criterion that a culture cannot provide out of its own resources; it needs to come from outside.

Innovation

Luther introduces the second criterion with these words, "In the second place I find something in Moses that I do not have from nature: the promises and pledges of God about Christ. This is the best thing. It is not something that is written naturally into the heart, but comes from heaven."[16]

If the law needs to be cast contextually, the gospel says: now that you understand where you are (which is the function of the law), it is time for a transformation, change; it is time for innovation. It is time for the book of the law—and every "book" is about the law—to be closed so that the living word of the gospel can be opened. Even as we respect our cultural bearings and are faithful to them, transformation comes from the outside, from the other, and the other is the one who announces, "Do not think that I have come to abolish the law or the prophets; I have come not to abolish but to fulfill. ... You have heard that it was said ... . But I say to you" (Mt 5:17–22). Paraphrasing, "I have come not to disregard your context, but to make it whole. ... You have learned to accept what resonates with you ... but I am daring you to do something new." This is Luther's hermeneutical *discrimen*, the critical and decisive moment that sets the limit to pertinence. While pertinence looks for resonance of a text in relation to a situation, innovation is attuned to the moment of dissonance in which novelty brings about transformation. This double task that entails both resonance and dissonance is biblically presented with perspicuity in a short parable closing the collection of parables in the Gospel of Matthew, the gospel that most evinces the concern for contextuality and pertinence. "And he [Jesus] said to them, 'Therefore every scribe who has been trained for the kingdom of heaven is like the master of a household who brings out of his treasure what is new and what is old'" (Mt 13:52). And what is new is the gospel, the good news, that which has not been there; it breaks in; it renews and disturbs.

Novelty brings people out of their comfort zone and calls for the boundaries of contextuality to be transgressed. Again I offer a biblical example. In the Gospel of John, chapter 20, we have the story of the disciples gathering in the upper room, with the doors shut for fear of the Judeans. It is the Sun-

---

[15] Luther, op. cit. (note 7), 169.

[16] Ibid., 168f. This is one of many examples in which Luther asserts the presence of the gospel in the Hebrew Scriptures.

day of Resurrection. Suddenly Jesus stands among them and says, "Peace be with you," and the disciples rejoice. All is cozy and everything is in order as long as they stay in the upper room with Jesus in their midst, as long as they stay in their reliable context. Now something interesting happens. Jesus has already wished them peace. But he says to them again, "Peace be with you." It is a salutation not much different from saying "good morning," or so the disciples thought. And you do not repeat a salutation unless, for some reason, the person to whom it was directed did not hear it. The repetition was necessary because they did not get it! The disciples where clueless as to what "peace" meant. So Jesus repeats it, "peace be with you," and, to make it clearer, he paraphrases it, "As the Father sent me, so I send you." That meant, get out of here, face your fear, and go for the new. In fact, novelty is always a source of anxiety and fear because it exposes us and disrupts that which we learn to administer in the quotidian of our contexts. The oldest of the gospels, Mark, in its probably original ending has the women at the tomb of Jesus on Easter Sunday being told that Jesus had resurrected and the final words of the gospel, arguably original, are, "… terror and amazement had seized them; and they said nothing to anyone, for they were afraid" (Mk 16:8). We know and are even trained to administer grief, but a surprise, even if wonderful, scares us because it is out of our control.

Cultures seek to represent their context. In theological language, this representation is called the law, the frozen image that purports to exhibit the way things are. But, the reality represented is dynamic, unstable and ever changing. So the moment a representation is displayed it is no longer faithful to the context it presumes to portray; it is no longer presence but representation. Novelty, the gospel, cannot be represented because it is presence; to use Paul's image, it is not the letter that is dead in its frozen state. It is the living word, *viva vox*. This presence is of Jesus himself by the power of the Spirit that breaks in and breaks out as the spirit is the breath that inhales and exhales.

In Greek, and so in the New Testament also, the word for "presence" is *parousia*. But this word has a vitiated and often false connotation referring to an eventual future return of Jesus, a "second coming," a *deutero parousia*, which is an expression never used in the New Testament.[17] *Parousia* is the presence of the gospel, that is, of Christ. This has an eschatological character to it. But it is an eschatology that is undistinguishable from the experience of the Christ breaking in and convoking us out of the familiar places we inhabit and learn to control by the mechanisms of representation described above.

---

[17] Probably was used the first time by Justin Martyr by the middle of the second century.

This is then the tension between pertinence and innovation. One defines our context and the other calls us out or brings about a transformation inside. Pertinence without innovation is blind legalism, but innovation without pertinence is empty spiritualism.

Transfiguration

Here we come to Luther's third criterion. It entails the healing of the malady of the archive that says that we can only be legitimate if we do it exactly as Moses, Jesus, Paul, Augustine, or Luther did, or else as this tradition has been conveyed by the German, Scandinavian, or North American readings of it. It is important to honor tradition in a similar way as Luther regarded the Scriptures, distinguishing what pertains to a context and what does not on the one hand, and the novelty for all that is the gospel of Christ's presence (*parousia*) on the other. But if only this distinction were to be applied, then I would just throw into the garbage all that does not pertain to me in my context, and end up with a hacked Bible and contempt for other contexts and traditions, and novelty, the gospel, becomes that which makes me feel good.

Luther thus introduces his third point by saying that we also "read Moses for the beautiful examples of faith, of love, and of the cross, as shown in the fathers, Adam, Abel, Noah, Abraham, Isaac, Moses, and all the rest. From them, we should learn to trust in and to love him [God]. In turn there are also examples of the godless …"[18] An example is what in literary theory has been called *figura*, a figure.[19] Figures describe emblematic characters, as the ones Luther mentioned, or events, which unlike concepts and doctrines are rooted in and belong to a context; they have a genealogy, a place, and a time to which they belong. Additionally, figures have the capability of migrating over time and space and find roots in other characters or events. A figure is the catalyst of different experiences in different times and different places. The Exodus of the Israelites from Egypt is the figure for many contemporary liberation struggles. Pharaoh is the figure for many oppressive and authoritarian rulers. Moses is the figure for revolutionary leaders. Peter is the figure for the papacy, Luther for resolute leadership, as in "here I stand," and so forth.

This is the practice of transfiguration. A figure that was part of a given context reemerges in another and is in this new one trans-figured. This figure becomes the host of contextual experiences different from the ones it was originally invested with, but in a certain way also consonant with it. Just as

---

[18] Luther, op. cit. (note 7), 173.

[19] Erich Auerbach, "Figura," in Erich Auerbach, *Scenes from the Drama of European Literature* (Minneapolis, MN: University of Minnesota Press, 1984), 11–78.

Luther suggested that we take the examples and emulate them, we also need to take the example of Luther when he witnessed the good news of Christ for us in our contexts. Luther needs to be transfigured as he often has been.

Take, for example, the story of Jesus' transfiguration as they are presented in the Synoptic Gospels. It seems to me that the passage needs to be read in the context of the preceding pericope, both in Mark and Matthew. Jesus asks the people as to who they said he was, and the answer he got was John, Elijah, or one of the prophets—even the greatest one, Moses. But Peter confessed him as the Messiah, the one who the others pointed to. Right confession! However, immediately thereafter Jesus starts narrating the suffering he had to undergo. Peter rebukes him because tradition had it that this would not be the lot of a blessed prophet, much less of the triumphant Messiah. Jesus' retort is, "Get behind me, Satan!" In other words, Jesus was saying, "Peter, don't flee from our context, Elijah is here, and so is Moses, it is also about them; they are also in me and with me. But I am who I am, and I am here under the present circumstances which are not those of any other prophet; let me be who I am." Indeed, Peter has the right confession. But, alas, the wrong context! Peter had archive fever. Precise orthodoxy, yet inept contextualization—this is a sign of the demonic.[20]

In the narrative of the transfiguration, which immediately follows, the same lesson is repeated. The figures of Moses and Elijah emerge from different times and contexts and their mantels are laid upon Jesus. Their figures were transmuted (*metamorphete* in Greek) to Jesus and in him they became again alive and present. When the disciples remind him that the scribes said that, before the Messiah, Elijah must come first, Jesus tells them that Elijah had already come but was not recognized. And they realize that he was talking about John the Baptist. Now Jesus was also the new Moses, the liberator of the people. Behold this marginal Galilean for he was claiming the staff of Moses when the high priests were those who sat in the chair of Moses. For the disciples, it was at that moment that Jesus became contextualized and his figure became the host of all the relevant and cherished experiences of that Jewish context and its traditions. Jesus was not the "Son of God" out of this world above the ambiguities of history. Jesus, the Son of God, was tied to the history of his people in that context; he was not the pristine "Son of God" as Peter seemed to believe. Jesus embodied the ambiguous and frail history of the context in which he was immersed and absorbed it, and ended up being killed by the context in which he did the weaving of his message. Luther applied the same principle to Jesus himself. So says Luther in the same text I have been using,

---

[20] Vítor Westhelle, *The Church Event: Call and Challenge of a Church Protestant* (Minneapolis: Fortress Press, 2009), 98–102

"For example in the account of the ten lepers, that Christ bid them to go to the priest and make sacrifice [Lk 17:14] does not pertain to me. The example of their faith, however, does pertain to me; I should believe Christ, as they did."[21]

Transfiguration is this practice by which a figure from a given context has the potential for being a catalyst of experiences for other contexts, or when a figure from a given context embodies the spirit of figures from another context. This is the reason why we say that these contexts are hybrid. They inject autochthonous materials in what used to be an alien figure. Another example for transfiguration is that of Harriet Tubman. She was called the Moses of the abolitionist struggle for nothing less than her transformative role in the abolitionist movement and in bringing slaves from the south of the USA to the north in what was called the Underground Railroad. Transfiguration tells the history of how the past comes alive, is metamorphosed into the present contexts. The malady of the archive does precisely the opposite, dissolves the present into a dead past. In Luther, Paul and Augustine were indeed transfigured, but he did not repeat them; he took upon himself their mantel, but on his own skin, in his own context, in order to preach Christ for the people of his time. That is what he meant by the term "apostolic." In his own words, "Whatever does not teach Christ is not apostolic, even though St Peter or St Paul does the teaching. Again, whatever preaches Christ would be apostolic, even if Judas, Annas, Pilate, and Herod were doing it."[22] And what Luther said about the Scriptures must also be said about Luther. Luther's example, his figure can be emulated insofar as he preached the precious good news, the words of novelty, even when some of his teachings given to his "dear German people" are not for us, even as the example is useful.

In the offing

Offing is originally a nautical term that designates a space between the horizon and the sea that can still be seen from the shore. It designates the place in-between what belongs to my context and that which lies beyond. This is a place that is neither ours nor anybody else's. It is where the rules and laws of navigation are ending and the new is still unseen. This text was woven in such offing. This is the space between pertinence and innovation in which transfiguration takes place.

---

[21] Luther, op. cit. (note 7), 174.

[22] Luther, op. cit. (note 7), 396.

Lutheran Hermeneutics and New Testament Studies: Some Political and Cultural Implications

Eve-Marie Becker

Investigating "Lutheran hermeneutics": Searching for traces

If we are to speak about Lutheran hermeneutics or Lutheran theology, we will first of all require some clarification since these expressions presuppose that we know what "Lutheran" actually stands for. Should Lutheran refer to the reading and interpreting of Luther's writings and theology, or, rather, imply further developing Luther's personal[1] impact on the development of theology and adopting this paradigm of innovation to our contemporary world? It is only in a general sense then that we are talking about Martin Luther's impact on the history of Protestantism and the Protestant churches when we use the term Lutheran. In order to be more concrete, we thus need to modify what precisely we mean by looking for Lutheran tendencies in recent Protestantism in European cultures and/or in a globalized world.

By doing so, I cannot and will not ignore that my approach to this topic and these questions derives from and always points back to my education and background as a European scholar. Luther's impact on history, culture and politics in the sixteenth century and beyond is part of our common European identity. This is especially true for Germany and the Nordic countries. In Aarhus, for instance, the 500th anniversary of Luther's posting of his theses in 1517 will generate intensive reflection on how Danish culture and society were and still are shaped by Reformation history and, in particular, by Martin Luther's influence on Danish politics and theology.[2]

---

[1] Gerhard Ebeling pointed out that Luther's paradigmatic role in the history of theology is based in his way of thinking theology and the hermeneutics of reading the Bible together. Gerhard Ebeling, *Luther. Einführung in sein Denken* (Tübingen: J. C. B. Mohr Siebeck, [4]1981), esp. 102–4.

[2] Cf. M. Schwarz Lausten, *Die Reformation in Dänemark*, Schriften des Vereins für Reformationsgeschichte 208, transl. L. M. Tönnies and ed. J. Schilling (Heidelberg: Gütersloher Verlagshaus, 2008). And see below.

In German discourses on church history, scholars are used to considering Luther as a theologian framed by the history of the late Middle Ages and, thus, as being restorative. He could, however, also be seen as the initiator of the so-called "modern era" (*Neuzeit*) in central Europe, and thus as a forward thinking individual, a modernizer or revolutionary. Depending on how we value Luther's place in history, we will understand his hermeneutics either as an anticipation of how to critique modernity and its approach to a critical reading of biblical texts, or as the initiation of the modern attitude of critique as we find it especially in the field of biblical studies.[3] Both perspectives and options are valid since Luther stood at the intersection of the late Middle Ages and the modern era. Which perspective we choose finally depends on how we look at Luther and for what purpose we use his role in history as a model of reference or contrast to our current debates on church history and politics as well as methodology in biblical studies and/or hermeneutics.

Nevertheless, we are not simply free to choose our approach to Luther since there are various discourses that have already been defined beforehand. These discourses result from the history of Luther reception and its theological as well as political implications, especially on twentieth-century theology. In 2009, the Vereinigte Evangelisch-Lutherische Kirche Deutschlands (VELKD) used Rudolf Bultmann's 125th birthday as an opportunity to discuss this issue by analyzing Luther's effect on Bultmann's theology and hermeneutics.[4] This is a most intriguing case study of Luther reception in the twentieth century. For various reasons, Bultmann is considered to be an eminent, if not the most influential, more recent German successor of Luther's theology in the field of New Testament studies—in a positive as well as a problematic sense.

By investigating Bultmann's relationship to Luther, the basic question arises as to whether and how we can find certain "Lutheran" elements in and behind Bultmann's hermeneutics (*Rezeptionsgeschichte* or *Ideengeschichte* [reception history/history of ideas]).[5] When and how does Bultmann make use of certain elements of Luther's hermeneutics? There can be no doubt that Bultmann explicitly referred to Luther. His 1957 article is most revealing in this respect. Bultmann proposes here his hermeneutical understanding of *Sachkritik* that is based explicitly on Luther's "was Christum treibet" ("what promotes Christ"):

---

[3] Recently, Ulrich H. J. Körtner has pointed to analogue distinctions. See below.

[4] Cf. Ulrich H. J. Körtner et al. (eds), *Bultmann und Luther. Lutherrezeption in Exegese und Hermeneutik Rudolf Bultmanns* (Hannover: Amt der VELKD, 2010).

[5] Cf. Ulrich H. J. Körtner, "Zur Einführung: Bultmann und Luther—oder: Wie lutherisch ist die Theologie Rudolf Bultmanns?, in Körtner, ibid., 18.

"This [principle] should, indeed, be Lutheran, and if that… is a risk, we should ask, Does any exegesis exist without any risk?"[6]

As we see here, Bultmann refers to a crucial Lutheran principle of interpreting biblical texts, i.e., *Sachkritik* (a critical assessment of what the biblical text says). Such a principle derives from Luther's theological emphasis on Christology, which leads to a critical attitude toward institutional as well as scriptural traditions. Here lies the foundation of what we could call the reformatory *Schriftprinzip* (*sola scriptura*). In this sense, Bultmann is an appropriate candidate for investigating the influence of Lutheran hermeneutics in New Testament studies in Germany as well as in Denmark[7] in the mid-twentieth century and beyond.

Such a Lutheran impact on contemporary theology, however, cannot simply be detected as a distinct and coherent or plausible concept. Already Bultmann himself was quite sensitive of the various dilemmas of Luther reception. He considers the fact that Luther's interpretation of Pauline texts does not only function as a helpful key to the interpretation of New Testament texts but also tends to conceal Pauline theology as a problem. In 1928, Bultmann said,

> Academic research is infinite because our terminology develops infinitely and therefore each generation is given the task of interpretation. Luther's exegesis of Paul may be based on a real understanding of Paul; but we cannot settle for it, since we first of all need to interpret Luther.[8]

In other words, the "Lutheran Paul" is a concept itself that is in need of critical interpretation or even revision.

At this point, it is important to acknowledge Bultmann's sensitivity to Luther's specific interpretative concept of Pauline theology since current scholarship tends to see Bultmann in close accordance with the "Lutheran Paul"[9]—an assessment that is not necessarily meant to be positive, especially

---

[6] Rudolf Bultmann, "In eigener Sache (1957)," in *Idem, GuV 3* (1993)[4] (Tübingen: J. C. B. Mohr Siebeck, Uni-Taschenbücher1762), 178–89, here 186: "Angesichts der innerhalb des NT vorhandenen Differenzen erscheint mir eine Sachkritik als unumgänglich, die ihren Maßstab an den entscheidenden Grundgedanken des NT, oder vielleicht besser: an der Intention der im NT erklingenden Botschaft (Luther: 'was Christum treibet') hat. Das dürfte in der Tat lutherisch sein, und wenn das—wie nicht zu leugnen—ein Risiko ist, so ist zu fragen: gibt es denn überhaupt eine Exegese ohne Risiko?"

[7] On Bultmann's impact on Danish theology, cf. P. G. Lindhardt, Johannes Sløk and K. Olesen Larsen. For references to this I would like to thank my colleagues in Aarhus, Lars Albinus and Ole Davidsen.

[8] Rudolf Bultmann, "Die Bedeutung der 'dialektischen Theologie' für die neutestamentliche Wissenschaft," in *GuV 1* (1993[9]) (Tübingen: J. C. B. Mohr Siebeck, Uni-Taschenbücher 1760), 114–33, 123.

[9] Cf. e.g., Magnus Zetterholm, *Approaches to Paul. A Student's Guide to Recent Scholarship* (Minneapolis: Fortress Press, 2009), e.g., 75.

when referring to Bultmann's *Theologie des Neuen Testaments.*[10] The critique of the Luther–Bultmann hermeneutical tradition is basically formulated for reasons of political suspicion. The basic question is, Do Bultmann's words such as "the meaning of the law finally is to lead humans to death"[11] recall "Lutheran anti-Judaism"?[12] This question relates to Luther's evaluation of Judaism as a contrast to the Pauline concept of justification, which in itself portrays Jews and Judaism in a negative light in general. Such a view is most problematical when seen against the background of the history of the twentieth century. Especially since World War II and the Holocaust, all issues related to anti-Judaism and anti-Semitism need to be treated with *Sachkritik* themselves, last but not least, for political reasons. In this respect, not only Luther's attitude towards Jews and Judaism and its possible influence on the *Wirkungsgeschichte* has to be looked at critically. Furthermore, we need to discuss whether the impact of Lutheran hermeneutics on Pauline studies is legitimate after all.

Consequently, in more recent scholarship, such as the "New Perspective on Paul," the discussion on the "Lutheran Paul" is controversial. As can be observed in and beyond Bultmann's case, the interpretation of the Jewish law and its consequences on Pauline scholarship is continuously under dispute. We should, however, not forget that Bultmann would not simply identify his reading of Paul with Luther's approach (see above). On the other hand, much scholarly work is done in order to reassess and/or to defend the concept of the Lutheran Paul again—both, regarding its historical foundation in sixteenth-century theology as well as with regard to its hermeneutical implications and effects on current theology.[13] Nonetheless, we should ask here to what extent these attempts of reestablishing the Lutheran Paul finally serve as strategies of defense and apologetics. In any case, the theological tradition stretching from Paul to Luther and from Luther to Bultmann and contemporary Protestant theology is hardly without problems, unambiguous and self-evident, but bears rather serious hermeneutical difficulties and challenges in it.

---

[10] Rudolf Bultmann, *Theologie des Neuen Testaments*, 9th edition revised by O. Merk (Tübingen: J. C. B. Mohr Siebeck, 1984, Uni-Taschenbücher 630).

[11] Ibid., "... Dann aber ist der Sinn des Gesetzes letztlich der, den Menschen in den Tod zu führen und damit Gott als Gott erscheinen zu lassen."

[12] Luther's anti-Judaism needs to be seen in close relation to his anti-Papism as well as his anti-Turkish attitudes. Cf. Ebeling, op. cit. (note 1), 153, with reference to *WA* 40, 1; 603, 5–11.

[13] Cf. e.g., Stephen Westerholm, *Perspectives Old and New on Paul. The "Lutheran Paul" and His Critics* (Grand Rapids: Eerdmans, 2004). Cf. also Alexander J. M. Wedderburn, "Eine neuere Paulusperspektive?," in Eve-Marie Becker/Peter Pilhofer (eds), *Biographie und Persönlichkeit des Paulus* (Tübingen: Mohr Siebeck 2005/2009, WUNT 187), 46–64.

This leads us to the following preliminary conclusion: Our dealing with Lutheran hermeneutics partly has enormous political implications. In this light, it becomes obvious that it is still a matter of debate to what extent Luther's theological focus on justification and its hermeneutical implications are, in principle, legitimate or at least useful. The difficulties in applying Lutheran hermeneutics to contemporary theology increase when we are aware that we are dealing here with a basic doctrine of Protestant dogmatics. Theologians such as Gerhard Ebeling have underlined the fact that Luther's idea on justification *sola fide* can by no means be seen as an "arbitrary preference of a favorite teaching..., but rather as a declaration of what the inner structure of all theological assertions is about."[14] In other words, by approaching the Lutheran Paul we are about to move into the material centre of Lutheran hermeneutics and carry out heart surgery.

Against this background, twenty-first-century Lutheran hermeneutics still faces a immense political dimension. It will have to figure out how the Pauline doctrine of justification can be based on New Testament writings in such a way that it finally stabilizes the peaceful coexistence of Judaism and Christianity in and beyond European culture(s). In contemporary discourse, Lutheran hermeneutics thus is continuously challenged and controlled by political ethics. It is a matter of biblical and academic hermeneutics then to provide a proper discursive frame for interpreting, assessing and exploring further basic tools of Luther's hermeneutics, such as the sharp contrast between law and gospel.[15]

Biographical views

In our quest to find traces of Lutheran hermeneutics in contemporary theology and culture we will always be influenced by certain modes of *Vorverständnis* [preconception] that guide our investigation. We can never escape our preconceptions. Our view on Lutheran hermeneutics is thus strongly influenced by our cultural setting(s) and political locations. It is to be expected then that my approach to these questions is partly defined by biographical data as well

---

[14] Gerhard Ebeling, *Dogmatik des christlichen Glaubens*, vol. I: Prolegomena—Erster Teil (Tübingen: J. C. B. Mohr Siebeck, 1987³), 32: "Aber ebenso ist der Hinweis auf die Rechtfertigung allein aus Glauben nicht etwa als willkürliche Bevorzugung einer Lieblingslehre vor anderen gemeint, sondern als Angabe dessen, was die innere Struktur sämtlicher theologischer Aussagen ausmacht. Dasselbe gilt von der dem Rechtfertigungsthema korrespondierenden Unterscheidung zwischen Gesetz und Evangelium... ." Cf. also Ebeling, op. cit. (note 1), 121.

[15] Cf. James A. Loader et al., "Gesetz und Evangelium" in Oda Wischmeyer (ed.), *Lexikon der Bibelhermeneutik* (Berlin/New York: Walter de Gruyter, 2009), 217–21.

as professional obligations. There can be no exegesis or theology without the involvement of the individual exegete.[16] Thus, biographical and autobiographical reflections serve to clarify academic discourse.[17]

My basic approach here is to consider Lutheran hermeneutics to be a valuable and helpful paradigm of Protestant theology. In what follows, I will thus work out some ideas on how I think that Lutheran hermeneutics still has a potential for enriching and stimulating theological work and cultural life. In particular, I will mention some aspects that seem to be crucial in this context and that are directly related to my academic biography and current status at a Danish university.

Luther's humanism

As a professor of New Testament exegesis, my primary point of interest in Lutheran hermeneutics still relates to methodological issues of text interpretation in the field of biblical studies. In this respect, Luther's exegetical studies as well as his philological works are of crucial importance. I consider Luther to be part of a broader humanistic milieu of the early sixteenth century in which the philologically based concept of *ad fontes* was as important as the recourse to ancient (literary) habits and traditions.[18]

At the same time, Luther was mainly interested in the development of the German language, a concrete result of which was his eagerness to provide the Bible in German by translating Old and New Testament texts on the basis of the Hebrew and Greek manuscripts that were available to him. The hermeneutical implication here is that all people should have access to biblical texts as well as to the results of exegesis and textual interpretation. This has formidable sociopolitical implications, which become evident when we look at recent African projects for Bible translation and their impact on African politics,[19] or at the Western academic ideas of "research communication" (see below). In other words, reading and interpreting biblical texts presupposes certain academic or scientific expertise, which should, however, finally also

---

[16] Cf. e.g., Eve-Marie Becker, "Die Person des Exegeten. Überlegungen zu einem vernachlässigten Thema," in Oda Wischmeyer (ed.), *Herkunft und Zukunft der neutestamentlichen Wissenschaft* (Tübingen/Basel: Francke Verlag, 2003, Neutestamentliche Entwürfe zur Theologie 6), 207–43.

[17] Cf. e.g., Eve-Marie Becker (ed.), *Neutestamentliche Wissenschaft. Autobiographische Essays aus der Evangelischen Theologie* (Tübingen/Basel: Francke Verlag, 2003, Uni-Taschenbücher 2475).

[18] Cf. e.g., the revival of the tradition of *laudatio funebris*: e.g., Philipp Melanchthon, *Oratio in funere reverendi viri D. Martini Lutheri* (1546).

[19] Cf. Gosnell L. Yorke, "Hearing the Politics of Peace in Ephesians. A Proposal from an African Postcolonial Perspective," in *JSNT 30* (2007), 113–27.

be used in order to bridge the gap between the ancient setting of the New Testament writings and the contemporary reader's mind.

The strength of Luther's translation policy is correlated to his interest in an "existential" theological interpretation of New Testament writings. Here, again, Luther appears as a theologian who might be best embedded in a broader humanistic milieu. Similarly, Erasmus of Rotterdam is not only interested in philological work even though he is one of the first scholars to have worked on a text-critical edition of the New Testament (1516).[20] Rather, Erasmus sought to move beyond the philosophical to the ethical or theological issues as evident in his *Enchiridion militis christiani* [The Manual of a Christian Knight], published in 1502 in Latin, and in 1524 in German.[21] This is true even if Luther obviously considered Erasmus as a contemporary who was not engaged in Reformation theology as much as he should have been.[22]

From these humanists and reformers we can discern considerable respect for the existential potential of ancient authors and their writings. The hermeneutical implication here is the following: Ancient texts—New Testament texts in particular—contain basic insights into human life and the quest for God so that they can challenge the understanding of contemporary living conditions in highly instructive ways. A similar approach to the theological understanding of New Testament writings that coincides with its sociopolitical implications can be found in recent African exegesis,[23] such as for instance in its search for political concepts of peace.[24] European scholars have to reconsider how the humanistic impetus of Lutheran hermeneutics can be applied to current cultural challenges in our societies which, I believe, are in the main characterized by processes of secularization.

The heritage of modernization

As a German theologian, educated during the last decade of the twentieth century partly in Marburg and partly in Erlangen, I was confronted with the effects of Bultmann's theology and hermeneutics on contemporary Prot-

---

[20] See *Novum Instrumentum*. Faks.-Neudr. der Ausgabe Basel 1516 mit einer historischen, textkritischen und bibliographischen Einleitung v. H. Holeczek (Stuttgart, 1986).

[21] Cf. Erasmus von Rotterdam, *Enchiridion militis christiani/Handbüchlein eines christlichen Streiters*, in Werner Weizig (ed.), *Erasmus von Rotterdam. Ausgewählte Schriften*, 8 vols, Latin and German (Darmstadt: Wissenschaftliche Buchgesellschaft, 1995), vol. 1, 55–375.

[22] Cf. e.g., Luther's letter to Erasmus, April 1524.

[23] Cf. Jean-Claude Loba-Mkole, *Paul and Africa?* (Manuscript submitted to the SNTS annual meeting 2011).

[24] Cf. Yorke, op. cit. (note 19); ibid., 10.

estant academia. In a typological sense, Bultmann might still be regarded as an influential representative of Lutheran hermeneutics. Because of the way in which he critically uses (see for instance Sachkritik above) the liberating political power of New Testament texts and applies it to contemporary life in church and society, it is not surprising that some aspects of so-called libera-tion theology—at least in the German context—can be regarded as a result of a post-Bultmannian hermeneutics (e.g. Luise Schottroff). Bultmann himself basically struggled with such an adaptation of New Testament writings to the modern world, which has until now provoked quite ambiguous reactions.

An essential part of this conflict was dealing with Bultmann's ideas on *Entmythologisierung* [demythologization], formulated in 1941 on the basis of lectures given at Frankfurt/Main and Alpirsbach (21 April and 4 June), entitled *Neues Testament und Mythologie* [New Testament and Mythology]. Recently, the historian Konrad Hammann contextualized this lecture as a consequence of Bultmann's contestation with National Socialism.[25] Only very few twentieth-century theological texts have been surrounded by such controversy as this article, which has been debated by theologians as well as philosophers.

What was it precisely that made this article so problematic? Bultmann in-tended to reflect on the modern appearance of the Protestant belief and gospel proclamation.

> You cannot use electric light and the radio and, in case of illness, make use of modern medicine and clinical treatment while, at the same time, believing in the New Testament world of demons and miracles. And everyone who thinks that they can do this for their own sake should know that if they take this to be the position of the Christian faith, they will render Christian proclamation incomprehensible and impossible.[26]

Bultmann's idea, therefore, is to interpret the mythical worldview and display of salvation, as represented in the New Testament texts, in such a way that mythical ideas and language can be construed "anthropologically or, better, existentially."[27] Demythologization thus means reading the New Testament mythology not with regard to its "objectifiable potential of ideas but, rather,

---

[25] Cf. Konrad Hammann, *Rudolf Bultmann. Eine Biographie* (Tübingen: Mohr Siebeck, 2009), 307–19.

[26] Rudolf Bultmann, *Neues Testament und Mythologie. Das Problem der Entmythologisierung der neutesta-mentlichen Verkündigung,* Nachdr. der 1941 erschienenen Fassung, ed. Eberhard Jüngel (München: Chr. Kaiser Verlag, 1988, Beiträge zur evangelischen Theologie 96), 16.

[27] Cf. ibid., 22.

regarding the understanding of existence which is articulated here."[28] In other words, Bultmann demythologizes the New Testament writings by taking them to an existential interpretation, which reminds us again of Luther's quest for an existential understanding of the gospel. The relevant question here is not whether Bultmann was right in his interpretation of myths. There are two main aspects implied in this approach: Bultmann's program of demythologization has huge political implications as we will soon see, and it was based on the idea of existential interpretation.

Do we thus meet Lutheran hermeneutics here—in fact, beyond some possible typological affinities between Luther and Bultmann? In an absolute sense, we could, of course, answer this question in the negative. Luther did not initiate a demythologization of biblical or New Testament texts where he would have had to eliminate any kind of mythical language or concepts. This was not part of his hermeneutical agenda. Nevertheless, what Luther did and what might still be considered a crucial point of Lutheran hermeneutics is the idea that New Testament writings—even if being read as authoritative texts—need to be interpreted in accordance with current needs and living conditions. *Sachkritik* plays an eminent role here.

Interestingly, Bultmann explicitly understood his program of demythologization as a continuation of Reformation theology. Ulrich H. J. Körtner indicates how closely Bultmann put himself into the tradition of Philipp Melanchthon as well as Wilhelm Herrmann. Bultmann applied Melanchthon's paradigm of *Christum cognoscere hoc est: beneficia eius cognoscere, non eius naturas et modos incarnationis intueri* (To know Christ is to know his benefits, not to contemplate his natures or the modes of his incarnation)[29] directly to his program of demythologization in that the latter is defined as a method of revealing critically what God did for us. Therefore, for Bultmann demythologization is seen "parallel to the Pauline Lutheran doctrine of justification *sola fide*."[30] According to Bultmann's understanding, the program of demythologization thus refers to the ideas of Reformation theology in general and elementary parts of Luther's theology in particular.[31]

---

[28] Ibid., 23.

[29] Cf. Philipp Melanchthon, *Loci communes*, (1521), 0, 13.

[30] Cf. Rudolf Bultmann, "Zum Problem der Entmythologisierung," in *KuM II* (Hamburg, 1952), 179–208, esp. 184f. and 207. To this, Körtner, op. cit. (note 4), 11f.

[31] Cf. Körtner's references to how Bultmann links his program explicitly to Luther's lecture on Romans in 1515/16, Bultmann, ibid., 203f.; Körtner, ibid., 12; Johannes Ficker (ed.), *Luthers Vorlesung über den Römerbrief 1515/1516* (Leipzig³, 1925).

The quest for political responsibility

There is another line connecting Luther's and Bultmann's hermeneutics. I would call this the line of sociopolitical implications and effects of New Testament hermeneutics. In his biography of Bultmann, Konrad Hammann has shown clearly that Bultmann's program of demythologization impacted politics in two particular directions. Bultmann aimed to override the myths of his time, especially the disastrous correlation between myth and history that was to be found in the sphere of National Socialism. On the basis of the *Barmer Erklärung*, Bultmann critiqued a natural knowledge of God [*natürliche Gotteserkenntnis*] as was proposed by the so-called *Deutsche Christen*, a group that tried to back up German policy in the Third Reich.[32] In his article, *Die Frage der natürlichen Offenbarung*, Bultmann claims that New Testament writings do not offer a clear or decisive reflection on history.[33] On the other hand, Bultmann's program of demythologization acts against certain tendencies also in the Confessing Church. Bultmann was anxious that this group of Christian resistance was concentrated on a repristination of the creed so that it was in danger of expressing Christian belief only in terms of an old-fashioned language and a worldview that was already outdated.[34]

---

[32] Jedes "*Phänomen der Geschichte ist zweideutig*, und keines offenbart als solches Gottes Willen. Und erst recht ist jedes *geschichtliche Phänomen der Gegenwart* zweideutig… Sind Gottes Forderung und Gottes Heiligkeit in ihrer Radikalität erfaßt, so schweigt die Rede von der Offenbarung Gottes in der Forderung des Guten und in der Geschichte; so muß das Urteil lauten, daß *der Mensch vor Gott Sünder* ist, und daß *seine Geschichte eine Geschichte sündiger Menschen* ist und deshalb Gott gerade verhüllt," Rudolf Bultmann, "Die Frage der natürlichen Offenbarung" (1941), *GuV 2* (Tübingen: J. C. B. Mohr Paul Siebeck, 1993[6], Uni-Taschenbücher 1761), 79–104, 92f. "Mit dieser eminent politischen Aussage gab Bultmann 1940/41 ein Exempel der theologischen Auseinandersetzung mit den aktuellen Mythen," Hammann, op. cit. (note 25), 309.

[33] They express the paradox, "daß Gottes eschatologischer Gesandter ein konkreter historischer Mensch ist, daß Gottes eschatologisches Handeln sich in einem Menschenschicksal vollzieht, daß es also ein Geschehen ist, das sich als eschatologisches nicht weltlich ausweisen kann… Die Verkündiger, die Apostel: Menschen, in ihrer historischen Menschlichkeit verständlich! Die Kirche: ein soziologisches, historisches Phänomen; ihre Geschichte historisch, geistesgeschichtlich verständlich! Und dennoch alles eschatologische Phänomene, eschatologisches Geschehen!," Bultmann, op. cit. (note 26), 63f.

[34] Cf. Hammann, op. cit. (note 25), 309. In January 1941, Bultmann said in a "Grußwort im Marburger Rundbrief zu Jahresbeginn 1941" to his students who were at war: "Liebe Freunde! Zu Beginn des neuen Jahres soll Euch ein Gruß dessen versichern, daß ich an Euch mit herzlichen Wünschen denke… Ich will Euch gestehen, daß mir die Absicht, Euch das Folgende zu schreiben, kam, als ich am Weihnachtsfest aus dem Gottesdienst nach Hause ging, - tief enttäuscht und deprimiert. Wohl hatte ich eine in der Form treffliche und in ihrem Inhalt dogmatisch höchst korrekte Predigt gehört. Aber es war keine wirkliche *Predigt* gewesen… so darf nicht länger gepredigt werden; sonst werden unsere Kirchen in der nächsten Generation völlig entleert sein," Rudolf Bultmann, "Grußwort im Marburger Rundbrief zu Jahresbeginn Januar 194," in Erika Dinkler-von Schubert (ed.), *Feldpost – Zeugnis und Vermächtnis. Briefe und Texte aus dem Kreis der evangelischen Studentengemeinde 1939-1945* (Göttingen: Vandenhoeck & Ruprecht 1993), 142–45, 142f.

We might say that Bultmann's well-balanced evaluation of how to articulate theological positions in times of a political crisis, recalls Lutheran hermeneutics in that Luther himself never looked for simple solutions such as was the case regarding the discussion of when to use force and violence during the Reformation period. In his dealings with Christian II of Denmark, Luther did not tend to argue one-sidedly in favor of one of his sympathizers, but remained distant and critical, relying on his personal and theological conscience. Even if he aimed to open up religious discourse for ordinary people also, he did not promote political revolution, but reminded people to act peacefully and to respect the (God-given) authorities.[35]

I shall not discuss here the complex question of to what extent people have to accept political authorities and at what point they should overturn a government—something at the time of this writing we have seen in various North African and Middle Eastern countries that should encourage us seriously to rethink our postmodern and rather easygoing European ideas on the legitimacy of political power. In thinking of Helmuth James von Moltke or Dietrich Bonhoeffer, who are still part of the recent German past, we should rather remind ourselves of how serious and difficult it is to deal with tyrannicide, especially from a Christian perspective. Nor will I judge to what extent Bultmann's role in the Third Reich might be compared to Luther's response to his own context. But I would like to claim that Lutheran hermeneutics always implies sensitivity to personal responsibility as well as the careful attempt better to understand New Testament texts as the basis for expressing theological thoughts and adapting them to contemporary life in the church as well as society. In this respect, it is sad enough to see how many German theologians, who understood themselves as Lutherans, could not live up to those expectations. Instead, they failed in the most complicated period of German and possibly European history, the Third Reich.

Lutheran hermeneutics and university policy

I will make some remarks on possible implications and effects of Lutheran hermeneutics on current university policy: How can contemporary Danish

---

[35] Cf. Luther's tractate on "Ob Kriegsleute auch in seligem Stande sein können" (1526) [Whether Soldiers, Too, Can be Saved] and to this, Schwarz Lausten, op. cit. (note 2), 27; cf. also, Martin Schwarz Lausten, *Christian 2. Mellem paven og Luther. Tro og politik omkring 'den røde konge' I eksilet og I fangenskabet (1523-1559)* (København: Alademisk Forlag (Kirkehistoriske Studier III./3); Carsten Bach-Nielsen and Per Ingesmann (eds), *Reformation, religion og politik. Fyrsternes personlige rolle i de europæiske reformation* (Århus: Aarhus Universitetsforlag 2003). Thanks, to my colleague Carsten Bach-Nielsen for these hints. Differently, e.g., Philipp Melanchthon, *An iure C. Caesar est interfectus* (1533).

culture be understood in light of Lutheran hermeneutics? To what extent do the cultural surroundings influence or even determine our work as theologians and New Testament scholars in particular?

In the following, I will refer to some observations that I have made since I came to Aarhus University in 2006—a public, non-denominational university run by the Danish state.

In September 2011, we had a discussion among the teachers of theology on whether we might in the future offer a kind of "university service." Many colleagues were hesitant fearing that the distinction between *academia* and *ecclesia* would be violated. Every engagement in church and ecclesial activity is first of all seen as a part of private life. This situation, indeed, seems to be ambiguous. On the one hand, Denmark has a national church (The Church of Denmark, a folk church) based on the Lutheran confession. On the other, we can observe a clear separation between the academic world and private religion—even if we as academic scholars are expected to contribute to the public discourse, i.e., to make the results of our research accessible to cultural and social life.

This ambiguity might have something to do with the reception of the Lutheran doctrine of the two kingdoms. According to this doctrine, political affairs and religious matters are to be separated from each other. This doctrine, however, is not consistent, neither in today's Denmark, nor in Luther's case as we saw earlier. This doctrine might have also influenced the church since nowadays the Church of Denmark has its own sociocultural identity rather than being driven by private religiosity or confessionalism. This is especially true in light of the high degree of secularism in Danish society. The American sociologist Phil Zuckerman, who some years ago carried out empirical studies on people's individual belief in Sweden and Denmark, basically came to the conclusion that these societies are characterized by a *Kulturreligion* [cultural religion][36] instead of individual piety. Can we thus say that in contemporary European societies Lutheran hermeneutics can affect processes of secularization and the loss of individual belief? And if so, What precisely is the impact and how should we assess it?

In central European societies, we can observe a trend toward secularization rather than a religious revival.[37] These processes of secularization are to some

---

[36] Cf. Phil Zuckerman, *Samfund uden Gud* (Højbjerg: Forlaget Univers, 2008), 169ff.

[37] To this discourse, cf. Friedrich Wilhelm Graf, *Die Wiederkehr der Götter. Religion in der modernen Kultur* (München: Beck, 2004); Jürgen Habermas/Joseph Ratzinger, *Dialektik der Säkularisierung. Über Vernunft und Religion* (Freiburg: Herder, 2005); Charles Taylor, *A Secular Age* (Cambridge: Harvard University Press, 2007); Michael Reder/Joseph Schmidt (eds), *Ein Bewußtsein von dem, was fehlt. Eine Diskussion mit Jürgen Habermas* (Frankfurt: Suhrkamp, 2008). Cf. also, Anton Hügli, "Jaspers Vorlesung die Chiffern der Transzendenz im Kontext seines Schaffens während seiner Basler Zeit," in Karl Jaspers, *Die Chiffern der Transzendenz. Mit zwei Nachworten*, ed. Anton Hügli and Hans Saner (Basel: Schwabe Verlag, 2011), 115–34, 115f.

extent a result of the Protestant questioning of ecclesial authorities and traditions. Similar processes can be observed in other European countries. In the case of Denmark, a comparatively small country with all in all a homogenous manifestation of Protestant denomination, religion is much less a matter of inter-Christian conflict or confessional debate, but at most a matter of defense against atheists and agnostics.

In the case of Denmark, we can observe how Lutheran hermeneutics can develop thought processes of cultural transformation and revision (see e.g., Grundtvig). We can see how Lutheran hermeneutics develops as a theological and cultural concept in a sociopolitical setting where until today other religions and/or Christian denominations have played only a minor role. We might call this a "monoculture" even if this may change in the future because of the increasing significance of Islam. I do not dare to venture a prognosis on how the Danish concept of *Kulturreligion* will react to these future challenges.

How does academic theology in Denmark deal with the boundaries prescribed by politics and culture—boundaries that might be considered as late and possibly mutated historical effects of Lutheran hermeneutics and its manifestation in how state and church are organized? I can see at least three factors which guide theology as an academic discipline.

- First, in Denmark, academic theology seeks to have a sound grasp of contemporary developments in culture and society. This factor certainly derives from Lutheran hermeneutics itself. Besides, it also mirrors external expectations. It is not accidental that theology today is expected strongly to define itself as a part of *Kulturvidenskab* [Arts]. So the faculty of theology at Aarhus University is right now moving into a bigger faculty of Arts.

- Second, academic theology is based on the principle of freedom of religion. Personal piety is thus strictly excluded from academic work, including obligations of research communication.

- Third, instead of looking for alliances with ecclesial institutions or asking for backing from the Danish Church, academic theology is eager to act as a field of humaniora—by accepting scientific criteria and paradigms of scientific policy only and by integrating itself into the broader frame of the Arts. It does, however, still consider itself as contributing something specific and indispensable to the field of humanities. Accordingly, the academic *proprium* of theology might be described as follows: on the one hand it rests in its academic tradition while, on the other, it has a formative task for Christian religion in its job oriented approach to academic education (education of ministers for the Danish Church).

It is precisely this academic milieu in which cultural studies as well as the history of religion and philosophy play a predominant role. This context creates the intellectual challenge for us as we try to provoke students to develop an interest in New Testament studies. Within this framework, it is necessary that Lutheran hermeneutics stand for a broader political and cultural vision. Such hermeneutics should contribute to Christianity as a whole and Protestant belief in particular which is able to meet the conditions of modern societies. In this way, Lutherans can actively contribute to cultural change through their emphases on the liberating as well as the critical and analytical power of Christian belief.

Challenges of globalization

While the implications and impacts of Lutheran hermeneutics have until now been deeply anchored in European Protestant culture and theology, they are under dispute and being tested continuously and extensively.

A major future challenge for European theology might be the question of how it can interact with Christian cultures in the Far East as well as in the global South. Hereby, all of us dealing with Protestant theology will increasingly enter a field of a globalized Christianity that is in strong competition with other denominations, religions and sects as well as various worldviews and political ideologies. In this respect, the worldwide reception of Lutheran hermeneutics might even provide a *lingua franca* that leads to an understanding among Christians and theologians beyond national, ethnic or cultural borders. Such a hermeneutics might also shape a common language among Lutherans who come from different cultures and contexts. In a geo-political sense, here might even lie the most essential task of reflecting Lutheran hermeneutics and depicting its sociopolitical potential. In that sense, the Lutheran World Federation plays a pivotal role and has, with the consultation on Lutheran hermeneutics of scriptural interpretation, taken a fundamental step in that direction.

Bible, Tradition and the Asian Context

Monica Jyotsna Melanchthon

To love. To be loved. To never forget your own insignificance. To never get used to the unspeakable violence and the vulgar disparity of life around you. To seek joy in the saddest places. To pursue beauty to its lair. To never simplify what is complicated or complicate what is simple. To respect strength, never power. Above all, to watch. To try and understand. To never look away. And never, never, to forget

— Arundhati Roy from a speech *Come September*

The locus

Meira Paibi ("torch bearers") of Manipur

Human rights violations by security forces engaged in counterinsurgency operations in the northeastern Indian state of Manipur have occurred with depressing regularity over the last five decades. Many have been killed either by armed forces or separatist militants that are seeking autonomy from the Indian state. Manipuris have long campaigned for the repeal of the Armed Forces Special Powers Act (AFSPA), which provides the troops with extraordinary powers during counterinsurgency operations.[1] Demanding that the Act be scrapped, human rights activist Irom Chanu Sharmila has been on hunger strike for nearly eleven years. Her protest began after the Assam Rifles gunned down ten civilians on 2 November 2000. She remains in judicially ordered custody, force-fed through a nasal tube. Sharmila says it is her "bounden duty" to protest in the most peaceful way.

Thangjam Manorama Devi, a thirty-two-year-old resident of Manipur state, was arrested by the paramilitary Assam Rifles on the night of 10 July 2004. Suspected of having links to an underground separatist group, the soldiers raided her home in Bamon Kampu village, tortured her and after signing an "arrest memo,"[2] took her away. The family was forced to sign a "no claims"

---

[1] This law was instituted by the Ministry of Home Affairs in 1958 and became applicable in the areas of present-day Nagaland and in the hill areas of Manipur.

[2] An official acknowledgement of detention put in place to prevent "disappearances."

certificate.[3] At 5:30 am on the morning of the next day her body was found about four kilometers from her home. She had been shot in the lower half of her body, raising suspicion that bullets had been used to hide any evidence of rape. The security forces function as though they were "judge, jury and executioner—and have become comfortable in adopting this role."[4]

After Manorama's killing, on 12 July 2004, several civil society groups called a fourty-eight-hour protest strike. Thirty-two organizations formed a network called *Apunba Lup* in a campaign to repeal the AFSPA. But the most heart-wrenching protest was by a group of Manipuri women between the ages of forty-five and seventy-three, members of the *Meira Paibi* ("torch bearers"),[5] who on 15 July 2004 stripped naked in front of the Assam Rifles camp in the state capital, Imphal, wrapped in a banner that said, "Indian Army Rape Us." Forced to respond, the state government ordered a judicial enquiry, and although a report was submitted, no action has yet been taken. The central government then ordered an enquiry of its own, and it seems that the committee ordered a repeal of the AFSPA but action remains to be taken. Political leaders and government officials may privately agree that Manorama's killing was unlaw-ful, but the Indian state has failed, yet again, to hold soldiers responsible and accountable for this serious human rights violation.

L. Gyaneshori was one of the women who took part in the protest. She told Human Rights Watch,

> Manorama's killing broke our hearts. We had campaigned for the arrest memo to protect people from torture after arrest. Yet, it did not stop the soldiers from raping and killing her. They mutilated her body and shot her in the vagina. We mothers were weeping, "Now our daughters can be raped. They can be subjected to such cruelty. Every girl is at risk." We shed our clothes and stood before the army. We said, "We mothers have come. Drink our blood. Eat our flesh. Maybe this way you can spare our daughters." But nothing has been done to

---

[3] Which states that they had no claims against members of the Assam Rifles who had searched the house and made the arrest; that the troops "haven't misbehaved with women folk and not damaged any property." Human Rights Watch, "*These Fellows must be Eliminated!*" *Relentless Violence and Impunity in Manipur* (New York: Human Rights Watch, 2008), 27, at **www.hrw.org**

[4] Ibid., 11.

[5] Also referred to as the "Mother's Front." One of two well-known women's groups in Manipur, whose concerns today center on two issues: human rights violations by the armed forces and the increasing use of drugs and subsequently the emergence of HIV and AIDS amongst the youth of Manipur. Anytime they hear of rape, torture, or the death or disappearance of a person, they gather in their hundreds and sometimes keep vigil all night. They cannot be easily deterred, as the government and the army have realized.

punish those soldiers. The women of Manipur were disrobed by AFSPA. We are still naked.[6]

In 2011, Manorama was remembered again on the seventh anniversary of her death and her family and the groups that called attention to her death are still waiting for justice.

Salient features of the Asian context[7]

This incident is one among many that are illustrative of the situation in India and perhaps other parts of Asia. An analysis of the social, political and economic conditions in India show that what is needed and urgently so, are:

- Defending human rights and freedom against state repression of various kinds and grades. Political authoritarianism and militarism, the gross violation of human rights, the recognition of a particular religion as state religion and the dominance of a single ethnic community are characteristic to many parts of Asia. Any expression of dissent is suppressed, protest squelched and people "made to disappear."

- Protecting the poor from the oppression of the market: There is an unprecedented gulf between the rich and the poor, growing unemployment and the pauperization of the peasantry. The suppression of workers, death by starvation and suicides, all these coexist with a growing culture of middle-class consumerism and apathy. These developments combined with the market economy have created problems of immigration, migration, displacement of people, trafficking of children and women and the commercial sale of human organs and many more.

- Creating and fostering just and inclusive communities in the face of increasing violence, conflict among various ethnic groups, caste and religious groups and among linguistic and regional communities. There is growing religious fundamentalism, Hindu fascism, Islamic fundamentalism and the exclusion of women and those suffering from HIV and AIDS.

---

[6] Human Rights Watch interview with L. Gyaneshori, President, Thangmeiban Apunba Nupi Lup, Imphal, February 26, 2008, as cited in, Human Rights Watch, op. cit. (note 3), 31.

[7] Cf. also, Felix Wilfred, *Asian Public Theology: Critical Concerns in Challenging Times* (New Delhi: ISPCK, 2010), xii-xv.

- Protecting the environment: The accelerated mode of development, propelled by technology, has resulted in an environmental crisis.

- Encouraging struggle and resistance against all forms of oppression and subjugation and to present them as signs of hope.

The call for organic intellectuals and biblical interpreters

Hence, many Asian theologians cognizant of the public nature of religion[8] and the Christian faith are stressing the need to take up issues of this kind, and to respond to them critically, theologically and biblically, taking "life for all" or "transformation" as the criteria of judgment. Biblical interpreters are also encouraged to be aware of the various strategies and methods employed by movements of resistance and for change, whether by groups or individuals. This requires that scholars provide interpretations of Scripture and tradition that are in some organic manner connected to the many communities that experience the problems highlighted above. These interpretations have to be different from traditional biblical interpretations, innovative, and constantly in dialogue with the new questions and issues as they emerge on the continent. The starting point for such a venture is the subaltern communities, the Dalits, the women, the tribals, the *adivasis*, the victims of human trafficking, those who suffer from HIV and AIDS; all those who need to overcome various forms of exclusion. In their struggles, aspirations and dreams we already see the shape of things to come for a just and egalitarian society.

The call for organic intellectuals and interpreters who give a transformative or life giving impetus to biblical study and interpretation has not been received with enthusiasm in many quarters, neither in the academy nor the church. I have been involved in the teaching of biblical studies for several years now at a Lutheran seminary in South India. Challenging traditional and orthodox ideas about gender roles, inequity, caste discrimination, corruption and power abuse in communities and the church, is still done with much hesitation and with a sense of breaking taboos. These views are considered personal, value laden and political, and do not belong in the arena of "faith" or "scholarship." Hence, there are many who still continue to exercise self-censorship and restraint, especially in the choice of research topics, employing perspectival methods or approaches to the reading of the biblical text. Yet, somehow, not paying attention to the realities and conditions of India or the world is not regarded as demonstrating personal, value laden and political views. Thus the

---

[8] Ibid., vii.

support of the *status quo* both within the church and the academy continues, and many issues are rejected, silenced or ignored. But, as systemic thinkers, we are aware that it is impossible not to communicate or call attention to this reality, and that which we are perforce communicating must be seen by any discerning hearer and student as condoning violence, narrowing options and not reflecting the unhappiness and frustrations that communities are experiencing.

In the wider academy (SBL, IOSOT, or even in consultations and study projects of the LWF), interpreters, particularly non-Western ones with commitments to "context" (of the interpreter or the community), have been received with varied levels of tolerance and acceptance. The academy is suspicious and sees contextual biblical interpretation as a "watering down" of the "academic" and "scholarly" nature of biblical studies. Our methods are considered flawed and biased. Contextual readings are seen only as "epistemological judgments" or driven by "value judgments" that are relative and significant only to the context of the interpreter and hence of little importance or significance for the wider academy.

But biblical interpreters from contextual geographies and the landscape of varying legitimate identities can participate in defining the discipline only when religious and biblical studies de-center their stance of objectivist positivism and scientific value detachment and become "engaged" scholarship and "organic." Not the posture of value detachment and apolitical objectivism but the articulation of one's social location, interpretive strategies and theoretical frameworks are essential and appropriate,"[9] in biblical and theological studies.

The makeup of contextual interpretations/readings

> "'O' for objective: a delusion which other lunatics share."
> Bertrand Russell, "The Good Citizen's Alphabet and History of the World" in *Epitome*, 1953

As we work toward a world where healing and justice are possible, we not only critique but also engage in constructive theological reflection that is public in nature.[10] In this venture, the Bible is a constant and, at the same time, an ever changing partner. The Bible, by virtue of its inherently diverse, polyphonic and

---

[9] Elisabeth Schüssler Fiorenza, "Changing the Paradigms," at **www.religion-online.org/showarticle. asp?title=439**.

[10] "The relationship of religion to society is viewed differently in Asia. This means that religion and society are not connected in terms of sacred and profane, religious and secular. Rather, public life includes also a place for religion," in ibid., xxi.

poly-contextual nature, is rich and a treasure for visual resources that offer a fundamental structure of critique that should inform all theological endeavors and expressions of communion.[11] The Bible is a resourceful mine for the ongoing vocation of liberated Christians living in their respective worlds and yet needy of critique itself as are all our human efforts to speak of God and the world.

There is a strong emphasis on relating biblical studies and theology to the real life crises of contemporary societies, including the breakdown of social structures, the struggles for life, power, dignity, change, justice, recognition, and the anguish caused to human life by these realities. In the effort to do justice to the interweaving of the three arenas of Bible, tradition and contemporary society—each a complex entity—concepts such as "transformation," "life in all its fullness," "justice," "resistance" and "liberation" founded in the gospel of Jesus Christ have served as hermeneutical lenses or focal points to provide coherence to a multilayered analysis, functioning almost like prisms that might refract the issues with all their complexities and intricacies.

There is interest in reflection that takes seriously not only the issues of the sociocultural context, but also the **systemic** (structural, economic, societal, judicial, political, media, etc.) and **systematic** distortions (meaning systems, religious symbol system, theological articulations, confessional creeds)[12] that are inherent to any and all contexts. They analyze and evaluate the roots of social construction and distortion discernible in social and cultural worlds, especially those that create, intensify, or reinforce discrimination, injustice and subjugation. The roots are often entrenched within a culture's symbol system, the realm of its world making imagination, including its religious imagination and its theology (i.e., casteism in India), and hence need to be unearthed and exposed.

One cannot miss discerning the strong ethical component in contextual biblical interpretation. In the midst of complex, contradictory and ambiguous realities and experiences, developing a moral and ethical outlook is a very challenging task, and hence might vary from context to context, which underlines the importance of conversation and dialogue with other religious traditions and movements of struggle and resistance at the grassroots level.

Commitments to justice, human dignity, equality, peace, reconciliation and wholeness have led the contextual interpreter and theologian to work with

---

[11] Cf. Barbara Rossing, "Diversity in the Bible as Model for Lutheran Hermeneutics," in Karen L. Bloomquist, *Transformative Theological Perspectives*, Theology in the Life of the Church, vol. 6 (Minneapolis/Geneva: Lutheran University Press/Lutheran World Federation, 2009), 39–50.

[12] Using concepts offered by William Schweiker and Michael Welker, "A New Paradigm of Theological and Biblical Inquiry," in Cynthia L. Rigby (ed.), *Power, Powerlessness and the Divine: New Inquiries in Bible and Theology* (Atlanta, Georgia: Scholars Press, 1997), 6.

surprising and unexpected partners. Interdisciplinary in approach and methodology, both the social reality and the biblical text are studied and analyzed with the assistance of other disciplines—economics, sociology, psychology, anthropology, human rights, political theory to name a few, and partners within other religious communities and ideological persuasions. The pluralistic world in which we live has made interreligious cooperation essential for addressing issues confronting the world today, and to take seriously the sacred scriptures of other religious communities and native resources/texts from within one's given culture—epics, myths, tales, poems, art, etc.

Biblical interpretation is emotive for me personally and it needs to be so. It should provide space for feeling, vulnerability, humility and charity on the part of the interpreter who is invested in biblical interpretation at the margins. There seems to be an unwritten taboo on the use of the heart, passion and feeling in biblical interpretation and academic work. Evocation of emotion may be disconcerting to the Western/dominant interpreter in the context of the academy because emotions challenge and counter the so-called "objective" approach and framework of biblical studies. Feminist scholars have been at the forefront in the effort to restore the emotional dimension to the current conceptions of rationality. Objectivity and unemotionality are often considered interchangeable and emotion has been discarded of its role in the creation of knowledge. Yet, inclusion of these in our endeavor perhaps would actually be helpful and effective. Alison Jaggar contends that feminist scholars as well as scholars from other oppressed groups have developed "outlaw emotions" that afford them the unique opportunity to create alternative epistemologies, ones that "would show how our emotional responses to the world change as we conceptualize it differently and how our changing emotional responses then stimulate us to new insights."[13]

Tradition—Lutheran or Indian?

An issue that confronts most of us from the global South is the place or the importance we should give to our own cultural and religious traditions—traditions which we have been distanced from owing to our conversion to Christianity. I do not intend to suggest that there needs to be a tussle between the "Lutheran" and the "Indian" tradition. I do not believe the two traditions need to be at odds with each other, although this might happen in some cases. Yet, the is-

---

[13] Alison Jaggar, "Love and Knowledge: Emotion in Feminist Epistemologies," in Alison Jaggar and Susan R. Bordo (eds), *Gender/Body/Knowledge* (New Brunswick: Rutgers University Press, 1989), 164.

sue for me is how we can give the two equal importance or use the richness of the two in our interpretation of the biblical text and in our theologizing?

For centuries now, Luther's writings and theology and their interpretations have been conveyed to the churches and its populace by missionaries and theological educators, primarily from the West. Luther's theology has been presented, encased, or packaged in a purely European wrapper and burdened with the history of interpretation. Few attempts have been made to unpack Luther for the Indian context or to expose the richness of Luther's work and theology for the Indian experience. Perhaps, this is the reason why it has not made a significant impact on theologizing or biblical interpretation in India. Because of the lack of tutored Indian exegetes or "experts" in Luther and the Lutheran tradition, familiar and equipped with the tenets of Lutheran dogma and theology, churches and academic institutions of theological training were and still are dependent on the West to tell us what Lutheranism is all about. In the current scenario, interpreters and theologians of the "contextual" kind seem to be keen on familiarizing themselves with the works of thinkers and reformers such as Ambedkar[14] and other Indian and subaltern leaders, and perhaps juxtapose the insights derived alongside traditional Christian theological concepts for the purposes of the church and the academy.

When pressed for Lutheran positions on something, there have been attempts to tie (sometimes rather loosely) their interpretations to the more popular or well-known Lutheran dictums such as the theology of the cross, the two realms, the doctrine of justification by grace through faith, the Lutheran understanding of the temporal authority or Scripture. These have, in my opinion, sometimes been misunderstood or received insufficient reflection and have therefore been impediments to the work of liberation and transformation. That Luther's political theory evolved under specific circumstances and his articulation of beliefs had radical implications is uncontested. His encouragement to the German nobles to begin dismantling the Roman power structures in his "Open Letter to the Christian Nobility of the German Nation" is received with enthusiasm by those who espouse a liberationist stance.

The cross, too, has been paramount in Indian theologizing, because it reverses all our expectations of what is effective, and challenges our very concept of power and understanding. It even alienates us from all we may believe about wisdom, religion and power politics of society. But then, so is the resurrection,

---

[14] Leader of the Dalit movement in India.

because it offers us a worldview that cannot be evaluated by any systematic predetermined way of thinking.[15]

But, most significantly, Luther's writings have not been helpful as starting points for interreligious dialogue since much of his writing is colored by the anti-Judaism of medieval Europe and the threat of the Turks. This is further complicated by the issues raised by popular renditions of *sola scriptura* or the centrality of Christ, the sacrament of baptism in a multifaith context.

I agree that my identity as a Lutheran should draw upon my Lutheran heritage. But I am also an Indian and a woman and all these should also figure in the manner in which I approach the Bible in my search for truths and strategies that would aid me in addressing not only my individual faith and my struggles but also the communities within which I am placed. How can one best address the complexities of the Bible, the Lutheran tradition and the Indian context without privileging any one in particular?

Reading in juxtaposition

Behind the proposals of multifaith or multicultural hermeneutics lies this basic notion that in reading together and in relation to one another we might discover traditions that transcend structures of oppression derived from diverse sources outside of our own. Acts of protests and liberative streams are found even among other religious traditions and communities, which might in fact sensitize the hermeneutical antennae of biblical interpreters and enable us to discover within the biblical tradition fresh insights to help us to implement the larger purpose in the story of God's liberation of both men and women in the totality of a reconciled humanity. This involves reading in juxtaposition. The uniqueness of juxtaposed reading is that the interpretation given by the reader is not the ultimate interpretation of the religious texts. The process of juxtaposed reading continues when the interpreted texts are read by multiple readers and interpreted in their own way. This is one of the basic principles of postmodern reading, where the production of meaning continues when the same text is read and reread.

An example: The Samaritan woman and Akkamahadevi

I have, for example, read John 4 alongside the life and writings of Akkamahadevi, a twelfth-century *bhakta* from Karnataka in India.[16] It was an attempt to

---

[15] Anthony C. Thistleton, *New Horizons in Hermeneutics: The Theory and Practice of Transforming Bible Study* (London: Harper Collins, 1992), 612.

[16] Monica J. Melanchthon, "Akkamahadevi and the Samaritan Woman: Paradigms of Resistance and Spirituality," in Devadasan N. Premnath (ed.), *Border Crossings: Cross-Cultural Hermeneutics*, Essays in Honor of Prof. R. S. Sugirtharajah (Maryknoll, NY: Orbis, 2007), 35–54.

uncover possible similarities, differences and shared insights between the two texts, which might contribute to our effort to reclaim images and traditions of protest and hope that transcend systems of subjugation and build alternative structures contributing to the dignity and subjecthood of women and men.

The *bhakti* movements of the twelfth century provided the opportunity and space for women, even to those from the so-called "untouchable" caste groups. Several of these *bhaktas* were extremely courageous and creative and claimed their right to control their own lives. They left behind a powerful and cultural legacy for us. This legacy constitutes a living tradition even today, not only in the sense that their songs are an integral part of popular culture in their regions,[17] but also because they are remembered and revered for having stood by their chosen ideals in defiance of the prevalent social norms. The work of these women and the legends surrounding them testify not only to their creativity but also to their joyous exploration of their own truth, even when this involved the radical departure from the life legislated for most women.

Akkamahadevi was born in Karanataka and was initiated into *Virasaivism* as a young girl. She was married to a Jain king whom she left in favor of Siva, who gives form to herself. She severed her ties with family and birthplace and set out in search of her Lord Chennamallikar juna, to whom she betroths herself.[18] The manner in which she handled her marriage is in some ways linked to the deeper question of her sexuality and her explicit attitude to the female body. She wandered across most of what is now Karnataka in search of her divine lover, covered only by the tresses of her hair.[19] She is not embarrassed by her body and does not consider her sexuality as an impediment. In fact, she sees her body as the instrument and the site through which her devotion is expressed. Her relationship with the Lord is set within the framework of bridal mysticism.[20] She confronts her body with a directness which is without parallel and, by confronting it the way she does, she forces the world around to do the same. Her brutal frankness sees no shame in stripping off conventional notions of modesty.[21]

The Samaritan woman meets Jesus at the well and water wells are contested sites in India. The location of this encounter is also significant because it ac-

---

[17] http://chnm.gmu.edu/wwh/modules/lesson1/lesson1.php?menu=1&s=7.

[18] Susie Tharu and K. Lalitha, *Women Writing in India: 600 B.C. to the Present*, vol. I: 600 B.C. to the Early 20th Century (New Delhi: Oxford University, 1993), 77.

[19] www.poetseers.org/the_great_poets/female_poets/spiritual_and_devotional_poets/india/mah.

[20] Tharu and Lalitha, op. cit. (note 18), 77.

[21] R. G. Mathapati writes, "However, she, defending her disregard for body and clothes says I have killed the cupid in myself and conquered this world. So I have no body. When I have no body, no sex where does exist the question of clothes?"; cf. www.ourkarnataka.com/religion/akka_mathapati.htm.

centuates two things: first, the need for water that draws both the characters to the well, which becomes the meeting point of two cultures, communities and religions. Second, the well is one that belonged to Jacob and hence it serves to underscore the common ancestry of these two individuals, Jesus and the Samaritan woman, who are now divided due to historical and social circumstances. I do not see this woman as one of ill repute nor do I judge her for having five husbands. I celebrate her agency and the role she played in perhaps opening the eyes of Jesus and sharing with her community the knowledge of Jesus. I do not see the Samaritan woman as a passive recipient of welfare but as an active promoter and facilitator of social transformations. Such transformations in general influence, of course, the lives and well-being of women, but also those of men and children. The Samaritan woman, after having had a few hard experiences, realized that she needs to come into her own so as to speak and therefore defy expected social norms and customs. Living with someone who was not her husband, she transcended barriers of gender and religion and made a space for herself that was characterized by freedom and agency. This was her way of protesting against these societal norms and expectations with courage, and she was willing to face the odds whatever they might be. Because she was not legally tied to a man, she was able to speak to Jesus alone or otherwise, and share the benefits of her conversation with the rest of the community. And for this she is remembered and celebrated. In arriving at this conclusion I am only valorizing her autonomy and agency. By striving for individual autonomy she strives also for the autonomy of all women, realizing it within the family, asserting it within the community and fostering change.

In comparing these two women, one discerns a structure of protest and transcendence. Although both defied convention in startling ways, neither of them was persecuted or dismissed, but respected during their lifetimes and incorporated into living and growing traditions. The two texts in my opinion showcase a tradition's capacity to make social space available for women with exceptionally outstanding abilities and courage, even when they have outrageously defied what are ordinarily considered the fundamental tenets of *stree dharma*, marriage, and motherhood.[22] These women represent illegitimate, subversive or transgressing relationships. These women, though victims of atrocity, attain new power by renewed transgression. Their sovereignty is expressed in the extraordinariness of their family situation.[23]

---

[22] Note the women mentioned in the genealogy of Jesus.

[23] Gabriele Dietrich, "Subversion, Transgression, Transcendence: 'Asian Spirituality' in the Light of Dalit and Adivasi struggles," in *A New Thing on Earth: Hopes and Fears facing Feminist Theology* (New Delhi: ISPCK, 2001), 246.

In order to move our society in the direction of greater justice and freedom we need to develop a creative relationship with the more humane and potentially liberating aspects of our cultural and religious traditions. My question now is what from within the Lutheran tradition can I place alongside these texts or which Lutheran hermeneutical principle could I use to interpret these two texts which would render it Lutheran? Do these two women show forth Christ? Do the women of Manipur, who cried, "We mothers have come. Drink our blood. Eat our flesh. Maybe this way you can spare our daughters," show forth Christ? I believe that the gospel and the good news can also be found in other biblical characters, in women and children, and they are worth unearthing and sharing. If biblical characters and Luther can be "transfigured" using Vítor Westhelle's use of this concept,[24] I think even figures from within our own cultural traditions, movements and other forms of "texts" can also be transfigured. We need them and we use them because they are pertinent and resonate with our experiences, challenge our faith, enrich our understanding of the biblical text, and open up new and innovative insights and strategies for addressing the realities of our time and place.

Luther: An experiential and contextual biblical scholar?

Luther was a man of his epoch, a product of his time, contextual and sensitive to the needs of his time, and by bringing this sensitivity to his work he energized a revolution. His formation as a scholar and theologian was most definitely influenced by his experiences and his theology was molded by the scholars under whom he was trained. The writings of Augustine, the sermons of John Tauler, the great German mystic, and the little book, *The German Theology*, written by an unknown mystic of the earlier part of the fifteenth century, the conciliarists,[25] all had an impact on his life and theology. All this helped shape his theology and response to the signs of his time. According to Walter Altmann, Luther,

---

[24] Cf. Vítor Westhelle, "Exploring Effective Context. Luther's Contextual Hermeneutics," in this publication.

[25] Luther had been fond of citing the conciliarist Nicolo de Tudeschi, known as Panormitanus, who said that "in matters touching the faith, the word of a single private person is to be preferred to that of a Pope if that person is moved by sounder arguments from the Old and New Testament." As cited by Roland Bainton, "The Bible in the Reformation," in Stanley L. Greenslade (ed.), *The Cambridge History of the Bible: The West from the Reformation to the Present Day* (Cambridge: Cambridge University Press, 1963), 2. But Luther went beyond the conciliarists arguing that infallible interpretations did not reside in councils any more than in popes.

caught in the midst of dramatic and, transitional events for the church and, indeed, for the Western world, Luther acted and reacted in what he thought were relevant and necessary ways, in response to the signs of the times and to the Word of God.[26]

His interpretations of the Bible were deeply informed by medieval methods of biblical interpretation. For example, in his early commentary on the Psalms (1513–1515), Luther combines the *quadriga* or the fourfold mode of reading (literal, allegorical, tropological and analogical) with the double literal sense of the French humanist Jacques Lefèvre d'Étaples to produce a hermeneutic of eight senses.[27] My question is, What are some of the cultural texts/resources that influenced Luther? To what extent did Luther engage local wisdom, cultural traditions, folklore and myths in his theologizing?

Contextual biblical interpreters seek to employ indigenous methods of interpretation and use resources also arising from within their own cultures. In doing so, they seek attempt to work within the meaning systems of the community to which they belong. Knowledge of what is important in a given culture enables the informed interpreter to use the symbolic meanings attached to that culture. The use of cultural metaphors inherent in poetry, proverbs, folktales and myths engages the interpreter and the listener and facilitates understanding and growth within a framework and patterning that is culturally congruent.

The challenges of contextual approaches to Lutheran hermeneutics

Our focus is the book of John and much has been said on what the "Word made flesh" means. Many pastors in India preach with an emphasis only on "the Word made flesh." This has engendered an individualistic and personal approach to the Christian faith, thereby promoting psychological dependency, political passivity and communal exclusiveness, particularly among Dalit Christians and other marginalized communities. Such a theology, according to Wilson, is built "upon the edifice of human weakness;" it nurtures a low self-image and a sense of helplessness. [28] This emphasis has neglected and sometimes even excluded the social realm and, therefore, any idea of social

---

[26] Walter Altmann, *Luther and Liberation* (Minneapolis: Fortress, 1992), vii–viii.

[27] Cf. Peter J. Leithart, *Deep Exegesis: The Mystery of Reading Scripture* (Waco, Texas: Baylor University Press, 2009), 13.

[28] K. Wilson, *The Twice Alienated: Culture of Dalit Christians* (Hyderabad, 1982), 26.

salvation; it has impacted the manner in which the church views economics, politics, culture, social relationships and international affairs. In light of the context of India, what is needed is an emphasis on the fact that "the Word which became flesh," also "dwelt among us,"—the historical Jesus who identified with the oppressed, who dwelt with us and lived a life of protest and struggle against forces of oppression.[29] This stresses the fact Jesus proclaimed in word and deed (Mk 1:15). Such an emphasis provides encouragement, provocation, empowerment, and the enabling of the oppressed to take responsibility for their own emancipation and liberation.

What we seem to be confronted with is how best to deal not only with the complexity of the biblical text but also the tradition, both Lutheran and cultural, and the contexts of which we are a part. Our situation is a shared planetary space comprised of diverse, often competing, communities and traditions. The entry of new players into a game sometimes changes the nature of the game. Contextual biblical interpreters have not only shaken the North American and western European dominance of biblical studies, but they have brought new agendas, new questions and new perspectives to the table. The discipline is fraught with divisions, arguments among scholars about theories, approaches, methods, hermeneutics; but these are not of themselves either dangerous or unexpected. Indeed, they are essential to the progress of understanding. Unity, if understood as homogeneity, provides safety. But, safety is not a place for adventure; it forbids life to be experienced directly. Homogeneity and safety are not conducive to the flowering of any discipline or reorganization of knowledge or perhaps for expressing communion.

We therefore need to think about the coherence and complexity of our situation, our diverse histories and lives. How do we achieve coherence in the midst of such a diversity of exegetes, thinkers, methods, hermeneutical strategies and contexts? Is there a singular principle that might aid us in this task? I think that any emphasis on a singular method or hermeneutical strategy is unhelpful given the diversity of the communion. Any singular systematic approach would be controlling. It is what Walter Brueggemann calls "a vested interest which is passed off as truth, partial truth, which counterfeits as a whole truth, a theological claim functioning as a mode of social control."[30] We are rich in our differences and in our diverse approaches, theories and hermeneutical strategies. And biblical interpretation has always involved multiple agents, varied skills and diverse commitments.

---

[29] V. Devasahayam (ed.), *Frontiers of Dalit Theology* (Chennai/New Delhi: Gurukul/ISPCK, 1997), 5.

[30] Walter Brueggemann, *Israel's Praise: Doxology Against Idolatry and Ideology* (Philadelphia: Fortress, 1989),111. Cf. also Rex Mason, *Propaganda and Subversion in the Old Testament* (London: SPCK, 1997).

But biblical scholars cannot afford to get lost in the intellectual ramifications of the discipline or tradition and neglect of the communities that they are a part of and should be addressing. Whatever the method—approach or hermeneutic—all are easily different ways of "reader-centredness" whereby every reader assumes the same right to a proper interpretation of a text. The challenge lies in achieving a balance between the complexity and the need for coherence/unity. What a contextual approach endorses is a multi-perspectival critique of society and its structures, a plurality of methods that would contribute to the recognition of oppressive systems and practices and help find ways to overcome them. This diversity, I believe, is an opportunity, an invitation to contend with each other and our particularities and our contextual interpretations of the biblical text. It is a call to openness and with openness perhaps there will come what Clarke and Ringe call the "capacity for interpretative elasticity."[31] Openness is a stretching of ourselves outside of our comfort zones, our safety nets, and stretching our hearts and minds to understand the text from the perspective of another resulting in "mutual fecundation,"[32] "cross fertilization," "acculturation," in order to formulate the Word of God for the self and for the communion.

We also have to pay attention to the histories of the reception of the Bible in the varied contexts and the circumstances surrounding the time when the Bible was first introduced to a particular community; the ordinary reader does not work with the Hebrew and the Greek text—we need to research into the politics of language and translations and how they affect the meaning of the text in that context.

Not a conclusion ...

There cannot be a conclusion to this endeavor. Because context is fluid and requires biblical interpretations that are dynamic and address the context in a particular moment and particular space. The public nature of biblical interpretation does not end nor can it have an end; it simply waits for another rendering and other performers. Biblical scholars need seriously to engage with the context in order to arrive at a critical appraisal of what current methods

---

[31] Sathinathan Clarke and Sharon Ringe, "Inter-Location as Textual Trans-version: A Study in John 4: 1–42," in Tat Siong Benny Liew (ed.), *Post Colonial Interventions: Essays in Honor of R. S. Sugirtharajah* (Sheffield: Phoenix, 2009), 59.

[32] Duane A. Priebe, "Mutual fecundation: The Creative Interplay of Texts and New Contexts," in Bloomquist, op. cit. (note 11), 91–104.

or hermeneutical principles or approaches signify as the future for the communities that we seek to serve. This engagement is necessary if the discourse wishes to stick to its goal of making a real difference in the lives of men and women even as it debates ways to go ahead.

The Role of Tradition in Relation to Scripture: Questions and Reflections

Dennis T. Olson

Remember the former things of old;
for I am God, and there is no other;
I am God, and there is no one like me.
   Isa 46:8

Do not remember the former things,
or consider the things of old.
I am about to do a new thing;
now it springs forth, do you not perceive it?
   Isa 43:18–19

"Tradition is the living faith of the dead, traditionalism is the dead faith of the living."
   Jaroslav Pelikan[1]

A host of questions naturally arise when thinking about the relationship of Scripture and tradition. I do not plan to answer all of the questions that can be raised when thinking about tradition and Scripture in the brief span of this one essay. What I plan to do is to raise three groups of possible questions and after each group of questions, provide some accompanying "reflections" related to that group of questions.

The first group of questions explores the meaning and function of tradition as a generic topic. These questions will touch on the idea of tradition not only in religious communities but tradition as it exists across varied disciplines, cultures and fields of study. The second group of questions will explore aspects of specifically religious tradition within the church, that is, the church catholic. The third set of questions will explore the peculiar issues that arise when examining the role of tradition within the specifically Lutheran com-

---

[1] Jaroslav Pelikan, *The Vindication of Tradition* (New Haven: Yale University Press, 1984), 65.

munion, that is, from a Reformation perspective. What is provided here is only a sampling and selection of issues.

Generalized studies of tradition

Questions

From a more generic and wide-angle lens perspective, how do we define a "tradition" in any culture or field of study? Are traditions inherently conservative and resistant to change? How does a tradition emerge? What are the benefits and the dangers in the use or abuse of traditions? Do complex traditions have clear boundaries and a uniform shape from whatever vantage point we view them? Or do traditions have fuzzy but identifiable boundaries and shape? Or do the boundaries and shape of complex traditions change completely, depending on who the observer might be?

Reflections

The term "tradition" is used in quite varied ways in different disciplines. In the social sciences such as anthropology, "tradition" is most often used of established folkways and social customs which are carried on without much explicit or conscious reflection and are often threatened by forces of modernity. In the areas of philosophy, religion, science and law, tradition refers to a body of ideas and practices that are more explicitly studied and analyzed in a self-conscious way as knowledge that is to be interpreted, sometimes consciously changed, and handed on from generation to generation. But even in these fields of more objective analysis of tradition, there remains operative what Michael Polanyi describes in his philosophy of science as "tacit knowledge" and the inevitability of personal commitments that enter into human ways of knowing.[2]

Some deconstructionist theorists take a skeptical view of tradition and see tradition as functioning primarily as authoritative ideology designed to preserve the status quo and the position of those who hold power in the society or group. Tradition for these theorists is often described as "invented tradition" which masks and supports the interests of those in power.[3] Such treatments sometimes appear to lump all traditions together in the same basket, often failing to distinguish traditionalisms that are genuinely repressive and abusive

---

[2] Mark S. Phillips and Gordon Schochet (eds), *Questions of Tradition* (Toronto: University of Toronto, 2004), ix–x.

[3] Eric Hobsbawn and Terence Ranger (eds), *Invention of Tradition* (Cambridge: Cambridge University Press, 1983).

of power from positive living traditions that are constructive, creative, empowering and open to new circumstances and the wisdom of other traditions.

The distinction of "tradition" versus "modernity" that often occurs is itself a false distinction. Modernity's Enlightenment rationalism, like any substantive set of beliefs and practices, is itself a tradition.[4] The quest for truth is not about choosing between tradition versus what is modern, but rather what tradition among competing traditions one chooses to follow or support. The same is true for oppositions like tradition versus innovation or tradition versus change. Tradition can as readily provide the fuel for radical change against current trends as it can support maintaining the present structures of thought or practice. The hermeneutical philosopher Hans-Georg Gadamer affirmed the importance of fruitful prejudices and tradition (closely bound to human language) as a necessary element of understanding within the human sciences. For the physical sciences, Thomas Kuhn promoted the importance of paradigms (as exemplary solutions to a core set of problems functioning as a kind of tradition) that provide the consensus foundation for new research and innovation.[5]

I have found Delwin Brown's book, *Boundaries of Our Habitations, Tradition and Theological Construction,* a helpful resource on the inevitable role of traditions (religious, academic, cultural) that shape our reading, thinking and action and on the role and function of a canon of authoritative documents (whether a canon of Scripture or creeds in a variety of religious traditions).[6] Brown presents a helpful metaphor for understanding how to think about any complex and "thick" tradition. Using astronomy as a metaphorical field, one can compare a substantive tradition to a galaxy, a galaxy of meanings, if you will. A galaxy lies on a spectrum somewhere between the one extreme of a planet and the other extreme of a constellation. A complex and deep tradition is not like a single planet that has an absolutely defined circular boundary that will always look identical from every angle, the same round shape from whatever vantage point in the universe that anyone stands and looks at the planet. A complex tradition is also not like a constellation of stars in the sky (the perceived pattern of stars in the night sky when standing on earth by which you can trace out various creatures and figures—Leo the lion, Orion the hunter,

---

[4] John Michael, "Tradition and Critical Talent," in *Telos* 94 (1993–94), 58.

[5] Thomas Kuhn, "The Essential Tension: Tradition and Innovation in Scientific Research," in C. W. Taylor (ed.), *The Third University of Utah Research Conference on the Identification of Scientific Talent* (Salt Lake City: University of Utah Press, 1959). This essay preceded his later well-known book, Thomas Kuhn, *Structures of Scientific Revolutions* (Chicago: University of Chicago Press, 1962). See Phillips and Schochet, op. cit (note 2), 22–25.

[6] Delwin Brown, *Boundaries of Our Habitations: Tradition and Theological Construction* (Albany: State University of New York, 1994), 75–76.

Pisces the fish, and the like). The thing about constellations is that they are arbitrary and can be seen from only one vantage point in the universe, that is, from earth connecting the dots among a random series of stars in the sky. Other hypothetical observers located elsewhere in the universe would not see the patterns an earthling would see.

A complex tradition (the creeds or the Lutheran Confessions might be examples), Brown argues, is better compared to a galaxy like the Milky Way. A galaxy of stars has a form and a certain material objectivity, a givenness, a three-dimensional thickness to it. A galaxy of stars exerts its own gravitational pull, its own inner drive in interaction with its own changing internal dynamics and in a back and forth interaction with external bodies outside the galaxy. At the same time, a galaxy will have some fuzziness around the edges, not an absolute boundary. The galaxy will have a consistent but dynamic three-dimensional shape to the whole that can be seen and identified from many vantage points, both from within it and outside of it. "At any given time," Brown writes, "and from any given perspective, a canon [or tradition] has a coarse and practical unity, though that unity is always differently construed from different perspectives."[7]

Thus, a thick, complex tradition will be amenable to some degree of proximate objective description that can be shared among multiple observers viewing the same Milky Way galaxy from different parts of the universe. On the other hand, its interpretation (the particular view of any one observer) will also depend in part on the vantage point. The particular view will depend in part on the web of other traditions in which one stands and by which one interprets the given complex tradition. One will see the same swirl of the Milky Way as other observers but from different angles.

Tradition and the church catholic

Questions

If we speak of the tradition of the church catholic, what is the proper relationship of Scripture and church tradition? Should we properly speak of one true apostolic tradition as the early patristic sources did? What, then, do we make of the multiple authoritative traditions, given the many denominational and theological divisions and differences within the church catholic? What was the early church's understanding of the rule of faith? How did it function? Does it have significance for us today? Does the proper use of the church's Scripture

---

[7] Ibid., 76.

and its creedal traditions also require a strong episcopacy with bishops whose primary task is to enforce adherence to the tradition, to right preaching and administration of the sacraments? Does some human body or group (bishops, theological commissions) have to act as police or judge in order for tradition to work effectively as a guide in the church?

Reflections

In the early centuries of the church, the "rule of faith" functioned as a guide to belief and interpretation to preserve orthodoxy and avoid heretical beliefs. Most scholars would trace the trajectory of the notion of a "rule" back to Paul's use in Galatians 6:16 of the noun κανών ("rule," the same Greek term which later came to be associated with a "canon" of Scripture). In Galatians 6, Paul speaks of the need for the Galatians to trust and boast only "in the cross of our Lord Jesus Christ . . . for neither circumcision or uncircumcision is anything, but a new creation is everything! As for those who will follow this rule (κανόνι)—peace be upon them, and mercy, and upon the Israel of God."[8]

Irenaeus (second century CE) was one of the first to use the phrase, "the rule of faith" (*Adv. Haer.* 1.9.4) explicitly in the sense of a standard or norm by which Christian truth is judged. Although a matter of some scholarly debate, the rule of faith and Scripture were closely associated (but often also distinguished) by several Church Fathers before the fourth century CE with the closing of the New Testament canon. The rule of faith or rule of truth was identified with the one true apostolic witness handed down in both written and oral firm in the early centuries of the church.[9]

In *Canon and Creed*, Robert Jenson argues for the mutual reciprocity of canon (Scripture) and creed (the formal catechetical-baptismal confessions of the church) **and** the less formal rule of faith that was the one true apostolic witness of the early church:

> The rule of faith, the *regula fidei*, was a sort of communal linguistic awareness of the faith delivered to the apostles, which sufficed the church for genera-tions. The gift of the spirit guided missionary proclamation, shaped instruction, identified heresy, and in general functioned wherever in the church's life a brief statement of the gospel's content was needed.

---

[8] William Farmer, "Galatians and the Second-Century Development of the *Regula Fidei*," in *The Second Century* 4 (1984), 143–70.

[9] Jonathan Armstrong, "The Rule of Faith and the New Testament Canon," in Ronnie Rombs and Alex-ander Hwant (eds), *Tradition and the Rule of Faith in the Early Church* (Washington: Catholic University of America Press, 2010), 47.

> We speak of "the" rule of faith, though there was no one text in general use, and indeed strictly speaking no *text* at all. The *regula fidei*, though directed and attuned to statement in language, was not itself written or even memorized… The early pastors and theologians who invoked the rule of faith …located the "rule" of this community's faith in its communal self-consciousness.[10]

Although the rule of faith and Scripture were distinguished, Scripture played a role similar to the rule of faith for later Christian interpreters: "In the era that followed, after the New Testament canon was fixed, we find that the Fathers appealed to the canonical Scriptures in the same way that they once appealed to the rule of faith."[11]

Alongside the early use of the phrase "rule of faith," the term "tradition" (παράδοσις) also appears in the early Church Fathers. In Everett Ferguson's study of the term "tradition" in ancient Jewish, Greek and Latin writings as well as early Christian writings, the following list of eight possible meanings for "tradition" emerged:

- The active sense of the act of handing over [process]
  1. The handing over of objects
  2. The handing over, betrayal, surrender of persons or a place.
  3. The passing on of teaching, especially by philosophers

- The passive sense of that which is handed over [content]
  4. Any item of information
  5. Ancestral customs
  6. Jewish interpretations and application of the Torah—*halakah* [oral Torah alongside written Torah]
  7. The Christian message—from God, Christ, or the apostles
  8. Apostolic or ecclesiastical practices—liturgical, organizational and disciplinary
  9. Erroneous or heretical teaching
  10. Content indeterminate from the context [miscellaneous].

Fergusson concludes his survey with this assessment:

> Neither *paradosis* nor *tradition* appears to have been a technical term in the earliest Christian literature. . . . Even where tradition appears in a theological

---

[10] Robert Jenson, *Canon and Creed* (Louisville: Westminster John Knox, 2010), 15.

[11] Armstrong, op. cit. (note 9), 45–46.

> context there is no specific content nor definite mode of delivery [oral versus written] prior to the fourth century. The earliest Christian authors use tradition in a wide variety of contexts and with varied meanings. . . . Tradition came to prominence in a polemical context, first in response to Gnostic claims and then in internal church conflicts. . . . But on many controverted issues it was a two-edged sword, with both sides claiming tradition in their favor. Where this was not possible, (as for Cyprian in the rebaptism controversy), tradition was subordinated to other standards [reason, custom, and the like].[12]

The councils and formal creeds of the church that emerged in the subsequent centuries (e.g., the Apostle's Creed, the Nicene Creed, the Athanasian Creed with their antecedents) solidified what could be called the emerging tradition of the church. Alongside the Scriptures of the Old and New Testaments and the creeds were collections of interpretations by the Church Fathers. The standard collection of these interpretations was the assembly of glosses or commentary that arose in the medieval period called the *Glossa ordinaria* ("the ordinary gloss/interpretation"), written in the margins of the Vulgate Bible. Luther regularly consulted and interacted with the *Glossa* in his own scriptural interpretation.[13]

The churches have continued to produce creeds and confessions as part of their expanding "tradition" over the centuries. Indeed, the production of creeds or statements of belief is a fairly distinctive element of the Christian tradition not shared by most of the other world's religions. Jews have gotten along for over 3000 years with the simple creed of the *Shema:* "Hear O Israel, the LORD our God, the LORD is one." Muslims are united over centuries with the sparse creed, "There is no God but Allah, and Muhammad is His prophet." Those suffice as shared statements of belief. Not so for Christianity. Yale historian Jaroslav Pelikan participated in the collection and editing of four volumes of Christian creeds and confessions from ancient to modern times.[14] His editorial team assembled over 2000 such creeds but had room to publish only about 200 creeds and confessions of faith in four volumes. In an interview about the project, Pelikan made these three interesting observations:

1) "The only alternative to tradition is bad tradition."

---

[12] Everett Ferguson, "Paradosis and Traditio: A Word Study," in Rombs and Hwant, op. cit. (note 9), 4, 28.

[13] Karlfried Froehlich, "Martin Luther and the Glossa ordinaria," in *Lutheran Quarterly* 23 (2009), 29–48.

[14] Jaroslav Pelikan and Valerie Hotchkiss (eds), *Creeds and Confessions of Faith in the Christian Tradition*, 4 vol. (New Haven: Yale University Press, 2003).

2) [In response to the interviewer's recollection of a remark that Pelikan had made in one of the volumes that one of the most remarkable aspects of the work of editing this collection of diverse creeds was to observe the "sheer repetitiveness" of all these creeds, Pelikan replied with this comment]: "You should try to proofread them all in the course of a few weeks, as we did, and then you discover just how repetitive—you wonder, didn't I just read this one yesterday?"

3) [The interviewer observed that "it's so interesting because I think that where someone goes when they hear that there are these thousands of creeds is that everybody's doing it differently all the time, and that's not really what you find. But I did want to dwell briefly on one that I sense is near and dear to your heart, which is this Maasai Creed from the Maasai people of Africa which was written around 1960, the Congregation of the Holy Ghost in east Nigeria." Pelikan responds:] "Oh yes…Like most creeds, it is designed on a threefold pattern of Father, Son, and Holy Spirit and comes out of the experience of Christians in Africa. [It reads in part,] 'We believe in one high God, who out of love created the beautiful world. We believe that God made good His promise by sending His Son, Jesus Christ, a man in the flesh, a Jew by tribe, born poor in a little village, who left His home and was always on safari doing good, curing people by the power of God, teaching about God and man, and showing that the meaning of religion is love. He was rejected by His people, tortured and nailed hands and feet to a cross, and died. He was buried in the grave, but the hyenas did not touch Him, and on the third day He rose from the grave."

"Now for one thing, the Nicene Creed as well as the Apostles' Creed go directly from born of the Virgin Mary to suffered under Pontius Pilate. And the whole story in the Gospels . . . is just leapt over. . . . You go from alpha to omega. And here, see, He was born, as the creed said, He left His home—the creeds don't say that—and He was always on safari in Africa. When I read that the first time, a student of mine who'd been a member of a religious order, she was a sister, and she had been in a hospital in east Nigeria, and that's the creed they recited at their liturgy. And so she brought it to me, and I just got shivers, just the thought, you know, the hyenas did not touch Him and the act of defiance—God lives even in spite of the hyenas. But it's a good example of this model that I quoted earlier, that it is not enough to Christianize Africa. We have to Africanize Christianity."[15]

---

[15] Transcript of an interview with Jaroslav Pelikan on Krista Tippet's "On Being," National Public Radio, March 20, 2008, rebroadcast of a 2006 interview, at **http://being.publicradio.org/programs/ pelikan/transcript.shtml.**

Pelikan's three observations highlight three key insights into the nature of tradition. First, humans are tradition-bound creatures who inevitably view reality through traditions (often multiple, competing traditions derived from many sources), some of which may be fruitful and good, and some of which may need review and critique from time to time. Secondly, the Christian tradition has retained a remarkable consistency in the midst of its expansions and rearticulations of creeds and confessions over a broad swath of time (centuries and millennia) and of geography (every major region of the world). The Christian tradition has a gravitas, a material reality that has had remarkable staying power in time and space. Thirdly, such repetition and consistency of the Christian tradition works alongside the need for robust translation and incarnation—linguistic, cultural and historical—into the peculiar idioms, metaphors and realities of the concrete contexts to which the Christian gospel moves. This latter insight is part of what Christian missiologist Andrew Walls calls the "translation principle" in Christian history, the capacity of Christianity to flourish most powerfully in contexts in which its gospel must be translated into new cultures, idioms and contexts.[16]

Tradition in the Lutheran tradition

Questions

If we narrow our lens down even further and specifically to the Lutheran church tradition, what constitutes the Lutheran tradition that we uphold alongside Scripture? Is it the Large and Small Catechisms, the Augsburg Confession, the Lutheran Book of Confessions? Does the tradition also include the hymns of the Lutheran tradition? Does tradition not only need to proclaim and declare in prose but also to sing and to recite in poetry? Are the shape of the liturgy, the administration of the sacraments, and other distinctive congregational practices also part of our Lutheran tradition that we share, and if so, what role do these elements play alongside others?

What is the function of tradition for Lutherans in light of the Reformation principles of *sola scriptura* (Scripture alone) and *sacra scriptura sui ipsius interpres* (Sacred Scripture is self-interpreting or Scripture interprets itself)? In what ways, if any, should the post-biblical history of interpretation, the church's creeds, and the confessions of other church traditions guide the reading and interpreting of Scripture? Do Lutherans have a particular responsibility within

---

[16] Andrew Walls, "The Translation Principle in Christian History," in Philip Stine (ed.), *Biblical Translation and the Spread of the Church: The Last 200 Years* (Leiden: Brill, 1990), 24–39.

the church catholic clearly to articulate a distinctive, solid and common Lutheran confession as its unique and fundamental contribution to the ecumenical conversation? Should Lutherans seek wisdom in theological formulations from other intellectual disciplines (for example, neuroscience, psychology, astrophysics, social sciences, studies of expanding digital and internet technology and the like) and adapt and reshape our Lutheran tradition in dialogue with these traditions? How do we decide what to hold onto and what to let go? Will the increasing democratization of knowledge and opportunities for collaboration through the expanding use of digital technology and the internet have any impact on the shape or role of the Lutheran tradition?

Reflections

Here I simply list a number of helpful or provocative quotations and principles as resources to help spur our thinking about Scripture and tradition in Luther and the Lutheran church.

The Protestant principle of *sola scriptura* ("Scripture alone") understood within a Trinitarian framework. The Protestant principle of *sola scriptura* did not suggest that Scripture should be interpreted apart from any confessional tradition. *Sola scriptura* assumed the use of Christian tradition to guide biblical interpretation. Luther wrote the catechisms as guides to the use of Scripture. As Gerhard Ebeling argued, *sola scriptura* affirmed that the primary authority mediated through Scripture was the concrete encounter with the person of Jesus Christ through the localized and oral proclamation of Scripture.

> The decisive fact [is] that the content of the *traditum tradendum* is not a doctrinal statement, nor a law, nor a book of Revelation, but the very person of Jesus himself as the incarnate Word of God, giving its authority to the Gospel and to the event of the authoritative Word of faith; and correspondingly we have the Holy Spirit as God's Presence in the faith-creating Word of preaching." In that encounter, the Gospel is revealed "not only as freedom *from* the false use of traditions but also and especially as freedom to use them rightly.[17]

"Christ alone" is the prior principle undergirding "Scripture alone." David Lotz has well observed that "*solus Christus* is the presupposition and ground of *sola scriptura*."[18] Scripture proclaimed in the community of faith is the place

---

[17] Gerhard Ebeling, "'Sola Scriptura' and Tradition," in Gerhard Ebeling, *The Word of God and Tradition* (Philadelphia: Fortress, 1964), 146–47.

[18] David Lotz, "*Sola Scriptura: Luther on Biblical Authority*," in *Interpretation* 35 (1981), 258–73.

where the living Christ encounters the church in the ministry of Word and sacrament.

Luther trusted that God would preserve the true church and authentic tradition in the midst of the broken images of both. Najeeb George Awad has observed that,

> Luther believed that, despite the erring nature of the visible church, God can miraculously preserve the true church in the midst of the broken visible image of it. The same belief is applicable to Luther's view of tradition and his acknowledgement of good and authentic elements in it. These elements exist in tradition because God can also preserve a message of salvation in the teaching that the church passes on from one generation to another. Because of this conviction, Luther had no problem in receiving elements related to the truth of faith from the "ecclesial tradition.[19]

Luther's stated intention was not to innovate but to recover the true early Christian tradition. David Steinmetz, in an essay on Luther's treatise, "On the Councils and the Church" (1539), argues that,

> both Luther and Calvin reject the notion that Protestant reformers are theological innovators who have disrupted a 1500-year-old consensus in Christian doctrine. Innovations have been introduced by the Catholic Church during the middle ages which were not found in the earliest Church . . . What the Protestants are attempting to do (at least as they understand it) is to persuade the Church to abandon its fascination with the theological and disciplinary innovations of the later middle ages and return to Scripture and the fathers, Scripture as the authoritative text and the fathers as helpful interpreters (not infallible but better far than the scholastics).[20]

Luther's exegetical optimism about the clarity of Scripture. In a study of the views of Luther and Calvin on Scripture and tradition, David Steinmetz concludes that,

> both Luther and Calvin reflect the exegetical optimism which marked early Protestantism. For a brief period, Protestants thought it would be possible to

---

[19] Najeeb George Awad, "Should We Dispense with *Sola Scriptura*? Scripture, Tradition and Postmodern Theology," in *Dialog* 47 (2008), 70.

[20] David Steinmetz, "Luther and Calvin on Church and Tradition," in David Steinmetz, *Luther in Context* (Grand Rapids: Baker, 1995), 95.

write a theology which was wholly biblical and excluded all philosophical and speculative questions. It became clear within a decade that such hope was not well founded. Nevertheless, Protestants remained optimistic about the clarity of Scripture and the simplicity and persuasive power of the truth which it contained. Protestants were not well prepared for the internal disagreements within Protestantism when the careful exegesis of one group of godly and learned men clashed with the exegesis of another group equally learned and godly. On the whole, Luther and Calvin seem to believe that good exegesis will drive out bad and do not provide a great deal of help in suggesting a practical mechanism for the reconciliation of conflicts. . . . Luther and Calvin are confident that, in every generation, the lively and living Word of God will create communities of obedient hearers and doers of that Word. The unity which the Church seeks beyond all theological and doctrinal strife is the unity which the Word itself creates through the action of the Holy Spirit: "for God's Word cannot be without God's people, and conversely, God's people cannot be without God's Word.[21]

Luther himself was embedded within and worked from a number of "traditions" (Christian, philosophical, methodological and cultural) as follows:

Luther scholar Christine Helmer describes the multiple influences on Luther's thought which included not only Scripture but also other non-biblical traditions:

My views on the relation of Bible to theology have changed a lot over the years. I can start here with Luther's Works. The first thirty volumes are on Luther's biblical interpretation; his works on theology and pastoral theology begin in volume 31. But when you look at the German edition of Luther's works (the Weimarer Ausgabe), the sequence is more or less chronological. So the "bias" that is written into the English translation of Luther's works is that the exegetical commentaries are the foundation of his theology, which is based on the Bible. This is a bias that needs to be critically examined about Luther, but also more broadly in view of the ways in which the Bible is contextualized and conceptualized in new contexts.[22]

Helmer notes the importance of other significant shapers of Luther's theology and way of interpreting Scripture.

---

[21] Ibid., 96–97.

[22] Christine Helmer, an interview on the book, *The Global Luther: A Theologian for Modern Times* (Minneapolis: Fortress, 2009), at **www.fortressforum.com/profiles/blogs/an-interview-with-christine-1.**

> I think we need to look at Luther's interpretation of the Bible in a complex matrix. First, philosophy plays a key role in Luther's interpretation of scripture. Take for example his love for specific biblical passages that highlight a symmetry in God. God is the one who "builds up and destroys." "God loves Jacob and hates Esau." The theological amplitudes that Luther drives into his doctrine of God are more than what he took from the Bible's prophetic corpus. Luther interprets the divine symmetry through his own intellectual formation in the art of disputation. Disputation trained logic in binary oppositions. But in my research on Luther's understanding of divine omnipotence, which Luther defines as the divine capacity to create and to destroy what is created, I discovered that Luther took this definition from William of Ockham. This gets to the question of which philosophical tools and resources Luther used to interpret the Bible.[23]

Another key element in Luther's breakthrough in interpreting the Bible involved his translations from the original biblical languages which opened new avenues of meaning in comparison to the traditional Latin Vulgate translations of the Bible in use at the time. The Vulgate was based on the Greek Septuagint rather than the more original Hebrew of the Old Testament. Luther used the resources of careful philology and translation to make fundamental theological claims through his translation of the biblical text.

> Luther made serious adjustments to the Christian Bible. He translated the Bible from the original Greek and Hebrew rather than from the Latin Vulgate, as was a practice during his time. With the turn to the Masoretic text as the Hebrew basis for his Bible translation, Luther made this text canonical, replacing the canonicity of the Greek Septuagint (the basis of the Latin Vulgate). Furthermore, he made use of Erasmus's critical edition of the Greek New Testament and appealed to the Hebrew scholarship of his day to improve his translation of the Old Testament. Theological issues in translation are intimately joined to grammatical and syntactical issues. . . .[24]

This attention to details of grammar and syntax led Luther to new insights into how Scripture pointed away from itself and to the referent who was Christ. If Christ is the true referent and meaning of Scripture, then one was free to criticize or reject certain parts of Scripture for the sake of the true referent

---

[23] Ibid.

[24] Ibid.

who is Christ. But at the same time, it is only through the proclamation of the Word mediated through Scripture that we encounter this living Christ.

A caution about making Luther into a petrified or legalistic tradition. If the true referent of Scripture is the living Christ, then Christine Helmer reminds us that we should not turn Luther's own words into a rigid traditionalism used primarily to preserve the past. Helmer notes that,

> an honest look at Luther's impact in a number of fields brings us to tensions, conflicts, disharmonies—to ambivalence, I say. The example of Luther's formidable impact on the German language is a case in point. He opened up possibilities of speaking about religious realities in many discourses. He introduced the use of vernacular terms in his Bible translation and even his academic disputations departed from a strict theological Latin to a Latin rich with novel formulations and exclamations. What Luther teaches us in this respect, then, is that thinking about religion is a linguistically creative enterprise. If theology is to be a living enterprise it is inherently bound up with the creation of new and living language. The ambivalence occurs when later generations of Luther fans petrify his language as authoritative, particularly distinct formulations, without regard for the abundance of words he used to depict a religious reality. So that the appeal to Luther as an ally for "scripture and tradition" is an appeal to remain locked in a historical discourse rather than to ask questions of what this discourse might mean to us today. The ambivalence arises when Luther's own living language is turned into authoritative discourse and as authoritative, it becomes a standard and norm rather than a living conversation.[25]

The role of tradition within Scripture itself: Illustrations from the Old and New Testaments

The study of the multiple traditions that were brought together to form the books of the Bible itself provides an intra-biblical case study of how early traditions are both preserved but also changed and even invented over time in new contexts. For example, recent studies that compare the different law codes that coexist within the present form of the Pentateuch, the first five books of the Bible (Genesis–Deuteronomy) provide an illustration of how legal traditions developed within the Bible. In a recent major study, biblical scholar David

---

[25] Ibid.

Wright argues that the earliest law code in the Bible, the so-called Covenant Code in Exodus 20:23–23:19, was probably written by an Israelite scribe trained in the language of Akkadian, a technical scribal language used by the reigning empire of the time, Assyria. The scribe adapted the biblical law code from copies of an older set of laws, the Old Babylonian laws of King Hammurabi, which had been preserved and handed down over centuries, including within Assyria. Remarkable parallels between Hammurabi's laws and the biblical laws of the Covenant Code suggest a literary dependence. Significant differences, however, also exist caused by differences in religion (Mesopotamian polytheism versus Israelite worship of one God alone) or differences in narratives of identity (general concern for justice for the "weak ones" in Hammurabi's code versus the Covenant Code's special concern for "resident aliens" or "foreigners" arising out of Israel's narrative experience and core identity of being foreigners as slaves in Egypt (Exodus 22:21—"You shall not wrong or oppress a resident alien, for you were aliens in the land of Egypt"). In this case, a "tradition" from outside the culture of ancient Israel formed the basis for Israel's distinctive Covenant Code which preserved large parts of the Mesopotamian tradition and yet also adapted and revised it for its own context and own ideological ends as an act of resistance to Assyrian imperial domination over Israel or Judah in the late eighth or early seventh century BCE.[26]

A second major step in the development of the legal traditions of the Pentateuch came with the revising and reinterpreting of the laws of the Covenant Code by a writer or small group of writers responsible for formulating the law code in Deuteronomy 12–26, who changed some of the laws to fit the needs of a new time and context within ancient Israel. For example, the Covenant Code assumes the existence of multiple worship sites and altars throughout the land (Exodus 20:23–26). In contrast, the laws of Deuteronomy insist that Israel should have only one place of centralized worship in the entire land of Israel, which is presumably the temple in the city of Jerusalem. Although Jerusalem is not named in Deuteronomy, it is assumed to be "the [one] place that the Lord your God will choose out of all your tribes as his habitation to put his name there" (Deut 12:5). These and many other subtle changes orient Israel's laws in new ways; the tradition is carried forward but also changed.[27]

A third stage in the trajectory of preserving and reinterpreting these biblical law traditions has been recently studied by Jeffrey Stackert as he demonstrates

---

[26] David Wright, *Inventing God's Law: How the Covenant Code of the Bible Used and Revised the Laws of Hammurabi* (New York: Oxford University Press, 2009), esp. 3–30, 286–321.

[27] Bernard Levinson, *Deuteronomy and the Hermeneutics of Legal Innovation* (New York: Oxford University Press, 1997).

how certain laws in the so-called Holiness Code of laws in Leviticus 17–26 repeat and revise laws from the Covenant Code in Exodus 20–23 and the laws of Deuteronomy 12–26 to create a new set of laws with its own distinctive perspective and ideology. Tradition is preserved to some extent, but invention and change are injected into the tradition as well.

A later narrative in Numbers 27:1–11 provides an explicit warrant for just such legal innovation and reinterpretation in the story of Zelophehad's daughters. The father Zelophehad dies before being able to inherit his assigned family land share in the land of Canaan. He also dies during Israel's wilderness journey without any sons, no male heirs. Normally the custom is that only sons inherit land, but the daughters of Zelophehad argue that they should inherit the land rather than more distant male relatives. Moses is stymied since no law in the tradition covers this unique case, and so Moses brings the case before the LORD for a ruling. The LORD agrees with the daughters: they should inherit their father's land, even though previous practice had limited land inheritance to male heirs alone. The story illustrates the Bible's own recognition that tradition is living, flexible and open to new interpretations.

In the New Testament, the preservation and influence of earlier gospels (like Mark) on later gospels (like Matthew and Luke) clearly suggests the wisdom of both preserving tradition (retaining Mark as the earliest gospel) while also updating and revising tradition for new contexts and circumstances (Matthew and Luke).

The apostle Paul likewise discerned his role in part as one who conveyed the tradition of the gospel which had been received or handed down as a tradition from Christ. Paul uses his claim of being the recipient of this received tradition in 1 Corinthians 15:3–5 as a basis for strengthening his claim to authority as a true apostle along with the other disciples of Jesus:

> For I handed on to you as of first importance what I in turn had received: that Christ died for our sins in accordance with the scriptures, and that he was buried, and that he was raised on the third day in accordance with the scriptures, and that he appeared to Cephas, then to the twelve.

New Testament scholar Oda Wischmeyer argues that this 1 Corinthians 15 text is an example of what Eric Hobsbawm calls "invented tradition," a tradition used to bolster authority or power in contexts of rapid social change and emerging new patterns of leadership and power.[28] In a similar way, Paul

---

[28] Oda Wischmeyer, "'Invented Traditions' and 'New Traditions' in Earliest Christianity," in Anders-Christian Jacobsen (ed.), *Invention, Rewriting and Usurpation: the Discursive Fight over Religious Tradi-*

in Galatians 1:12 makes a strong bid for his reception of the gospel tradition directly from Christ:

> For I want you to know, brothers and sisters, that the gospel that was proclaimed by me is not of human origin; for I did not receive it from a human source, nor was I taught it, but I received it through a revelation of Jesus Christ.

I would take the term "invented tradition" to mean simply that Paul was the first human in this chain of tradition; it was not passed to him by another human individual or community. This need not be understood as being in contradiction to Paul's claim that Christ was the originator of the tradition.

On the other hand, the apostle Paul also testifies to traditions that seem to fall more clearly under the category of genuine communal traditions that were pre-Pauline and that Paul had received from other believers, although Paul does not always acknowledge the identity of those who have passed the tradition on to him. For example, Paul hands on the tradition of the words of the Lord's Supper which originated before Paul in the upper room with the disciples on the eve of Jesus' crucifixion. The words of the Lord's Supper were subsequently remembered and passed down, "For I received from the Lord what I also handed on to you, that the Lord Jesus on the night when he was betrayed took a loaf of bread …" (1 Cor 11:23).[29]

The ways in which the various books of the New Testament, whether the gospels or Paul's epistles or other New Testament witnesses, use and reinterpret Old Testament "traditions" in contrast to various Jewish appropriations of the Hebrew Bible or Old Testament provide additional examples of the dynamic character of the traditioning processes within the Bible itself and then carried on vigorously in post-biblical interpretations as well.

In conclusion, it is clear that the topic of "tradition" and its relationship to Scripture from a Lutheran perspective is also subject to misunderstandings and contestations. It is hoped that what is provided here may provide some useful resources for an ongoing dialogue together on developing a living and dynamic scriptural hermeneutic for our time and context. Such a hermeneutic would be both informed by the rich resources of the Christian tradition while at the same time being open to the voice of the living God in Jesus Christ who works through the power of the Holy Spirit to "make all things new" (Rev

---

tions in Antiquity (Frankfurt: Peter Lang, 2011). My thanks to Professor Wischmeyer for sharing this essay with me in its prepublication form and to Professor Eve-Marie Becker for bringing the essay to my attention. See Hobsbawn and Ranger, op. cit. (note 3).

[29] Ibid.

21:5). This essential tension in the preserving of tradition alongside the invention and reinterpretation of tradition is captured in the dual commands from God to the Jewish exiles in Babylon in Isaiah 40–55. On the one hand, God commands, "remember the former things of old" (Isa 46:8). On the other, God urges, "Do not remember the former things, nor consider the things of old. I am doing a new thing. Do you not perceive it" (Isa 43:18–19).